REFLEXIVE COMMUNICATION IN THE CULTURALLY DIVERSE WORKPLACE

John F. Kikoski
Catherine Kano Kikoski

Westport, Connecticut
London

The Library of Congress has cataloged the hardcover edition as follows:

Kikoski, John F.
    Reflexive communication in the culturally diverse workplace / John
F. Kikoski, Catherine Kano Kikoski.
      p. cm.
    Includes bibliographical references and index.
    ISBN 0–89930–955–0 (alk. paper)
    1. Communication in personnel management—Social aspects—United
States. 2. Diversity in the workplace—United States—Management.
3. Intercultural communication—United States. I. Kikoski,
Catherine Kano. II. Title.
HF5549.5.C6K55   1996
658.3′041—dc20   95–45398

British Library Cataloguing in Publication Data is available.

A hardcover edition of *Reflexive Communication in the Culturally Diverse
Workplace* is available from Quorum Books,
an imprint of Greenwood Publishing Group, Inc. (ISBN 0–89930–955–0).

Library of Congress Catalog Card Number: 95–45398
ISBN: 0–275–96630–5 (pbk.)

First published in 1996

Praeger Publishers, 88 Post Road West, Westport, CT 06881
An imprint of Greenwood Publishing Group, Inc.
www.praeger.com

Printed in the United States of America

The paper used in this book complies with the
Permanent Paper Standard issued by the National
Information Standards Organization (Z39.48–1984).

10 9 8 7 6 5 4 3 2 1

To our children,

John, André, and Nicole

and their generation
who hold the promise of a better world.
May you create the common ground.

Contents

Acknowledgments

We acknowledge the assistance and support of a number of individuals in the research and writing of this book. We owe a deep personal as well as intellectual debt to Allen Ivey of the University of Massachusetts, Amherst. For more than two decades he has had an impact on our attempts to better understand face-to-face communication. His scholarly research and personal example have inspired us in our individual and joint endeavors to improve understanding among individuals.

A number of colleagues have been kind enough to read selected chapters of this book and provide us with valuable comments. Lynn Hoffman's long-time friendship and support have sustained our energies in completing this project. Her keen insights and valuable feedback on the women's chapter are greatly appreciated. Josh Miller's observations and notes on both the African American and the Hispanic chapters were constructive and beneficial. Orlando Isaza made helpful comments on the Hispanic chapter. We value Shi Juan Wu's discerning remarks on the Asian American chapter. We also are deeply indebted to the individuals who anonymously but willingly shared their experiences and insights with us in our qualitative field research.

Our special thanks to our colleagues and administrators at Sacred Heart University and Saint Joseph College for their support — Gary Rose, Tom Corrigan, Tom Trebon, and Ed Malin as well as Dorothy Zeiser and Martin Snyder. We appreciate beyond words the congenial assistance of librarians at the two colleges — Dorothy Kijanka, Carol Clark, Linda Geffner, Don Gustafson, and, especially, Kathleen Kelly. We also thank our students who helped by sharpening our ideas in class discussions and providing research assistance.

It has been a pleasure to work with two special people at Quorum Books. Eric Valentine's encouragement and acumen kept us on task. We so much appreciate Ellen Dorosh's patience and incisive editorial talents.

To John, André, and Nicole, whose provocative ideas and candid discussions around the dinner table over the years have enriched and deepened our understanding about so many issues, our thanks, love, and hope for a world of concord.

Introduction

Diversity has become an increasingly important issue to every individual, manager, and organization in America. White males already are a rapidly shrinking percentage of the work force while the numbers of women and minorities are increasing. This demographic shift has generated a dramatic response. Numerous publications and training approaches have flooded the market in an effort to meet the challenges that changing demographics pose to the workplace.

We, too, have been drawn to the challenge that diversity presents. This book is a response. It is the result of traditional scholarly research as well as reflections and conversations that were leavened by the qualitative research that we have conducted.

The participants who were interviewed represented the major demographic groups of the American work force. They varied by gender, ethnicity, race, and position. The interviewees were white collar executives and managers from informational, service, financial, and manufacturing organizations in the northeastern United States. To encourage candor and genuineness of response, the participants were assured of confidentiality and anonymity. Therefore, any contextualizing or identifying information has been altered to conceal the identity of these individuals and organizations.

During these interviews, the researchers were struck by the participants' levels of frustration and eagerness for change. Both women and minorities frequently registered their disappointment with the exclusionary climate that generally prevailed where they work. This left them on the periphery despite their wish to become fully contributing members of their organizations. Many white males also expressed their frustration with the difficulties they experienced with diversity, particularly dealing with individuals on a one-to-one basis. All felt stymied by their organizations' endeavors to address these emerging issues effectively. This book addresses the genesis and problems that diversity poses and suggests a process for change. They are:

The demographic trends transforming the United States. These trends need to be honestly and factually addressed without hyperbole, on the one hand, or denial, on the other, both of which hinder reasonable and timely adaptation. Demographically, the face of the United States is changing quickly. The sense of urgency necessary to deal with these shifts is masked by the size of the baby boom generation. Behind these shifts lies a different America. Diversity is a reality that needs to be reckoned with.

The general impact of culture on human behavior. This is a phenomenon that many Americans in their continental country have yet to address. Culture shapes behavior. As America is demographically transformed, the operational impact of culture increases because culturally diverse contexts generally complicate face-to-face communication.

The concept of cultural paradigm. The components of a cultural paradigm or communication paradigm are the cultural historical background, the culturally-specific central values, nonverbal communication behaviors, and verbal communication behaviors of each major demographic group in the work force — white males, white females, African Americans, Hispanics, and Asian Americans. This concept can help members of each ethnic group become aware of their own as well as other groups' communication paradigms.

The larger American historical setting. The American national experience includes discrimination and exploitation, but its larger historical experience is one of inclusion and assimilation of new entrants into its work force and society. Just as dynamic convergence has been the experience of ethnic groups in America, so it will be the experience of differing communication styles converging to create a new order of talk.

The theory of reflexive communication. Reflexive communication is a practical and pragmatic approach to mitigate the problems of stereotyping that frequently and spontaneously emerge when we encounter diversity. The goal is not only to acknowledge but also to transcend cultural generalities through the process of reflexive communication to access the individual better. In today's diverse workplace, effective communication is more than information transmission, it is mutual understanding.

We have seen America change for the better during the past 30 years. We hope to contribute to the continuing transformation of the United

States by reinforcing what are, perhaps, its most profound ideals — the equality and worth of the individual.

Chapter 1, "Demography: New Realities, New Imperatives," examines the demographic trends that forecast a more ethnically and racially diverse twenty-first–century America. Readers will come away knowing that white males comprise about one-third of labor force entrants, not the widely misunderstood 15 percent; the law of thirds is used in planning for the U.S. work force through the first decades of the twenty-first century (one-third white male, one-third white female, and one-third black, Hispanic, and Asian American); and about one-half of today's work force is white, largely male baby boomers who will begin retiring early in the twenty-first century, and, as that happens, the U.S. workplace will rapidly come to resemble its younger and more diverse ranks of today.

In Chapter 2, "Culture, Communication, and Management," face-to-face communication is a central activity of managers. It also is an activity that culture complicates. This chapter explores the impact of cultural diversity on interpersonal communication in the workplace. It proposes that effective communication in any organization involves a common order of talk as a requirement for personal and organizational effectiveness. Individuals who represent the increasingly diverse work force are often as unfamiliar with the mainstream rules for discourse as are mainstream workers. Differing communication modes create new misperceptions and problems among workers.

To address this problem, Chapter 2 highlights the impact of culture upon face-to-face communication. We propose the concept of cultural or communication paradigm to help individuals realize the linkage between culture and communication. We find that grasping each demographic group's cultural paradigm is an essential first step to help individuals communicate more effectively across gender and ethnic lines.

Chapter 3, "Reflexive Communication," proposes a new epistemology of interpersonal communication in the diverse workplace. Here we introduce the premises, stances, and skills that foster reflexive communication. We believe that reflexive communication allows one to transcend stereotypical tendencies by accessing the uniqueness of each individual. It encourages participants to talk about what constitutes their individual realities; share their perceptions, feelings, and meanings about the way they perceive their situation; and make sense of it. No two individuals perceive the same situation similarly, especially when they come from different backgrounds.

Reflexive communication is particularly suited to the diverse workplace where the disparity of perceptions is likely to be high. Stereotyping fosters miscommunication. Reflexive communication can help communicants mutually abandon misleading stereotypes and, instead, focus on

ongoing transactions. Coworkers can tap into the differing understandings that each might impute to the same reality or experience. The
only antidote to stereotyping is to know each other as individuals. While
acknowledging the specifics of each cultural paradigm in the chapters
that follow, our goal is to transcend them and establish more effective
communication between individuals.

In Chapter 4, "Microskills for Reflexive Communication," we introduce a set of hands-on communication skills called microskills. Microskills are the tools everyone needs to implement reflexive communication. Microskills are comprised of nonverbal and verbal attending
behaviors. The nonverbal attending behaviors include eye contact, body
language, vocal qualities, and verbal tracking. The verbal attending
behaviors include open questions, closed questions, paraphrase, reflection of feeling, reflection of meaning, and summarization. The successful
use of these skills prepares individuals to generate information and
promote deeper understanding of one another, thereby maximizing
communication. The microskills provide the tools to address the
challenges that diversity brings to the workplace and encourage effective
communication.

Chapter 5, "The White Male Communication Paradigm," addresses the
White Anglo-Saxon Protestant cultural paradigm that has dominated U.S.
business for nearly 400 years. It is the antecedent and single most
powerful cultural paradigm in the corporate world. Since World War II it
has evolved into what we call the white male cultural paradigm. This
chapter is important because, even today, the white male paradigm
provides the basic template for managerial behavior in the United States.
The chapter examines the values (the most outstanding of which is hyper-
individualism) as well as the verbal and nonverbal communication styles
that characterize this paradigm. Women and minorities face the challenge
of navigating within its parameters. The goal of this chapter is in keeping
with our position that while the white male communication paradigm
remains predominant, it cannot, in the long run, dictate the order of talk.
Other voices need to be heard as well.

Chapter 6, "The Women's Communication Paradigm," addresses
women's roles, positions, and behaviors in the demographically changing
workplace. It reviews the inequities and barriers they confront and
examines the traditional assumptions about women that still prevail in
our society. The chapter explores the new assumptions about women that
are rapidly emerging. It is the struggle between these assumptions that
helps to explain the tension between the genders and among women
today. This chapter also explores women's values, the most central of
which is connectedness. The focus is to create a place for the women's
communication paradigm in the new order of talk.

Chapter 7, "The African American Communication Paradigm," emphasizes the history of forced group migration. The achievement of African Americans is particularly important given the heritage of slavery. Demographic and economic indicators also are examined. This chapter addresses the African American communication paradigm and its values as well as nonverbal and verbal communication styles. While the white male individualistic value is "I think, therefore I am," the single most important African American value may be "We think, therefore I am." Many blacks particularly value community and kinship.

Chapter 8 discusses the Hispanic communication paradigm. Today, much of America's Hispanic population is immigrants. A sketch of Latino American achievement demonstrates their continuing and growing contribution to U.S. society. The Hispanic communication paradigm accords a central place to the value of self-worth in terms of the inner qualities that give an individual self-respect while earning the respect of others. Ignoring the Hispanic's dignity assaults the core of his person-hood and integrity and plays an important role in relationships. As the Hispanic population increases this paradigm will assume a larger role in the evolving order of talk in the workplace.

Chapter 9, "The Asian American Communication Paradigm," begins with discussions of group migration and outstanding Asian Americans who have made important contributions to America. Special attention is given to the many waves and cultures from which Asian Americans come. The paramount Asian American values are hierarchy and interpersonal harmony. This helps explain why some individuals may erroneously typify the quiet, self-effacing Asian American communica-tion style as technical rather than as the indirect, consensus-seeking style it actually is. An understanding of how the Confucian value system contributes to the Asian American communication style in subtle and powerful ways can help colleagues avoid misunderstanding each other.

Chapter 10, "The Communication Paradigm of the United States in the Twenty-first Century," is a dispassionate examination of U.S. history indicating that, from 1607 through World War II, the dominant English White Anglo-Saxon Protestant mainstream first expanded to include other northern European Protestant white males. After World War II, the mainstream again expanded to include yesterday's ethnics — Catholic and Jewish, Irish, Italian, Greek, and Slav. Now, in the late twentieth and early twenty-first centuries, the same historical dynamic is unfolding to expand the mainstream to include today's minorities.

It is important for the reader to grasp a critical point before reading this book: cultural behaviors are shared behaviors that are generalizable to a group and do not necessarily describe any single, unique individual. Because cultural behaviors are shared behaviors, they provide the basis for the synchronized, out-of-consciousness behavior that is required for effective common action in groups. In an America that is becoming so diverse, it is critical for each one of us to be aware of the behaviors that every gender and ethnic group brings with them to the workplace.

What has not been studied adequately is the process by which gender and ethnic values as well as verbal and nonverbal behaviors differ and the impact they have on the communication process, each in their own unique way. Here, the ultimate goal is the development of a new order of talk, one that is informed by the gender, racial, and ethnic representations of U.S. workplaces. Only then can we realize the twin goals of a maximally effective workplace and the contributions of everyone to it.

The stakes are higher today than ever before because of diversity and the information revolution. The U.S. work force is becoming diverse with a scope and scale that are unprecedented. Simultaneously, the information revolution brings an unheralded speed and complexity to the workplace, requiring collaboration, partnership, and joint efforts.

As we experience the shifts to a global and informational economy, we are both heartened and saddened — heartened because they will usher in an era of great opportunity and wealth for those who have the education and skills to participate and saddened because of the dislocations and hurt it will cause and the increasingly bifurcated societies it is creating, not only in America but also in societies around the world. This era is similar to the shift from the agricultural economy to the industrial economy that Marx wrote about with all of its sufferings and successes. However, we firmly believe that the organizational need for the best talent, regardless of its gender, ethnicity, or race, coupled with America's longstanding commitment to its core values of individuality and equality will not only enable but also strengthen the continuation of America's process of inclusion in the workplace. Indeed, because of the richness that accompanies it, America's diversity should be a source of advantage in tomorrow's global competition.

In this book we propose an applied communication theory that we hope enhances mutual understanding across gender and ethnic divides. Our efforts have been informed by a postmodern constructionist approach that we believe is congruent with the requisites of our culturally-diverse and information era society — egalitarianism and collaboration. Concordantly, the thesis of this book is that the only antidote to stereotyping and discrimination is to know each other as individuals. Accordingly, the object of this book is to help the overlapping common ground emerge where individuals can understand and then transcend cultural differences to work together more collaboratively and effectively. This critical juncture provides us with the unique opportunity to bring together the threads for weaving the fabric of a new community in which individuals can communicate in ways that promote effective working relationships and benefit themselves and their society.

The following quotation reflects the vision of this book:

> The critical problem . . . in human relationships is not to eliminate diversity but to understand how diversity can be integrated into some form of unity. The differences between male and female, white and non-white, young and old, better educated and less educated are perennially the focus of social conflict. . . . The critical question is how to use these tensions and diversities to create a richer, fuller human society instead of a narrow, frightened and suspicious society.
>
> —Andrew Greeley*

---

*Andrew M. Greeley. (1971). *Why can't they be like us? America's white ethnic groups* (p. 16). New York: E. P. Dutton.

Reflexive Communication in the Culturally Diverse Workplace

1

Demography: New Realities, New Imperatives

Don't be cynical about the American experiment because it has only now begun.

— Kurt Vonnegut, Jr.[1]

America has always been a diverse society. Throughout its history men and women of every race and ethnicity have contributed to America's story.

Hardworking Dutchmen and Poles were among the earliest settlers of the English colony of Jamestown in 1608.[2]

Revolutionary War patriot Paul Revere's French Huguenot father bore the name Apollos Rivoire.[3]

Molly Pitcher, of Revolutionary War fighting fame, actually was a German American woman, Maria Ludwig.[4]

The second U.S. census, conducted in 1800, indicated that 20 percent of the population was black, as was 10 percent of Lincoln's Civil War troops who won 21 Congressional Medals of Honor.[5]

It was no accident that the first two states to legally recognize the equality of women by providing them the vote were Wyoming in 1869 and Colorado in 1893 — western frontier states where harsh conditions, hard work, and danger were blind to gender.[6]

The most highly decorated combat unit in U.S. military history is World War II's Japanese American 442nd Regimental Combat Team.[7]

During the 1990–91 Persian Gulf conflict, 16 percent of the U.S. military forces in the theater of operations were women.[8]

Women and men of all races and ethnicities have built the United States. In the past, it was principally the contributions of white Anglo-Saxon Protestant males that were recorded and taught as our U.S. history. The contributions of women and other ethnic groups were under-reported and underappreciated. Only recently have the contributions of women and other ethnic and racial groups begun to be recognized and appreciated.

Kurt Vonnegut may have been prescient in suggesting that the American experiment is only beginning because an America that has been (and perceived itself as being) white is becoming more African American, Hispanic, and Asian American within a relatively brief period of its history.

Many may be unaware that the United States has entered a new era. During this era the demographic composition of this country is changing. The nature of this change is both far-reaching and profound. In its scale, scope, and velocity this demographic transformation will create a new and different America. Few factors in human affairs are as predictable and powerful as demography. Paradoxically, few are as surprising. Demography often is thought of in terms of dry statistics. However, captured in those statistics are the dynamics of powerful trends that will reshape the United States. Those who prospectively and clearly discern these demographic trends will comprehend the forces shaping their personal future as well as the futures of their organizations and their nation. Few of us really comprehend the speed or scope of change that is upon us.

DEMOGRAPHY AND AMERICAN SOCIETY: FROM THE TWENTIETH TO THE TWENTY-FIRST CENTURY

The America of *Saturday Evening Post* illustrator Norman Rockwell, of an overwhelmingly white America with only a small and recessive minority presence, is fast disappearing. Consider that during the 1970s, only about one American in eight was black, Hispanic, or Asian American; during the 1990s, approximately one in four is black, Hispanic or Asian American; by 2010, one in three will be black, Hispanic, or Asian American; and by 2050, one American in two is forecast to be black, Hispanic, or Asian American.[9] Consider also that in 1989, New York City reported a higher percentage of foreign-born residents than at any time since 1910; the population of Washington, D.C., is two-thirds black;

Miami is two-thirds Hispanic; and one-third of San Franciscans are Asian American.[10]

Examining this profound demographic shift, the respected British news weekly, *The Economist*, concluded: "People of 30 and older will increasingly have the experience of growing up in one kind of country and growing old in another. In some parts of the United States, Americans will thus share the experience of new immigrants simply by staying at home."[11]

Two forces are driving this demographic transformation — different birthrates among ethnic and racial groups and changes in legal and illegal immigration. Currently the size of the largest U.S. age group, the baby-boomer generation, is shrouding these changes. The immense wave of baby boomers — who comprise approximately one-third of the U.S. population but about one-half of its work force — means that generations are changing their racial and ethnic mix at varied rates.[12] What these trends forecast is that within the next 50 years, native-born whites will constitute less than half of the U.S. population.

In the year 2000 nearly 80 percent of Americans over age 45 but 63 percent of U.S. children below age 8 will be native-born Caucasians. Examining these developments, demographer Martha Farnsworth Riche concludes: "These trends signal a transition to a multicultural society. If you count men and women as separate groups, all Americans are members of at least one minority group. . . . The trend is clear. If current conditions continue, the United States will become a nation with no racial or ethnic majority during the 21st century."[13] Few of us really comprehend the speed, scope, or certainty of the transformation that is upon us.

MISUNDERSTANDING *WORKFORCE 2000*

The public first became aware of these population and work force shifts with the publication in 1987 of *Workforce 2000*.[14] This study quickly became mandatory reading for executives, educators, and politicians throughout the United States. *Workforce 2000* was the first major study forecasting that America and its work force would become much less white male and much more female, African American, Hispanic, and Asian American. Before we began our interviews, we were told that everyone understood those demographic changes. We have found that not everyone clearly understands these demographic changes. In fact, our interviews indicated a need to clarify some significant misunderstandings about the demographic future of the United States. Often, those who least understand these demographics are most resistant to their own organizations' efforts to promote diversity in the work place.

After hearing our forecasts a human resources executive for a Fortune 500 company told us: "I'm very glad I met you. Knowing these points will affect my human resource strategy and help make me much more effective in preparing my company for the coming work force." Our six forecasts are:

1. Many still believe that white males comprise only 15 percent of new entrants to the labor force, but, in fact, white males will comprise one-third of new labor force entrants.

2. The white male share of the work force is sharply decreasing, but, for the foreseeable future, white males still will comprise the largest single category of workers.

3. The law of thirds will continue to explain the composition of the work force for the foreseeable future.

4. Women will comprise one-third of the labor force through 2005.

5. Another one-third of the U.S. work force will consist of blacks, Hispanics, and Asian Americans — the only demographic segment that is growing.

6. When baby boomers begin to retire after the year 2005, the composition of the U.S. work force will become even more diverse.

Workforce 2000's most famous forecast caught everyone's eye. "White males, thought of only a generation ago as the mainstays of the economy, will comprise only 15 percent of the *net additions* to the labor force between 1985 and 2000"[15] (emphasis added). However, this forecast is the source of a widespread myth. Seven years later even *Fortune* magazine was still reporting that "Nearly 85% of the 25 million entering the labor pool would be women, minorities, or immigrants, . . . only 15% of new entrants would be white males."[16] *Workforce 2000* did not state that "only 15% of new [work force] entrants would be white males." By subtracting the number of native-born white male retirees and others who leave the work force from the number of first-time entrants, the forecast technically (and correctly) categorized native-born white males as 15 percent of net additions to the work force.

If we ask what percent of actual entrants to the work force white males will make up — the sort of question chief executive officers must ask for recruitment or planning purposes — another answer emerges. As Bureau of Labor Statistics demographer Howard Fullerton stated: "The demise of the white male worker . . . has been greatly exaggerated. . . . The composition of the labor force is changing, but not as dramatically as the 85 percent figure suggests. . . . Between 1990 and 2005, white men will make up 18 million entrants to the labor force, *about one-third (32 percent) of all entrants*"[17] (emphasis added). For the foreseeable future, nearly one-third, not 15 percent, of work force entrants will be native-born white males.

Widespread misunderstanding exists about the number of white males in the overall work force. Some executives we interviewed believed that white males would all but disappear from the work force. A disinterested reading of the demographics indicates that white males will play a significant role in the workplace in the foreseeable future.

During the 20-year period from 1985 to 2005 the number of white males in the labor force has dropped and will continue to drop precipitously from just under one-half in 1985 to a little over one-third in 2005 — an unprecedented decline of about 0.5 percent per year. The percentage of white males in the work force actually declined from 47 percent in 1985 to 43 percent in 1990 and is forecast to drop to 38 percent in 2005.[18] Thirty-eight percent of the work force is hardly an insignificant presence. One of the shrewdest observers of diversity management, Taylor Cox, concluded: "American white males will continue to be the single largest gender/race identity group in the U.S. work force for many years."[19] However, he correctly questions the viability of what he terms the traditionally white male "monolithic organization."

We suggest that managers envision the labor force according to an approximate law of thirds — one-third white male, one-third white female, and one-third minorities (African Americans, Hispanics, and Asian Americans) — while remembering that the white male third is shrinking. Let us examine the growing two-thirds of the work force.

Surprisingly little change is forecast for the second-largest component of the work force — native-born white females. Women comprised about one-third of the labor force in 1992, will make up approximately one-third of the entrants between 1992 and 2005, and are estimated to comprise about one-third of the labor force in 2005.[20] Therefore, in 2005 approximately two-thirds of U.S. work force entrants will be native-born and white — one-third male and one-third female. The total work force will have the same approximate composition.

Youthful minorities already are entering the work force in increasing numbers and are creating a more diverse labor force. Little change is expected for blacks in the labor force. They comprise approximately 11 percent of both the 1992 and 2005 labor forces and about 12 percent of labor force entrants. The Hispanic share of the labor force will increase from 8 percent in 1992 to 11 percent in 2005 and will make up 15 percent of entrants. Asian Americans will comprise close to 8 percent of work force entrants during that period.[21] Therefore, from 1992 to 2005 minorities are forecast to make up 35 percent of work force entrants.

WHAT DOES ALL THIS MEAN TO THE MANAGER?

What does this mean to the manager who is planning for the future? Table 1.1 shows that in 2005 white males and white females will comprise 73 percent of the work force — 65 percent of entrants (native-born white females will comprise approximately one-third of the work force as well as its entrants); blacks, Hispanics, and Asian Americans will make up 27 percent of the work force — approximately 35 percent of entrants. Therefore, white women and minorities will make up approximately 69 percent of work force entrants.

TABLE 1.1
America's 1992–2005 Labor Force
(in percent)

	1992 Labor Force	2005 Labor Force	1992–2005 Entrants	Movement
White males	42.5	38.0	31.4	Decreasing
White females	35.3	34.9	33.7	Steady
Blacks	10.8	11.0	11.9	Increasing
Hispanics	8.0	11.0	15.2	Increasing
Asian Americans	3.4	5.0	7.7	Increasing

Source: Howard N. Fullerton. (1993, November). The American Workforce, 1992–2005: Another look at the labor force. *Monthly Labor Review*, p. 36.

The shift to a more diverse work force already is occurring. A 1992 survey of 578 private companies and nonprofit organizations found that: "More than half of the organizations surveyed reported increases in women and minorities in their workforces over the past five years. The role of women in management has increased dramatically, and more than a third of companies report increases in minority managers." Women are making strides. Almost 60 percent of organizations surveyed reported increased numbers of women among their employees, and nearly 70 percent reported more women managers. The number of individuals of color also increased. More than 50 percent of private companies and 71 percent of public and nonprofit organizations surveyed reported increases in the number of minority employees. Sixty-two percent of nonprofit organizations reported increases among minority managers.[22] The number of women and minorities in the labor force will accelerate even faster after 2005.

Post–World War II baby boomers (approximately 78 million persons born between 1946 and 1964) comprise the largest age cohort the United

States has ever seen — almost one-third of the U.S. population and one-half of its labor force.[23] As baby boomers reach age 60, in 2006, and begin to retire, what is already a strong current of twentieth-century demographic change will become a twenty-first–century torrent. The size of the baby-boomer generation currently masks the scale, scope, and velocity of change that demography makes imperative in twenty-first–century America.

Because corporate cultures change slowly, organizations that do not begin to adapt now will be overwhelmed by the consequences of diversity. Proactive and farsighted organizations will forge ahead. Wise managers will prepare themselves and their organizations today.

Diversity is not a question of yesterday or tomorrow but of today. Blayne Cutler quotes Patricia Cross, leading diversity consultant, as saying that "Change is here. . . . When 60 percent of the work force is other than white male, you have already got change."[24]

These demographic shifts pose a twofold challenge to America's managers.

PROACTIVELY ANTICIPATING
DEMOGRAPHIC CHANGE

Many managers believe they understand that the future American population and work force will become less white male, and more female, more black, more Hispanic, and more Asian American. But few managers truly comprehend the challenge that lies ahead. Because of the scope, velocity, and depth of that demographic change, sensible organizations will recruit and promote the most able individuals who are women, black, Hispanic, and Asian American as well as white male. To do less will jeopardize the success as well as viability of that organization. Now is the time for managers and organizations to proactively implement the changes that America's new demography makes imperative.

FACE-TO-FACE COMMUNICATION
IN THE DIVERSE WORKPLACE

Managers confront a second challenge — learning how to manage and communicate effectively with colleagues who are becoming more diverse. Managers will not necessarily communicate, decide, delegate, negotiate, act, or manage as they have in the past — uniformly and similarly. Occasionally and consciously, then daily and unconsciously, managers will find it prudent and then necessary to take gender and cultural differences into account. As Audrey Edwards put it: "The labor force is going to look and be different. The challenge, then, is in learning how to manage this difference. And the manager who can successfully do so will be as indispensable to corporate management as working capital."[25]

CONCLUSION

The wave is rising. Managers today can feel the first swells — low- and mid-level managers the most, upper-level managers the least. That wave will rise during the late 1990s, then curl, crest, and only begin to break during the early twenty-first century. A rising sea change is altering the demographic and cultural composition of the American work force and managers and, therefore, how they manage. The wise manager will be culturally prepared.

NOTES

1.   People in the news. (1990, May 28). *Hartford Courant*, p. A2 reporting on Vonnegut's commencement speech at the University of Rhode Island.

2.   Phillip Barbour. (1964). The identity of the first Poles in America. *William & Mary Quarterly, 21*, 77–92. Barbour points out that the Dutchmen whom Captain John Smith reported landing at Jamestown actually may have been Germans and even included one Swiss. See also the more popularized Louis Adamic. (1944). *A nation of nations* (pp. 287–288). New York: Harper & Brothers.

3.   Esther Forbes. (1942). *Paul Revere and the world he lived in* (pp. 1–17). Boston: Houghton Mifflin.

4.   Frederick Harling, & Martin Kaufman. (1976). *The ethnic contribution to the American revolution* (p. 30). Westfield, MA: Westfield Bicentennial Committee and The Historical Journal of Western Massachusetts.

5.   Thomas Sowell. (1981). *Ethnic America: A history* (pp. 193, 196). New York: Basic Books.

6.   Katherine Harris. (1987). Homesteading in northern Colorado, 1873–1920: Sex roles and women's experience." In Susan Armitage and Elizabeth Jameson (Eds.), *The women's west* (pp. 165–178). Norman: University of Oklahoma Press; Elizabeth Jameson. (1987). Women as workers, women as civilizers: True womanhood in the American west. In Susan Armitage and Elizabeth Jameson (Eds.), *The women's west* (pp. 145–164). Norman: University of Oklahoma Press.

7.   Bill Hosokawa. (1969). *Nisei: The quiet Americans* (p. 410). New York: William Morrow.

8.   John A. MacDonald. (1990, March 24). Kennelly urges another look at issue of women in combat. *Hartford Courant*, p. A15.

9.   Juanita Tamayo Lott. (1993, January). Do United States racial/ethnic categories still fit? *Population Today*, p. 7; U.S. Bureau of the Census. (1994). No. 18. Resident population by Hispanic origin status, 1980 to 1992, and projections, 1993 to 2050. In *Statistical abstract of the United States*. Washington, DC: Government Printing Office.

10.   Edward B. Fiske. (1991, March 22). Minorities a majority in New York. *New York Times*, pp. 81–82; U.S. Bureau of the Census. (1994). No. 46. Cities with

100,000 or more inhabitants in 1992. In *Statistical abstract of the United States*. Washington, DC: Government Printing Office.

11.   Poor men at the gate. (1991, March 16). *The Economist*, p. 9.

12.   Paul C. Light. (1988). *Baby boomers*. New York: W. W. Norton; Howard N. Fullerton, Jr. (1991, November). Outlook: 1990–2005 labor force projections: The baby boom moves on. *Monthly Labor Review*, p. 40; Diane Crispell. (1993, May). Where generations divide: A guide. *American Demographics*, p. 9.

13.   Martha Farnsworth Riche. (1991, October). We're all minorities now. *American Demographics*, pp. 26, 28, 29; see also Kevin M. Pollard. (1993, July/August). Youth on the cutting edge of diversity trend. *Population Today*, p. 3.

14.   William B. Johnston, & Arnold E. Packer. (1987). *Workforce 2000: Work and workers for the 21st century* (p. 95). Washington, DC: Government Printing Office.

15.   Ibid., p. 95.

16.   Faye Rice. (1994, August 8). How to make diversity pay. *Fortune*, p. 79.

17.   Howard Fullerton. (1993, May). Labor-force change exaggerated: One-third of new workers will still be white men. *Population Today*, p. 6.

18.   Johnston, & Packer. *Workforce 2000*, p. xxi; Fullerton. Labor-force change exaggerated, pp. 6–7.

19.   Taylor Cox, Jr. (1991). The multicultural organization. *Academy of Management Executives*, 5(2), p. 39.

20.   Howard N. Fullerton. (1993, November). The American work force, 1992–2005: Another look at the labor force. *Monthly Labor Review*, p. 36.

21.   Ibid., p. 36.

22.   The Olsten Forum on Human Resource Issues and Trends. (1992). *Workplace social issues in the 1990's* (pp. 1–3). Westbury, NY: The Olsten Corporation.

23.   Diane Crispell. (1995, January). Generations to 2025. *American Demographics*, p. 4.

24.   Blayne Cutler. (1993, May). Business reports: When Cross talks to the boss. *American Demographics*, p. 12.

25.   Audrey Edwards. (1991, January). The enlightened manager: How to treat all your employees fairly. *Working Woman*, 16(1), p. 46.

2

Culture, Communication, and Management

In some contexts — in offices, businesses, bureaucracies, educational establishments, etc. — knowing the order of talk required is a part of one's social competence as an adult.

— John Shotter[1]

The sort of business meeting that will occur more and more frequently in twenty-first–century America is described here. Mike is a middle class, white American male. Miguel is an immigrant Mexican American male. Both are mid-level executives in different corporations. They have met for the first time in Miguel's office. Mike has come to propose that Miguel's sales force add Mike's corporation's product line. Neither one is aware of the impact of his own or the other's culture.

Both men have been sitting in Miguel's office for some time growing more and more impatient.

MIKE (to himself): Why aren't we getting on with it?

MIGUEL (to himself): Why aren't we getting on with it?

MIKE (to himself): It's quarter-to-twelve. I've been here with Miguel for 45 minutes already, and I haven't even begun to talk business. I know that both me and this proposal are new to Miguel, but how can I count on this guy when all he does is ask me questions about myself, my background, my interests, my family, my "philosophy!" Why does he have to be so nosey? I don't know him well enough yet to get into that personal stuff. I know he's just invited me to have lunch with him, but it's a 30-minute drive to the 1 o'clock appointment I scheduled, and I have to be on time. All I wanted to achieve was to run through this proposal quickly the first time, see if he had any interest and if he did come back again to see about doing business. Sometimes I think that all these Hispanics want to do is talk about anything but business.

MIGUEL (to himself): It's quarter-to-twelve. I've been here with Mike for 45 minutes already, and he won't talk about anything important. How can I know if I want to do business with him unless I know something about him and the kind of man he is? But I feel like a dentist pulling teeth. And he doesn't want to know anything about me! Where I come from, we don't like to do business with strangers. We like to know something about the other person, and feel we can at least begin to trust them before we start to talk business seriously. If this were Monterrey, Mexico, and not Monterey, California, I probably would take a little longer. But given the pace of business here, one has to find out what he can in just hours. It's too bad that he's turned me down for lunch. I think I can trust him, and really am interested in his product line. With a little more time, I think we could do business. But first I've got to feel at least a little sure about who I'm doing business with. Sometimes I think that all these Anglos want to talk about is business.

MIKE (to himself): Oh well, I've never had any luck doing business with Hispanics before. Why should it be any different this time?

MIGUEL (to himself): Oh well, I've never had any luck doing business with Gringos before. Why should it be any different this time?

MIKE: Thanks for the invitation to have lunch with you Miguel, but I've got to get along to my next appointment. Here's my card. Maybe we can do business next time.

MIGUEL: Oh that's alright, Mike. We'll have lunch another time. Come back again. I'd like to get to know you better. Maybe we can do business next time.

There is nothing new in two individuals misunderstanding and, therefore, miscommunicating with each other. When things go wrong at work we all have the same explanation: It was a communication problem. And often we are right. Good communication and effective outcomes are difficult to achieve, especially when we deal with so many people on so many different levels every day. However, something else was at work here. This time the problem was different. Neither Mike nor Miguel communicated as the other expected. Neither one got through to the other. And neither one consciously understood why because this time the problem was culture. Let us briefly look at what happened.

When Mike meets someone for the first time, he expects — according to his mainstream American business culture — to spend a few perfunctory minutes getting to know one another and then getting right down to business. Professional and private lives are separate. One does not inquire into another's personal life or family. If the client relationship with Miguel develops into something more friendly, Mike expects it will be as a result of and after their business relationship, not before. Mike's cultural attitude is: Business is about money. Time is money. So let us get down to business.

When Miguel meets someone for the first time, he expects — according to his Mexican American culture — to spend a fair amount of time getting acquainted with the other individual. For Hispanics, work and personal life are closely joined. The human relationship holds a higher priority than is generally true among gringos. Miguel wants to find out at least a little about Mike's background and character first. Miguel expects that a relationship of trust should exist between them prior to, not after, the business relationship. Miguel's cultural attitude is: Business is about money. That is why I want to feel I can trust Mike before I go any further. But business also is about life. And people are life. So let us get to know one another.

This scenario will be repeated more and more frequently through the United States in years to come. Every manager needs to address these issues. Mike and Miguel's encounter is just a snapshot of the paradox that will confront every manager in every organization well into the twenty-first century.

THE PARADOX: DIVERSITY AND ORGANIZATION

John Shotter's quotation, which opened this chapter, and Mike and Miguel's difficulty in face-to-face communication frame the paradox that diversity poses to every manager in America today, one between the consequences of a more diverse work force and the necessity that colleagues in the workplace know and share a common "order of talk" as part of their social competence. \

In both numbers and power, today's mainstream white males have long dominated the key positions of the U.S. work force. With no reason to do otherwise, they overwhelmingly dealt with each other through their own order of talk — common values as well as common verbal and nonverbal communication behaviors that made for "fit" in U.S. offices and executive suites.

A much more diverse twentieth- and twenty-first–century America is changing all that. As time passes, millions of males and females who are white, black, Hispanic, and Asian American often will find themselves in pressured, face-to-face management interactions on a daily and hourly basis.

The consequences for interpersonal communications are profound. In their life cycle, women traditionally have possessed a number of roles and statuses — mother, daughter, sister, and wife. Similarly, men have been father, son, brother, and husband. Each gender may feel it knows how to relate and communicate with the other. However, men and women may be less familiar with relating to each other as colleagues and superiors in the workplace. A woman's touch in the relationship of daughter or sister may be intended to convey support; the same woman's touch could have a sexual meaning to a male colleague in the workplace. The consequences of misinterpretation could range from a damaged working relationship to a sexual harassment suit.[2] Similarly, African Americans, Hispanics, and Asian Americans have gained admission to some U.S. corporate suites only recently. They, too, have discovered that their new status has created problems in relating to and communicating with others.

Managers know that Shotter is right when he says that knowing the order of talk is part of one's social competence in every organization. Knowing the order of talk is recognized as crucial to personal effectiveness and group productivity. Research by linguists indicates that those who share common traits, such as gender, race, ethnicity, or culture, tend to communicate more effectively with each other than those who do not.[3] What textbooks call the interpersonal skills of being able to get along with or "fit" with others are crucial to personal effectiveness and group productivity. As Chester Barnard wrote in his 1938 management classic, *The Functions of the Executive,* fit involves sharing such traits as "education, experience, age, sex, personal distinctions, prestige, race, nationality, faith, politics, sectional antecedents; and such very specific personal traits as manners, speech, personal appearance, etc."[4] Generally, sharing such similar attributes helps to create that ready-made fit to which Barnard referred.

Today women and minorities have discovered that fit remains a critical issue as they climb the executive ladder. The challenge in today's workplace is how to create that fit. One may ask if all of Barnard's attributes are necessary for a fit to occur. Obviously, not in a society that promises to be so diverse. We believe that this condition of diversity presents the greatest challenge that confronts managers and workers in the United States. For that fit to take place, it is necessary for all of us to move beyond such objective attributes and work to develop a new common order of talk. To do so, we begin by developing a general awareness of each other's cultural and historical backgrounds. While this is necessary to our goal, it is not sufficient. It is imperative that we come to know our uniqueness as individuals as well as the skills required to communicate effectively and work together. Such an ability will become the prerequisite for workers and managers to do their jobs well.

In the past, Barnard's notion of fit was simple and operative. Until recently, in America's organizations there was one dominant culture with an accompanying single order of talk — white, Anglo-Saxon, Protestant male. However, today's world is far different from 50 years ago. Demographically, tomorrow's world will be even more different. The higher one goes in any organizational pyramid the more important fit becomes. Today, the problem is not limited to corporate headquarters, but encompasses every level of every organization in the United States. Our solution to the problem of fit must evolve.

Developing a solution is more critical and complex than ever before. The attributes that once were operative have become less significant in a more democratic and diverse society. We do not propose following the same rationale — lengthening or shortening the list of attributes to create fit. Rather, what we propose may require a major restructuring of the process. To establish any semblance of a common order of talk, we must begin by learning about each other so that we can work toward shedding the stereotypes that we all hold. Mike and Miguel will not be able to establish a business relationship successfully unless they do away with the mutual stereotypes that control their thoughts and behaviors as they attempt to communicate with one another. Many managers in U.S. organizations are experiencing similar problems.

Redefining fit no longer means using the broad attributes of Barnard but, rather, seeking a deeper sense of knowing and understanding one another. That is, the more we get to know who we all are as individuals, the less stereotyping we engage in and the more we treat each other equally and respectfully. These are the preconditions that engender the common goodwill to work and live together in this world of ours. It will no longer be an imposed fit to which we all must adhere. Rather, it will be a free-willed fit that we will have developed collaboratively. The ultimate goal of the process is that, once fit is redefined and established, a new common order of talk will evolve within the new matrix of the workplace.

We believe that U.S. managers face a paradox between increasing diversity, on the one hand, and the need for a common order of talk, on the other. Transcending this paradox is, perhaps, the greatest challenge facing managers. To accomplish this entails developing a general awareness as well as specific knowledge of the ways in which America's gender and cultural groups communicate. Such an ability will become no more and no less than a precondition to managers doing their own jobs well. Managers can prepare themselves for effective face-to-face communication in the workplace by exploring the emerging problems in face-to-face communication; frontiers of corporate culture; and cultural historical paradigms of white males, white females, African Americans, Hispanics, and Asian Americans.

PROBLEMS IN FACE-TO-FACE COMMUNICATION

Few aspects of organizational life are more important than inter-personal communication. One of the most valuable skills that a manager can possess is the ability to communicate effectively with others. In a classic study, Henry Mintzberg found that managers typically spend 78 percent of their time on the job verbally communicating with others.[5] Another often-cited study concluded: "Half the time what the manager thought he was giving as instructions or decisions was being treated as information or advice."[6] The major conclusion to be drawn is that interpersonal communication is among the most central, yet least effective, activities of organizational life. Even relatively simple monocultural white male organizations echo too frequently to the refrain of communication failure: "But I thought I told you to —" followed by, "But I thought you said that —." All of this becomes more complicated when groups become more heterogeneous.

Academic research supports this view. Fred E. Fiedler found that culturally and linguistically heterogeneous groups experience greater tension and more communication difficulties on certain tasks than culturally homogeneous groups.[7] Ivan Steiner concluded that more heterogeneous work groups were associated with less effective inter-personal communication.[8]

The University of Michigan's authority on diversity, Taylor Cox, Jr., concluded: "There is reason to believe that the presence of cultural diversity does make certain aspects of group functioning more prob-lematic. Misunderstandings may increase, conflict and anxiety may rise, and members may feel less comfortable with membership in the group. These effects may combine to make decision making more difficult and time-consuming. In certain respects, then, culturally diverse workgroups are more difficult to manage effectively than culturally homogeneous workgroups."[9]

In our field interviews, white male and female, black, Hispanic, and Asian American managers repeatedly referred to feeling out of sync or finding it more difficult to work with a colleague from another demo-graphic group. Experienced as well as relatively new managers expressed the same problem.

An upper-level white woman executive said: "It seems to get worse, not better as I go up the ladder. With every promotion I get, intangibles like 'fit' become more important. But somehow I don't 'fit' with the men like the men 'fit' with each other. And every day the strain gets greater. I don't know what I'm going to do. I may just leave the company or even the corporate world." A young black executive shortly out of college told us: "I don't know about corporate life. I've got a big problem with this company. I've got to 'act white' inside these corporate walls. But the problem is, I don't know all of their rules, and they don't know all of mine. Result: there's a lot of tenseness. Older African Americans here say it gets easier with time. But it never goes away." A middle-aged, upper-level Hispanic female executive related:

It's exhausting for me to be with almost exclusively white males all day. Just exhausting. Oh, I've learned the "ropes." I've learned how to deal with all those white males. I was quiet a lot until I figured things out. I had to think about what to say, what not to say, how, and how not to act. The fact that they expected me to be polite and quiet helped get me through those first few years. It's easier now that there are more women at my level. But I still have to be careful that little things I say or do won't be misinterpreted and make some male manager to either be turned off or make a pass at me.

What these managers may not have realized is that culture could be a source of their difficulties.

CULTURE

Few managers realize the influence of culture on behavior. Like time or distance, culture is one of those concepts we all know but find difficult to put into words. On one level, cultures can be as palpably different as bagpipes or jazz, western business suits or Arab robes. Many of us have experienced the differences between cultures and know that having grown up in one culture or another has had a powerful impact on us. We just do not know how powerful. Let us examine some key aspects of culture as they apply to the workplace.

The Power of Culture

Ethnic studies pioneer Monica McGoldrick wrote: "Ethnicity patterns our thinking, feeling and behavior in both obvious and subtle ways. It plays a major role in determining what we eat, how we work, how we relax, how we celebrate holidays and rituals, and how we feel about life, death and illness."[10]

Sociologist and priest Andrew Greeley provides scholarly and personal resonance to these points.

Some of the research . . . indicates that Italians are much more likely to give free expression to feelings of pain than are Irish . . . that there is a great deal more fatalism . . . among Italians than there is among white Anglo-Saxon Protestants. Blacks insist that "soul" . . . is not to be found among most white ethnic groups. . . . At one time in my career I was required professionally to show up at an almost infinite number of weddings. My impressions, subject to confirmation or rejection by further research, were that Irish wedding receptions were marked by drinking (and eventually, frequently by singing); Polish receptions by endless dancing; Bohemian receptions by prodigious consumption of food; and Jewish receptions by much food and prodigious and interminable conversation.[11]

Culture's Impact on Perception

Psychologist James W. Bagby determined that culture may even determine what we see. In a cross-cultural experiment, Bagby exposed one eye of Mexican and American subjects to a Mexican scene (a Mexican peasant or a bullfight) while he, simultaneously, exposed the other eye to a U.S. scene (a U.S. businessman or baseball game). The results were striking. What the overwhelming majority of subjects reported seeing was determined by their culture: Mexicans saw the bullfight while Americans saw the baseball game. Bagby's conclusion: in 70 percent of the instances "national cultural differences appear critical in affecting perceptual predominance."[12]

Culture Means Multiple Socialization

Socialization is the process by which we learn how to become human in our cultural group. For example, identical new-born Vietnamese twins separated by the 1975 baby airlift to the United States just prior to the fall of Saigon would be very different human beings if they met at age 21 in 1996, one having grown up in Vietnam and the other in the United States. During the process of socialization we unconsciously internalize the synchronous "action chains" of bowing or shaking hands upon meeting or when to gaze at or away from a superior during conversation. According to Erik Erikson, this helps account for the "secret familiarity of identical psychological construction" that Freud saw as the core of ethnicity.[13] Socialization teaches us the unconscious synchrony of successful intracultural communication.

As part of a powerful, lifelong process, we Americans are socialized to share the overarching and common values of our nation. In addition, we also are socialized into varied subcultures of gender, ethnicity, social class, religion, and region (male, African American, middle class, Baptist, New England); general profession or business (computers or military, automobiles or insurance); more specific corporate or organizational culture (Digital Equipment Corporation or U.S. Navy, Ford Motor Company or John Hancock Insurance Company); very specific occupational culture (software developer or Navy Seal, Mustang product marketer or life insurance actuary).[14]

There is a culture unique to each one of these areas. In addition, organizational cultures can differ as much as a ponderous, bureaucratic, government agency or a fluid, entrepreneurial startup, high-tech firm.

Corporate subcultures can differ as much as the purchasing and the research departments of the same organization. These brief examples highlight the many sorts of socialization that can have an impact on even one individual and the many unique variations that any single individual may embody. Being American, male or female, of one or another race or ethnicity matters. This book is built on that assumption.

It is important to keep in mind that each one of us is a unique individual no matter what our culture or gender. We never will forget one roundtable discussion at a professional conference we attended. At the end of a long session dealing with race, the sole African American present spoke to her white colleagues. She said she had listened very attentively and quietly during the last 90 minutes to all that we had had to say about black culture in general. She had only one point to make to all of her friends there — "But I am more than that."

Culture as Shared Design

Culture is an invisible, shared design that unconsciously patterns the actions of people so that they can interact and achieve together.[15] This shared design or script establishes certain culturally-governed rules for interpersonal interaction — conscious or unconscious compliance with the rules brings approval and ignorance of the rules brings misunderstanding. Our daily lives are governed by shared, implicit, and unconscious expectations of behavior of ourselves and others of which we may be only dimly aware. How do we decide each morning what is appropriate to wear that day? What do we deem appropriate to eat or drink at a business luncheon?

In society at large, and especially in organizations, these culturally-governed rules for behavior script daily routines. Consequently, in their own society or organization members are able to perform the many and necessary seemingly individually-determined group actions in unison with others and without conscious thought. Without these unconscious and shared designs for action, effective organizations could not achieve the goals for which they exist and strive.

Culture is one of the great social inventions of mankind. It helps solve the problem of how we as a society or as an organization can achieve individual as well as group goals while living together and interacting. Culture is a pervasive, shared, and unwritten consensus that helps pattern and make predictable the lives of people who interact and achieve together. It determines what is acceptable behavior for working in that group by establishing certain rules or codes, conscious or unconscious obedience to which brings approval and violation of which brings punishment. Business has only recently discovered the power of culture.

THE DISCOVERY OF CORPORATE
CULTURE — NEW FRONTIERS

Only in the 1980s did business come to recognize culture as applicable to organizations and as a key to organizational performance. The term "corporate culture" did not enter the mainstream vocabulary of business executives and scholars until 1979.[16] Two developments made corporate culture a business buzzword. First, Tom Peters and Robert Waterman's 1983 bestseller, *In Search of Excellence*, drove home the point that a strong corporate culture is crucial to the long-term success of any outstanding organization.[17] Second, U.S. business attempted to understand the global success of Japanese companies during the 1980s.[18] Since then, corporate culture has been viewed as a powerful factor in determining business performance. Perhaps, the increasing diversity of the workplace necessitates a reconceptualization of corporate culture. Let us look at this notion from two positions.

In their classic study, *Corporate Culture and Performance*, Harvard Business School professors John Kotter and James Heskett characterize today's orthodox view of corporate culture.

Once established, organizational cultures often perpetuate themselves in a number of ways. Potential group members may be screened out according to how well their values and behavior fit in. Newly selected members may be explicitly taught the group's style. Historical stories or legends may be told again and again to remind everyone of the group's values and what they mean. Managers may explicitly try to act in ways that exemplify the culture and its ideals. Senior members of the group may communicate key values over and over in their daily conversations or through special rituals and ceremonies. People who successfully achieve the ideals inherent in the culture may be recognized and made the heroes. The natural process of identification may encourage younger members to take on the values and styles of their mentors. *Perhaps most fundamental, people who follow cultural norms will be rewarded but those who do not will be penalized*[19] (emphasis added).

However, corporate culture can be seen and experienced from a very different position. From his position as an African American executive, Edward W. Jones, Jr., attributed an entirely different meaning to corporate culture. He wrote:

One of the phenomena that develops in every corporation is a set of behavioral and personal norms that facilitates communication and aids cohesiveness. Moreover, because this "informal organization" is built on white norms, it can reinforce the black-white differences just mentioned and thus reject or destroy all but the most persistent blacks. The informal organization operates at all levels in a corporation and the norms become more rigid the higher one goes in the hierarchy. While this phenomenon promotes efficiency and unity, it is also restrictive and very selective. It can preclude promotion or lead to failure on the basis of "fit" rather than competence.[20]

In these passages, different meanings were drawn from the same reality. What do these different meanings suggest for the future focus of corporate culture? Yesterday the focus was on the organization's culture within the workplace while tomorrow the focus will be on the diverse and antecedent cultures that employees bring to the workplace. Yesterday the focus of corporate culture was on common corporate cultural values, and tomorrow the focus will be on differing cultural values and behaviors that employees use in face-to-face communication. One executive succinctly stated yesterday's view of corporate culture when he called it: "The way we do things around here."[21] Edward Jones might respond (and the executive concur) that the way we do things might have to change. A change in focus would not necessarily mean excluding one view in favor of the other but, rather, supplementing the existing focus of corporate culture with an overlayer that strengthens both. Change is strengthened by continuity. This means, for example, paying attention to the vital, face-to-face, managerial interaction where culturally different communication styles converge.

CULTURAL INFLUENCES ON
FACE-TO-FACE COMMUNICATION

Culture was not an issue in the American work force as long as it was largely white male, especially toward the top of the organizational pyramid. However, culture has become more of an issue as work groups have become more diverse. Research demonstrates that differences exist between the communication styles of demographic groups.

In conversations with individuals from other groups, some Asian Americans have been found to be more verbally reserved and inhibited.[22] Some blacks reverse the gaze sequence of whites — white listeners tend to look at speakers who are making their points while blacks tend to look away. A white colleague might say that his black colleague is untrustworthy because he never looks him in the eye, whereas a black may interpret such eye contact as an attempt to intimidate.[23]

Leading scholars of intercultural communication Rosita Albert and Harry Triandis recognized the impact of culture when they wrote: "In many countries, the population is polyethnic. This is the case in the United States, where a number of distinct groups (i.e. blacks . . . Latin Americans, to mention just a few) enjoy cultural traditions that are different from the traditions of the white, Anglo-Saxon or melting-pot-produced majority. . . . Such . . . cultures lead members of a cultural or ethnic group to behave in characteristic ways and to perceive their own behavior and the behavior of others in a particular manner."[24]

Edward Hall, perhaps the most famous living U.S. anthropologist, was even more explicit about how culture can cause misunderstanding, especially in an area as subtle as nonverbal behavior:

Humans are tied to each other by hierarchies of rhythms that are *culture-specific* and expressed through language and body movement. . . . Several years ago when my students and I were working with blacks under controlled conditions, we uncovered great differences in the kinesic and proxemic, linguistic and other behavior patterns between working-class blacks and a wide range of whites (working-class to upper middle class). *Such unconscious differences may well be one of the sources of what blacks feel is the basic racism of white society.* . . . Whites do not move the way working class blacks do or the way Puerto Ricans move or Mexicans or Pueblo or Navajo Indians, Chinese or Japanese. Each culture has its own characteristic manner of locomotion, sitting, standing, reclining and gesturing[25] (emphasis added).

Culture also has an impact on the communication styles of the genders. Consider the conclusion of Deborah Tannen:

Much as I understand and am in sympathy with those who wish there were no differences between women and men — only reparable social justice — my research, others' research and my own and others' experience tell me it simply isn't so. There are gender differences in ways of speaking, and we need to identify and understand them. Without such understanding, we are doomed to blame others or ourselves — or the relationship — for the otherwise mystifying and damaging effects of our contrasting conversational styles. . . . This book shows that many frictions arise because *boys and girls grow up in what are essentially different cultures, so talk between women and men is cross-cultural communication*[26] (emphasis added).

Astute managers of both genders and every ethnicity are coming to realize that they need to learn more about each other's cultural values and communication styles.

CULTURAL PARADIGMS

Cultural paradigms combine the cultural values and communication styles of white males, white females, African Americans, Hispanics, and Asian Americans. Henceforth, the terms "cultural paradigm" and "communication paradigm" will be used interchangeably. By cultural paradigms we mean the subconscious, shared values and behaviors that guide our daily interactions with others.[27] We usually are unaware of the unwritten values and rules that determine our behavior. Common action with those who share our cultural paradigm is seemingly natural and comfortable until we encounter another individual who acts on the basis of a different cultural paradigm and who violates or deviates from what we call natural behavior in a face-to-face interaction. It is then that our own cultural paradigm springs into consciousness and common action becomes conscious, strained, and uncomfortable — as Mike and Miguel discovered. Each cultural paradigm encompasses a full panoply of values and behaviors (rules) for face-to-face communication.

We will explore the values of each major demographic group in the U.S. work force in later chapters. There are two channels for face-to-face communication — verbal language and nonverbal (body) language. "Body language" encompasses such nonverbal ways of communicating as facial expressions and gaze behavior, body movements (what anthropologists call kinesics), spatial proximity (proxemics), and vocal tones and rhythms (paralanguage) — all subconsciously and complexly synchronized and all differing from one culture or subculture to another.

Perhaps one can better understand cultural paradigm after reading the following excerpt from Joel Arthur Barker.

One of the stories . . . told of how the author would run a little experiment when she was talking to corporate audiences that were mixed — including white men, women, and minorities. She would ask the audience to do a simple task: "Please list," she would request, "the rules needed to be successful in a white male society."

Immediately the women and the minorities would begin to write down all the things they had to do to "fit in." Meanwhile, the white males in the audience just sat there, doing nothing, looking around at the women and the minorities writing for all they were worth. After about two minutes, the author said, the discomfort of the white males began to rise to such a level that sometimes she would have to stop the exercise just to keep them from panicking. Paradigms are like water to fish. They are invisible in many situations because it is "just the way we do things." Often they operate at an unconscious level. Yet they determine, to a large extent, our behavior. As a white male, I cannot write down all those rules. My wife can. My minority friends can.[28]

One of the purposes of this book is to help all Americans in the workplace understand the values and rules for more effectively communicating with each other. Each cultural paradigm will be discussed in succeeding chapters.

Table 2.1 lists some of the chief values and behaviors that are characteristic of different cultural paradigms in the workplace, contrasted with the dominant white male paradigm.

TABLE 2.1
Values and Behaviors of Five American Cultural Paradigms

Paradigm	Values	Behaviors
White women	Connectedness	Maintain more eye contact in conversation; stand/sit closer together
White males	Hyperindividualism	Maintain less eye contact in conversation; stand/sit farther apart
Blacks	Community	Look at another when talking/away from another when listening
White males	Hyperindividualism	Look away from another when talking/at another when listening
Hispanics	Personal relationships	Prefer to establish relationship before doing business
White males	Hyperindividualism	Prefer to "get right down to business"; relationship (if any) only after doing business
Asian Americans	Hierarchy	Ambiguous, subtle interpersonal communication; more meaning derived from body language than words. Value indirectness.
White males	Hyperindividualism	Words "mean what they say"; most meaning comes from words themselves; little from nonverbals. Value directness.

The U.S. work force increasingly will be comprised of individuals with differing cultural paradigms who will have not only their own unique styles of interaction and modes of communication but also their unique frames of reference and their own perspectives on reality.

ISION OF CATEGORIES:
ACE, AND CULTURE

y have noticed a somewhat varied use of central terms, race, and culture. In part, this is because of the inherent h categories. For example, in 1980 the editors of the

Harvard Encyclopedia of American Ethnic Groups pointed out that, while they listed American Indians as one ethnic category, there could have been 170 separate tribal entries.[29]

The fact that American Indians of the 1980s are today's Native Americans brings out another point: the continuous interplay of the names by which racial or ethnic groups are known. Early in the twentieth century when the National Association for the Advancement of Colored People was established, colored was the preferred term by which individuals from this group wished to be known. Since then, colored has been supplanted by negro, Negro, Afro-American, black, Black, African-American, and, now, African American. The same interplay has been true for many other ethnic groups. Within this rich and variegated human community, different individuals prefer different appellations.[30]

We usually use U.S. Bureau of the Census terms for racial and ethnic groups — white, black, Hispanic, and Asian American. We use other terms for these groups for literary variation. Therefore, we might substitute African American for black, or Latino for Hispanic. We also use additional terms for greater precision — Mexican American or Puerto Rican, Chinese American or Japanese American. We have not addressed Native Americans or Pacific Islanders in this book because of their small numbers in the work force and this book's space limitations.

The words "ethnicity," "race," and "culture" demand treatment, not in the sense of definitive scholarly definition but in the sense of the operational way in which we use these concepts. We wish to be as precise and consistent as we can in our own use of these terms, while recognizing their inherent imprecision and inconsistency.

Ethnicity

In everyday terms ethnic or ethnicity usually refers to white cultural groups — the Catholic Irish as well as the Italians, Greeks, Slavs, Jews, and others whose ancestors came to these shores from southern or eastern Europe from the 1840s to the 1920s. These are the groups that traditionally have been termed the "ethnics" of America. In the past, blacks, Hispanics, and Asian Americans have not been called ethnics. Likewise, the long-time dominant white, Anglo-Saxon, Protestants, those whose ancestors generally came earliest and from the British Isles, Scandinavia, and Germany, are not called ethnics.

However, we feel that all Americans have ethnicities. That is why we refer to every group as ethnic including African Americans, Hispanic Americans, Asian Americans, and white, Anglo-Saxon, Protestants. Our reasons are simple and pragmatic. All these groups possess ethnicities. Further, we opt to follow the convention demonstrated by the editors of the *Harvard Encyclopedia of American Ethnic Groups* who, confronted with the same dilemma, demonstrated consistency in the title of their publication.

Race

Race denotes individuals who share color. Not (as one of our good friends might suggest) in the nineteenth-century sense of the "Irish race."

Culture

The last term is "culture." We feel that each and every ethnic group possesses a culture — a unique set of shared values and patterned behaviors. In certain general ways, Italian Americans are different from African Americans, and Mexican Americans are different from Japanese Americans. However, they also share similarities. Every ethnic group shares in an overarching American culture such that each ethnic group is a subculture of a larger U.S. culture. The African American who travels to Africa learns the same lessons as the Irish American who travels to Ireland. To the natives, he is not the African American or the Irish American, but simply the American. By values, behavior, and culture, he is different from today's Irishman or African. One African American Peace Corps volunteer was surprised to be called *oyimbo* (white man) by the Sierra Leonese because of his U.S. verbal and nonverbal behaviors.[31] Cynthia Greggs Fleming reports an African American recalling his 1964 tour of West Africa with other Student Nonviolent Coordinating Committee staff: "That's when I found out how American I was and that 's when I found that I was at that time much closer to Bill Hanson, who was a white fella from Arkansas. . . . I was much closer to him than anybody, any of the Africans."[32]

We refer to the cultural paradigm, communication paradigm, or culture of each of the demographic groups we treat — white males, white females, blacks, Hispanics, and Asian Americans — for reasons of literary economy and their inherent conceptual imprecision. Each time we do so we mean subculture in the American context. We think it important that we state this point clearly and early because of the widespread use of the term "multiculturalism." We do not know the precise definition of multiculturalism. If it means the inclusion in our history books and school books of all Americans who contributed to our heritage, we agree with it. If it means a truly inclusive and meritocratic system in which each person can rise on the basis of his or her own hard work and merit, we support it. If it means recognizing and appreciating the richness that the many ethnicities contribute to this country, we endorse it.

However, the multiculturalism that sees the United States as a "quilt country," that emphasizes separate, subsidiary cultures at the expense of an overarching common American culture, can cause grave problems. Lebanon and what was called Yugoslavia are tragic proofs. We all should remember that during the 1984 Winter Olympics the host city of Sarajevo was described as a model of multiculturalism. Sarajevo was under siege and wracked by ethnic hatred and savagery during the writing of this book.

It is no more possible for organizations than for nations to build strong cultures by emphasizing only differences. Strong cultures respect differences while building on commonalities. The rationale undergirding our approach is to acknowledge the differences that complicate communication while stressing the similarities that join us. We hope this endeavor and the suggested techniques help build those commonalities by bridging differences to reach the common ground where we become individuals to each other.

SHOUTING AND WHISPERING: OUR NEED TO TALK RATIONALLY

> Racial discussions tend to be conducted at one of two levels — either in shouts or in whispers. The shouters are generally so twisted by pain or ignorance that spectators tune them out. The whisperers are so afraid of the sting of truth that they avoid saying much of anything at all.
>
> — Ellis Cose[33]

Cose, a high-powered black journalist, is tragically correct. Communication between racial, gender, and ethnic groups does tend to oscillate between the extremes of those who shout and those who whisper. The human tragedy is that both extremes of communication simply perpetuate or replace one stereotype with another: "Whites are —" "Women want —" "Blacks are—" "Hispanics want —" "Asian Americans are —" are too easily conveyed by shouts or whispers.

We do not wish to shout or whisper. We wish to talk. We wish to converse. We believe that it is time to take another road. In view of the demographic changes sketched in Chapter 1, it is time to literally, matter-of-factly, and rationally begin to talk and converse about racial, gender, cultural, and ethnic differences and similarities, especially in the workplace. However, there is a problem — the difficulty and even the toxicity of discussing diversity issues.

GENDER, RACE, ETHNICITY, AND CULTURE: TOXIC TOPICS

Few topics are more toxic than those that this book addresses — gender, race, ethnicity, and culture. Few areas are more open to pride or denial, assertion or accusation. Gender, race, ethnicity, and culture provide profoundly conscious as well as subconscious needs for personal identity, a larger group membership, and connection with a temporal tradition that extends both before and after one's own existence.[34] Indeed, speaking of ethnicity, Irving Levine states: "Ethnicity can be equated along with sex and death as a subject that touches off deep unconscious feelings in most people."[35] The difficulty of addressing these topics was captured by the cover of a professional journal that read: "Multiculturalism: Has It Got Us All Walking on Eggshells?"[36] Additionally, there is the fear of being labelled sexist or racist for merely suggesting that different subcultures exist and that certain groups of people tend to act differently because of them.

Could such topics place managers in a double-bind whereby they are either passively managed by cultural diversity because it cannot be discussed or begin to actively manage cultural diversity by openly discussing and acquiring the skills to deal with it?[37] Most important, it is time for all of us to talk rationally and collaboratively.

CONCLUSION

In this chapter we examined the role that culture plays in our lives, in our organizations, and, specifically, in our workplaces. Our intention was to highlight the importance of culture as a force that we need to reckon with. Culture is part of us, and we are part of culture. It is important that we acknowledge its presence and influence.

But then we need to transcend culture by finding a common process through which we can learn how to lead common lives together. Transcending culture is particularly difficult but especially important in the workplace where we find the impersonality of the office, on the one hand, and the near-intimacy of family, on the other. Our only avenue is conversation. The more we converse, the more we come to know each other and, thus, begin to dissolve the myths and stereotypes that separate us. Only then can a common order of talk begin to emerge. Only then can we become maximally functioning individuals in our workplaces and society. America's mix of cultures brings brilliance to our lives. We face an important choice: living life in vivid color or choosing a monochromatic version of it.

NOTES

1. John Shotter. (1993). *Conversational realities: Constructing life through language* (p. 4). London: Sage.

2. Danielle J. Dolin, & Melanie Booth-Butterfield. (1993, Fall). Reach out and touch someone: Analysis of nonverbal comforting responses. *Communication Quarterly, 47*(4), pp. 383–393.

3. Michael Burgoon, Frank G. Hunsaker, & Edwin Dawson. (1994). *Human communication,* 3rd ed., (pp. 49–50). Thousand Oaks: Sage.

4. Chester Barnard. (1938). *The functions of an executive* (p. 224). Cambridge, MA: Harvard University Press.

5. Henry Mintzberg. (1973). *The nature of managerial work* (p. 38). New York: Harper & Row.

6. Tom Burns. (1954, February). The directions of activity and communication in a departmental executive group. *Human Relations, 7*(1), p. 94.

7. Fred E. Fiedler. (1966). The effect of leadership and cultural heterogeneity on group performance: A test of the contingency model. *Journal of Experimental Social Psychology, 2,* pp. 237–264.

8. Ivan D. Steiner. (1972). *Group process and productivity* (pp. 105–130). New York: Academic Press.

9. Taylor Cox, Jr. (1993). *Cultural diversity in organizations: Theory, research & practice* (p. 39). San Francisco: Berrett-Koehler Publishers.

10. Monica McGoldrick. (1982). Ethnicity and family therapy. In Monica McGoldrick, John K. Pearce, & Joseph Giordano (Eds.), *Ethnicity and family therapy* (p. 4). New York: Guilford Press.

11. Andrew M. Greeley. (1971). *Why can't they be like us? America's white ethnic groups* (pp. 48–50). New York: E. P. Dutton.

12. James W. Bagby. (1957). A cross-cultural study of perceptual dominance in binocular rivalry. *Journal of Abnormal and Social Psychology, 54–55*(1–3), pp. 331–334.

13. Erik Erikson. (1963). *Childhood and society,* 2d ed., (p. 281). New York: W. W. Norton.

14. Daniel Charles Feldman. (1981). The multiple socialization of organization members. *Academy of Management Review, 6*(2), pp. 309–318. See also the interesting study of Peter A. Andersen, Myron W. Lustig, & Janis F. Andersen. (1987, June). Regional patterns of communication in the United States: A theoretical perspective. *Communication Monographs, 54,* pp. 128–143.

15. Clyde Kluckhohn. (1951). The study of culture. In Daniel Lerner & Harold D. Lasswell (Eds.), *The policy sciences: Recent developments in scope and method* (p. 85–88). Stanford, CA: Stanford University Press.

16. Andrew M. Pettigrew. (1979, December). On studying organizational cultures. *Administrative Science Quarterly, 24*(24), pp. 570–581.

17. Thomas J. Peters, & Robert H. Waterman, Jr. (1982). *In search of excellence: Lessons from America's best-run companies.* New York: Harper & Row.

18. Richard Tanner Pascale, & Anthony G. Athos. (1981). *The art of Japanese management: Applications for American executives.* New York: Warner Books.

19. John Kotter, & James Heskett. (1992). *Corporate culture and performance* (p. 7). New York: Free Press.

30   Reflexive Communication in the Culturally Diverse Workplace

20.   Edward W. Jones, Jr. (1973, July–August). What it's like to be a black manager. *Harvard Business Review*, p. 114.
21.   Terrence E. Deal, & Allen A. Kennedy. (1982). *Corporate cultures: The rites and rituals of corporate life* (p. 59). Reading: Addison-Wesley.
22.   James Morishima. (1981). Special employment issues for Asian Americans. *Public Personnel Management Journal, 10*, pp. 387–389; Colin Watanabe. (1973, February). Self-expression and the Asian-American experience. *Personnel and Guidance Journal, 51*(6), pp. 390–396.
23.   Marianne LaFrance, & Clara Mayo. (1976). Racial differences in gaze behavior during conversations: Two systematic observational studies. *Journal of Personality and Social Psychology, 33*(5), pp. 547–552.
24.   Rosita D. Albert, & Harry C. Triandis. (1985). Intercultural education for multicultural societies: Critical issues. *International Journal of Intercultural Relations, 9*, p. 320.
25.   Edward T. Hall. (1977). *Beyond culture* (pp. 74–75). Garden City: Anchor Press/Doubleday.
26.   Deborah Tannen. (1990). *You just don't understand: Men and women in conversation* (pp. 17–18). New York: William Morrow.
27.   Thomas Kuhn. (1970). *The structure of scientific revolutions*, 2d ed. Chicago: University of Chicago Press; Edward T. Hall, & Mildred Reed Hall. (1990). *Understanding cultural differences* (pp. 3–4). Yarmouth, ME: Intercultural Press, point out that "culture is communication."
28.   Joel Arthur Barker. (1992). *Future edge: Discovering the new paradigms of success* (pp. 124–125). New York: William Morrow.
29.   Stephen Thernstrom, Ann Orlov, & Oscar Handlin. (1980). Introduction. In Stephen Thernstrom, Ann Orlov, & Oscar Handlin (Eds.), *The Harvard encyclopedia of American ethnic groups* (p. vi). Cambridge, MA: Belknap Press.
30.   Ibid., pp. v–ix.
31.   Ian F. Hancock. (1974, Spring/Fall). Identity, equality and standard language. *The Florida FL Reporter*, p. 104.
32.   Cynthia Greggs Fleming. (1992). African-Americans. In John D. Buenker & Lorman A. Ratner (Eds.), *Multiculturalism in the United States: A complete guide to acculturation and ethnicity*, (p. 22). Westport, CT: Greenwood Press.
33.   Ellis Cose. (1993). *The rage of a privileged class: Why are middle-class blacks so angry? Why should America care?* (p. 9). New York: HarperCollins Publishers.
34.   Harold Isaacs. (1975). *Idols of the tribe: Group identity and political change.* New York: Harper & Row.
35.   Irving Levine, personal correspondence to Monica McGoldrick in McGoldrick, Ethnicity and family therapy, p. 4.
36.   Cover. (1994, August). *Family Therapy Networker, 18*(4).
37.   Nancy J. Adler. (1986). *International dimensions of organizational behavior* (pp. 77–78). Boston: Kent Publishing.

3

Reflexive Communication

Nothing that God ever made is the same thing to more than one person. That is natural. There is no single face in nature, because every eye that looks upon it, sees it from its own angle. So every man's spice box seasons his own food.

— Zora Neale Hurston[1]

The passage emphasizes fundamental principles of anthropological theory — people are products of their culture, culture creates different angles of vision, and the anthropologist studies, compares, and interprets those visions.

— Robert E. Hemenway[2]

In Chapter 2 we met Mike and Miguel as they ended their meeting unable to transact business. Their basic problem was misinterpreting each other's behavior because neither realized or understood the other's cultural paradigm. As America's demographics and workplaces change, many more misunderstandings and communication failures are likely to occur among not only many more Mikes and Miguels — the white males and Hispanics of the workplace — but also among white women, African Americans, Hispanics, and Asian Americans, the diverse array of Americans who will increasingly make up our nation. How can Mike, Miguel, and the rest of us communicate more effectively with one another?

The first and conventional response is the cultural awareness approach: Mike and Miguel need to know more about each other's culture to communicate better. The cultural paradigm embodies the principles of the cultural awareness approach. Certainly the richness of America's ethnicities should be acknowledged and valued. However, this approach only takes the first step in the journey toward better communication in an increasingly diverse workplace.

Knowledge of each other's culture is a necessary, but insufficient, first step toward effective face-to-face communication. If we value cultural differences, we should value individual differences.

VALUING CULTURAL AND INDIVIDUAL DIFFERENCES

The cultural awareness approach may heighten knowledge of cultures. It also can raise the toxic level of diversity issues, reinforce cultural stereotyping, or deny the uniqueness of the individual. Some experiences with diversity training indicate that it may raise toxic issues, which can make interpersonal communication more difficult. Frederick Lynch reported: "Diversity workshops may impart cultural sensitivity, but they can also generate alienation or bitter, lasting divisions."[3]

When we look at individuals solely through the lens of culture, we see only the patterns that are common to that culture. Dealing with culture alone logically can lead us to generalize by saying: "Whites are —," "Blacks are —," "Latinos are —," "Asian Americans are —," which simply is not true. Even brief contact with individuals from any of these cultures indicates just how different each one of us is. Culture alone does not explain the different values and behaviors of a Harold E. Doley, Jr., first African American to buy a seat on the New York Stock Exchange, or a Jay Rockefeller, white, Anglo-Saxon Protestant senator from West Virginia.

Culture provides us with the vista — the broad context — from which individuals have come. However, culture alone does not necessarily reflect each individual's uniqueness. While culture provides the context, it does not account for an individual's behavior. Each of us also embodies the sum of our gender, education, social class, occupation, region, and religious experiences and identities as well as our unique set of personal life experiences. We also should take into account such mediating factors as the length of time one needs to become acculturated into American society or to be socialized into the cultures of U.S. workplaces. The totality and interplay of all of these factors accounts for an individual's values and comportment. These factors can lead individuals to see the world differently.

Mike, Miguel, and all of us need to break through our general cultural misperceptions and stereotypes. Only then can we access each other as individuals. We can access each other only by engaging in dialogues that allow individuals to talk about what constitutes their realities and, then, to share perceptions, feelings, and meanings about the way each one of us perceives a situation and makes sense of it.

One could ask Mike and Miguel how relevant this understanding is to their business transaction. The response is, surprisingly, quite relevant. In their earlier interchange, Mike and Miguel were mutually typifying each other. Neither one was talking to the other as a person. Each was making an effort to do so but somehow completely missed the connection with the other. What was real to Mike, the mainstream "Anglo" businessman, was not real to Miguel, the Hispanic businessman. In fact, without the awareness of Mike or Miguel, two cultures were talking to each other, not two individuals.

Characteristically, their initial face-to-face interaction was reciprocally unsatisfying and frustrating. Mike acted in accordance with his business creed of impersonal efficiency by getting right down to business before relaxing and getting to know Miguel. On the other hand, Miguel attempted to initiate a trusting relationship that, according to his culture, is a prerequisite to actually doing business. Mike felt frustrated that Miguel was encroaching on his personal life, rather than staying with what Mike's culture dictated as the business reason for their meeting — discussing his proposal. Reciprocally, Miguel felt frustrated that Mike, the typical "cold Anglo" would not allow the precondition to be established that Miguel's culture required as necessary to their doing business — establishing a trusting relationship.

Sadly, Mike and Miguel parted anonymous strangers. Their knowledge of each other will remain mutually incomprehensible unless they can find a way to access each other's culturally-conditioned, but individually-developed view of the world. The only antidote to stereotyping and discrimination is to know each other as individuals.

In one sense, Mike and Miguel's problem is cross-cultural. As Americans, they share a common culture. However, communicating from different subcultural paradigms (in this case, Hispanic and white male) still led to their failure to do business. Neither one understood the other's cultural paradigm, and neither one came close to knowing the other as an individual.

ACCESSING THE INDIVIDUAL
IN THE CULTURAL CONTEXT

How can Mike and Miguel transcend their difficulties? Communication theorist Allen Ivey has proposed three models that operate when one communicates in a culturally diverse context (Figure 3.1). These communication models depict not only the individuals who are communicating but also their cultural paradigms. Model A results in the most effective communication.[4]

FIGURE 3.1
Not Two People, but Four "Participants" — Ivey Model

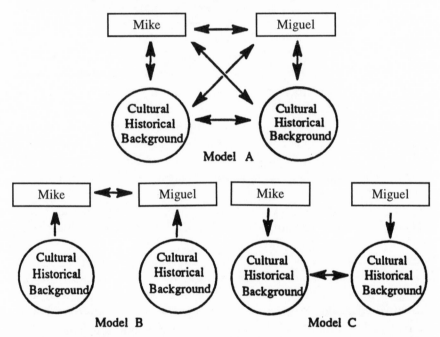

Source: Adapted from Allen E. Ivey, Mary Bradford Ivey, & Lynn Simek-Downing. (1987). *Counseling and psychotherapy: Integrating skills, theory and practice*, 2d ed., (pp. 94–97). Englewood Cliffs, NJ: Prentice Hall. Copyright © 1987 by Allyn and Bacon. Adapted by permission.

Model A presents the interaction most likely to lead to effective communication in a setting of diversity. In Model A, Mike and Miguel are aware of each other's general cultural paradigms as well as their own. They also can access each other's unique individuality for fuller understanding. In this model, Mike and Miguel can come to know one another as unique individuals each conditioned by his different cultural paradigms.

Model B presents two conversants communicating with each other as individuals, mutually unaware of each other's cultural historical backgrounds. To seek to communicate with everyone as an individual Model B may be admirable but also minimizes, if not ignores, the powerful impact of culture and history on an individual. Only limited understanding is possible because neither party can fully comprehend the essence of the message when the cultural context is missing. This was the fate of Mike and Miguel. Had they been aware of each other's cultural paradigm, they might have bypassed some of the cultural impediments to their business interaction.

Model C presents two cultural paradigms communicating with each other to the exclusion of the individuals involved. In such a situation, stereotyping is more likely to occur because of the inability to mutually access each other's individuality.

It is one thing to propose a model for more effective communication in the diverse workplace and quite another to provide the actual steps and procedures to accomplish it. Mike and Miguel can communicate more effectively only when each can begin to understand the other's perspective. This will occur only when each can begin to access the other's general cultural paradigm as well as specific individuality.

How can Mike and Miguel merge their culturally and individually differing views of the world to construct a mutual reality? We propose an approach that we call "reflexive communication for constructing mutual realities."

REFLEXIVE COMMUNICATION FOR
CONSTRUCTING MUTUAL REALITIES

Constructionism holds that the beliefs and meanings we develop about the world are socially constructed through ongoing communication.[5]

Reflexive communication assumes that different individuals have different views of the same reality and, therefore, derive different meanings from the same situation.[6] Mutual understanding of any single situation can only result from construction of a convergent view of that situation. Therefore, the actual process of communication — conversation itself — becomes important. Conversation using the process of reflexive communication helps individuals realize the multiple views and meanings that they have of any single situation.

Reflexive communication may be envisioned as a figure eight that reflects and folds back upon itself bringing more information to each conversant.[7] Reflexive communication is an active process that is particularly useful in understanding persons who come from different cultural contexts. Among individuals in an increasingly diverse society, there may be more than one understanding, more than one meaning of a single reality. Individuals who come from different cultural paradigms or different hierarchical positions may perceive the same situation differently and draw different meanings from it.

Tom's curiosity about reflexive communication is responded to in this conversation:

TOM: What's this new bit about reflexive communication in the workplace? What's so different about it?

TANYA: Well you see Tom, what makes this approach different is that the two people involved establish a better mutual understanding of a situation or a problem through conversation.

TOM: What do you mean? If I understand a problem, it's a matter of explaining it clearly.

TANYA: I daresay it's more than that. Communication is not a one-way street, but a two-way street. Reflexive communication assumes that. It also assumes that no two individuals see a situation the same way. If I really want my employees to work with me on a situation, I need their input. But they also need mine. I believe that only through our ongoing conversations can we bring our different perspectives together.

TOM: Well, I'm old-fashioned. The responsibility rests with me. I know the how to. After all, I've been managing for years. Are you telling me that a newcomer can tell me how to do things?

TANYA: Not exactly. To find the best solution, we need the greatest number of perspectives. To do that you need to be able to see it the way I do. And I need to understand where you're coming from. In fact, the more we talk about it, the clearer the situation becomes to both of us. And the better the outcome of our work will be.

TOM: Well, O.K. But how about another situation? How about when I'm having a conversation with a person who is culturally or ethnically different from me? Can we ever share in any perspectives then? Isn't that too much of a reach?

TANYA: Exactly! Talking is the forum where our divergent notions begin to crystallize into something that will become more similar than different. Only through reflexive communication that is open, accepting, and respectful of each other can we begin to work together to develop common perspectives and, thus, transcend those paralyzing stereotypes.

TOM: Fine, but how do we do that?

TANYA: First, you have to familiarize yourself with the process of reflexive communication. This means coming to understand, first, the premises for constructing common realities; second, the general stances you need to adopt; and third, the specific skills.

There are three components to this process of reflexive communication: premises, general stances, and microskills. The premises and general stances are discussed in this chapter. The microskills are discussed in Chapter 4.

Premises

The four premises for constructing mutual realities follow. These premises and their corollaries provide the basis for reflexive communication.

Premise 1

PREMISE: Reality always is viewed from a position or background; as one's position changes, so does one's view of reality.

COROLLARY: Reality always is viewed from a position that is the nexus into which flow the general cultural paradigm and the individual-specific experiences that comprise that person at that point in time.

Mike and Miguel each viewed their meeting quite differently because their respective cultural paradigms and individual experiences were different. Because each viewed the situation differently, he was unable to establish the common ground for understanding and conducting business with the other. What each saw and responded to was quite different.

Premise 2

PREMISE: Mutual understanding of reality becomes progressively clearer with the exchange of different perspectives.

COROLLARY: We come to know human and organizational realities through conversations with each other.

In the following performance appraisal interview, Jane's boss is criticizing her management style.

JAKE: While you work very hard and seem to have a smoothly running team, you let your people get away with murder.

JANE: Please tell me how you see that.

JAKE: One example. You have such relaxed rules that I can't remember the last time I saw all of your team at work at the same time. It goes way beyond flextime.

JANE: When someone is not there I always know the reason. It is always a valid one.

JAKE: What do you mean valid?

JANE: For example, Simon was off for two days last week to help his wife with their new baby.

JAKE: You give staff time off for that? I've never heard of it. I wouldn't do that.

JANE: As a woman, I understand how important it is for both Simon and his wife to be together as they make the transition to parenthood. Moreover, when he came back to work, Simon was a very relaxed and focused employee. I believe that this has a positive impact on employee productivity and helps us keep good people, don't you?

JAKE: You know Jane, I never saw the situation from that perspective. You may have a point. You seem to have a different take on this. Let's talk more.

This short vignette makes it evident that understanding the reality of a situation becomes clearer as differing views are exchanged. We recognize that such productive dialogues do not always occur. The only way that individuals can work through their differences is through conversations that allow for the mutually free expression of perspectives.

In this short dialogue, Jake was better able to understand Jane's values, thoughts, and meaning behind her actions. Consequently, Jake did not typify Jane as a soft-hearted woman but as an astute manager. Similarly, Jane came to realize that Jake was not an inflexible, hard-nosed, closed-minded boss.

Premise 3

PREMISE: Separate, uncommunicated realities divide us.

COROLLARY: Co-created realities that are shared provide a common understanding and a common reality so that common vision, purpose, and action can evolve.

Jake and Jane each viewed the situation differently. Therefore, their realities were separate and distinct. Only through the give-and-take of face-to-face conversation were they able to make their perspectives available to each other. Only through a mutual process of continuous interchange, modification, and clarification of subjective meanings could they generate a common reality, thereby establishing common understanding.

Premise 4

PREMISE: Reflexive communication is a process-focused approach.

COROLLARY: This process of communication brings about the folding back of different views, meanings, and positions so that they eventually overlap and begin to converge.

Many managers are solution-focused and inclined to solve problems rather than discuss them. They often walk into a meeting, voice the problem, and immediately move the group to solve it. Premise 4 may seem to run against the grain of most managers' mode of operation.

Reflexive communication focuses more on the process of communication than on the result of communication and generates more expressions of multiple views and understandings of a problem than a solution-focused approach. Reflexive communication triggers new ideas, which, in turn, evoke multiple perspectives for looking at a problem. These perspectives generate multiple ideas for the construction of possible solutions. This premise emphasizes the use of reflexive questions, which evokes different meanings about a situation and is likely to generate new ways of thinking and acting.[8] Such an approach involves the difference between asking "This is how I see the situation. Do you agree?" and "From your position, how would you see this situation developing?"

General Stances

Three general stances facilitate reflexive communication: not-knowing, curious, and collaborative. They provide a way for individuals to explore, express, and share the views and meanings of situations that, otherwise, can drive them apart. Let us examine each in turn.

Not-knowing Stance

This stance involves taking the nonexpert position of not knowing.[9] Taking this stance encourages communication by levelling the hierarchies of position and knowledge. While hierarchies exist in all organizations, emphasizing them discourages communication; deemphasizing them encourages conversation. Reflexive communication emphasizes equal participation rather than hierarchical power, thereby bringing about a shift from hierarchy to collaboration.

Most communication is characterized by content and relationship aspects. We all are aware of the content aspect of communication — the information that a message is intended to convey. We may be less conscious of the relationship aspect of communication — the relationship between sender and receiver that imposes behavior and delineates the hierarchy among communicants. For example, the question Do you think the report might be ready by tomorrow? conveys a different connotation if made by a superior than by a subordinate. It may be received as a command by the former or a request by the latter. In either case, the relationship aspect determines an expectation of behavior.[10] The egalitarian ethic of reflexive communication eliminates the positions of hierarchy and power in the communication process.

A not-knowing stance conveys the message that everyone is equally qualified to generate ideas, opinions, and perspectives about a situation or a problem. This means that the manager enters into the dialogue without any preconceived notions or ideas. The not-knowing stance also encourages listeners to attend to both the "outer" conversation of others as well as to their own "inner" conversation. The outer conversation is what others in the group are saying. The inner conversation consists of one's own thoughts and ideas that are triggered by the interactions. And to articulate them. This egalitarian approach encourages each participant to contribute to the mutual exploration of ideas. This criss-crossing triggers new meanings that continually unfold into additional new meanings.[11] Let us compare the impact of the following statements on team members:

Before I make my decision, let me hear your solutions to the problem;

and the same manager asking in a "not knowing" way,

Would it be a good idea for all of us to talk about this problem and decide how to handle it?

It is evident that the first statement implies a command emerging from a hierarchical position. Such a request constricts the respondent who may feel the need to make the answer correspond to the boss's ideas. Communication in such instances is strained and limited. The second statement is more democratic and relaxed. It encourages participation and has the tenor of a brainstorming session where every idea is equally welcome. In such an instance, communication is more open and rich.

Curious Stance

The curious stance simply means that one expresses one's ideas in a tentative manner.[12] A dogmatic or assertive expression of ideas often hinders the creative process, but a tentative or nonjudgmental mode of expression encourages others to take, leave, or develop ideas at will without vesting or territoriality. This climate encourages the free exchange of ideas on their own merit and without threat of penalty. Taking this stance helps to multiply varying perspectives on a problem and, naturally, leads to an evolved solution. A final advantage is that emergent solutions are usually not only the best thought-out and most fitting but also explored and designed by the individuals who will implement them.

We express our curious stance by asking questions rather than making statements as well as by beginning our questions with expressions that convey tentativeness — perhaps, possibly, or could it be. For example, "I wonder what the outcome might be if we implement Plan B instead of Plan A?" or "It's just an idea, but what would happen if we don't take any action right now?"

Collaborative Stance

This stance is the result of the two preceding stances. The shared perspectives, ideas, and meanings contributed by the conversants evolve into common knowledge.[13] This process filters many levels of perceptions and triggers deep involvement among participants making possible the co-construction of a jointly-owned outcome. Joy and Karen's conversation illustrates how this process unfolds.

JOY: I am glad you suggested we talk about this topic. You know, Karen, it has been very difficult for me to function in those team meetings. . . . I somehow draw a blank and find myself unable to contribute to the discussions.

KAREN: Well, you know, I, too, find it uncomfortable when no one seems to hear what I am saying. I somehow feel disqualified.

JOY: I am surprised to hear you say that. I always felt that, perhaps, it is my way of expressing myself. As a black woman, I tend to feel dismissed even before I open my mouth.

KAREN: Somehow I feel this way, too. But I always thought it happened because I am a woman.

JOY: You might be right, Karen. It could be a gender as well as a color issue that we are dealing with here.

These premises and stances undergird the process of reflexive communication. They bring about better understanding among individuals whose culture and gender may create varying perceptions of the same reality.

IMPLEMENTING REFLEXIVE COMMUNICATION

There is nothing simple about dealing with diversity. Diversity is one of the most complex and refracted areas of management because it involves the intimacy of the self with the impersonality of the workplace.

The first step in implementing reflexive communication in a work setting is to form small, voluntary, diverse groups. Participants can come from either the same office or a variety of divisions. There are only two rules for membership in the group — commitment and confidentiality. Participants must commit themselves to the long-term process of reflexive communication.

One quickly comes to realize that the premises and stances of reflexive communication are not part of our normal communication repertoire. We have learned to function in the hierarchical worlds of home, school, and, particularly, the workplace. In these settings we do not always relate to one another on an egalitarian basis. Much less accepted is the practice of communicating with others, whether colleagues or superiors, from a curious or not-knowing stance. Furthermore, assuming a collaborative stance in our dealings with one another is not an everyday occurrence either.

One achieves competence in reflexive communication through learnable skills that require patience and practice. One trains individuals in reflexive communication by introducing each premise and stance and allowing time for discussion and practice. The individual being trained acquires the command of one skill before moving on to the next. It may be difficult to begin the training by talking about diversity issues. To create a conducive climate, groups might begin by discussing work-related or other relatively neutral matters because such topics are more familiar and potentially less explosive. Reflexive communication is a general theory that lends itself to any communication context. Therefore, in any setting or on any topic, the process of reflexive communication will evoke multiple points of view and generate mutual self-awareness for the participants. Finally, the us versus them polarization that sometimes characterizes diversity can be transcended by having the group concentrate on a common task. Jointly concentrating on common tasks is an excellent way to begin diversity training, as Colgate-Palmolive and IBM have learned. In both cases, emphasis on teams and task performance aided diversity training efforts.[14]

With practice, the process of reflexive communication will engender a sense of trust among its participants. The structure of reflexive communication creates an environment wherein participants can freely exchange their views and, eventually, communicate with one another on deeper and more meaningful levels.

CONCLUSION

Reflexive communication is a new approach to face-to-face communication. It offers a process by which one can access the uniqueness of each individual as well as each individual's cultural paradigm. Through this approach, individuals can better generate information and co-construct those mutual realities that lead to enhanced problem solving. Reflexive communication is particularly useful to individuals from different cultures who wish to establish a common ground for mutual understanding and action.

The premises and stances of reflexive communication provide the vehicles to help realize the goal of more effective communication in the most diverse workplace in mankind's history.

NOTES

1. Zora Neale Hurston. (1984). *Dust tracks on a road: An autobiography*, 2d ed., (p. 61). Urbana: University of Illinois Press.

2. Robert E. Hemenway. (1984). Introduction. In Zora Neale Hurston, *Dust tracks on a road: An autobiography*, 2d ed. (p. 21). Urbana: University of Illinois Press.

3. Frederick R. Lynch. (1992, October 26). Manager's journal: Multiculturalism comes to the workplace. *Wall Street Journal*, p. A16.

4. Allen E. Ivey, Mary Bradford Ivey, & Lynn Simek-Downing. (1987). *Counseling and psychotherapy: Integrating skills, theory and practice*, 2d ed., (pp. 94–97). Englewood Cliffs, NJ: Prentice Hall.

5. Peter L. Berger, & Thomas Luckman. (1966). *The social construction of reality: A treatise in the sociology of knowledge*. New York: Anchor Books/ Doubleday; Kenneth J. Gergen. (1985, March). The social constructionist movement in modern psychology. *American Psychologist*, 40(3), pp. 266–75; Lynn Hoffman. (1990, March). Constructing realities: An art of lenses. *Family Process*, 29(1), pp. 1–12; John Shotter. (1989). Social accountability and the social construction of "you." In John Shotter & Kenneth J. Gergen (Eds.), *Texts of identity* (pp. 133–151). London: Sage Publications.

6. Vernon E. Cronen, Kenneth M. Johnson, & John W. Lannamann. (1982, March). Paradoxes, double binds, and reflexive loops: An alternative theoretical perspective. *Family Process*, 20, pp. 91–112; Frederick Steier. (1991). Introduction: Research as self-reflexivity, self-reflexivity as social process. In Frederick Steier (Ed.), *Research and Reflexivity* (pp. 1–11). London: Sage; Frederick Steier. (1991). Reflexivity and methodology: An ecological constructionism. In Frederick Steier (Ed.), *Research and Reflexivity* (pp. 163–185). London: Sage.

7. Lynn Hoffman. (1991, Fall/Winter). A reflexive stance for family therapy. *Journal of Strategic and Systemic Therapies*, 10(3, 4), pp. 4–17.

8. Karl Tomm. (1987). Interventive interviewing: Part II. Reflexive questioning as a means to enable self-healing. *Family Process*, 26, pp. 167–183.

9. Harlene D. Anderson. (1995). Collaborative language systems: Toward a postmodern therapy. In R. Mikesell, D. D. Lusterman, & S. McDaniel (Eds.), *Integrating family therapy: Handbook of family psychology and systems theory*. Hyattsville, MD: American Psychological Association; Harlene Anderson, & Harold Goolishian. (1992). The client is the expert: A not-knowing approach to therapy. In Sheila McNamee, & Kenneth J. Gergen (Eds.), *Therapy as Social Construction* (pp. 25–39). London: Sage Publications.

10. Paul Watzlawick, Janet Beavin Bavelas, & Don D. Jackson. (1967). *Pragmatics of human communication: A study of interactional patterns, pathologies, and paradoxes* (pp. 51–54). New York: W. W. Norton & Company.

11. Harlene Anderson, & Harry Goolishian. (1988). Human systems as linguistic systems: Evolving ideas about the implications for theory and practice. *Family Process*, 27, pp. 371–393; Harlene Anderson. (1990). Then and now: From knowing to not-knowing. *Contemporary Family Therapy Journal*, 12, pp. 193-198.

12. Harlene Anderson, & Susan Swim. (1993). Learning as collaborative conversation: Combining the student's and teacher's expertise. *Human Systems: The Journal of Systemic Consultation & Management*, 4, pp. 145–160.

13.   Kenneth J. Gergen. (1985, March). The social constructionist movement in modern psychology. *American Psychologist*, *40*(3), pp. 266–275.

14.   Shari Caudron. (1994, September). Diversity ignites effective work teams. *Personnel Journal*, pp. 54–63.

4

Microskills for Reflexive Communication

The process of identification and selection of specific skills . . . is called the microskills approach. Using the microskills approach, we can break down the complex interaction of the . . . interview into manageable and learnable dimensions.
— Allen E. Ivey, Mary Bradford Ivey, & Lynn Simek-Morgan[1]

We believe that a more diverse America creates a new context for face-to-face communication. We suggest that, in an increasingly diverse cultural context, there may be more than one understanding, more than one meaning of any single reality. Individuals from differing cultural paradigms or positions may perceive the same situation differently and draw different meanings from it. Reflexive communication is the process by which these different perspectives and views of reality can overlap and create the common ground for understanding. To implement this general process requires a set of specific skills. We call them the microskills for reflexive communication.

The microskills, the skills of how to communicate more effectively, were developed more than two decades ago by University of Massachusetts communication theorist Allen Ivey and attempt to make explicit what is presently largely implicit. Since then, thousands of executives, diplomats, and civil servants have been trained in the use of the microskills. The effectiveness of the microskills has been proven by more than two hundred studies in Western and non-Western cultures in the United States, Europe, Asia, Africa, and Latin America.[2]

The microskills are a set of hands-on, one-at-a-time, learnable, communication skills. They help individuals transcend their own cultural paradigm and gain access to another's culturally-based thoughts, feelings, values, and meanings. In a nutshell, the microskills can help one individual access the culturally-general but individually-specific world of another.

The microskills are comprised of nonverbal attending skills and verbal attending skills. Nonverbal attending skills include eye contact, body language, vocal qualities, and verbal tracking. Verbal attending skills include open and closed questions, paraphrasing, reflection of feeling, reflection of meaning, and summarization.

NONVERBAL ATTENDING SKILLS

Listening is the most basic skill in communication. It is a seemingly simple skill with profound implications. The goal of listening is to attend to the other person. One's patterns of eye contact, body language, vocal quality, and verbal tracking are behaviors that can encourage communication. Attending skills are simple but powerful ways to generate more communication with others. Nonverbal communication is taken for granted. When we talk about communication, we generally think only of its verbal component. However, nonverbal signals occupy a primary position in interpersonal communication. Some of the founding scholars of the field estimate that between 65 percent and 90 percent of face-to-face communication occurs through our nonverbal behavior.[3] It is safe to estimate that at least half of face-to-face communication takes place by way of nonverbal channels. Thus, nonverbal communication is as important, if not more important, than verbal communication.

Eye Contact

Eye contact is a nonverbal attending behavior. In the workplace where white, middle-class, cultural norms predominate listeners tend to look at the speaker during face-to-face communication. This indicates that one is interested in what is being said. Often, a break from the normal gaze pattern or looking away may indicate discomfort, distress, or even deceit.

Body Language

Body language is a nonverbal attending behavior. In most business contexts, the white, middle-class norm is to stand an arm's length (approximately 20 inches) from another while conversing. If seated, a slight, forward lean of the upper body expresses interest. Shifts and changes in body posture may be indicative of discomfort. Facial behavior, such as furrowed eyebrows or tightened lips, may indicate dislike and even anger.

Vocal Qualities

The voice is an instrument that communicates the feeling one has toward a person or situation. Changes in vocal tone, pace, or volume convey the same messages as body posture or eye contact. The meaning of a statement is very much embedded in the tone of voice in which it is conveyed. "Good job" conveys very different meanings when uttered in an upbeat tone of voice rather than a sarcastic one.

Verbal Tracking

Staying on the topic is a very important attending behavior. Verbal tracking helps the speaker tell us what needs to be said. That is why we all unconsciously utter such simple verbal trackers as "uh-hmmm" or "ah-ha". Our attending behavior encourages the speaker to go on. The power of these skills to improve or diminish conversation becomes apparent if you imagine conversing with another person who stands six to nine inches away or, if seated, leans backward while continually looking away and speaking to you in a grating voice.

If we are to be effective in our attending behavior, we must become more aware of cultural differences in face-to-face communication. Many Hispanics and people from Mediterranean cultures stand closer than other Americans when conversing. When listening, some African Americans are more likely to look away from than at the speaker.[4]

VERBAL ATTENDING SKILLS

Verbal attending skills involve listening attentively to another and then generating more communication by means of the appropriate use of verbal techniques. The use of verbal attending skills not only helps establish comfortable relationships with others but also encourages them to share information with us more openly.

Open Questions and Closed Questions

We all know that it is necessary to ask questions to secure information. However, few of us realize the power of different types of questions to elicit different responses. There are two types of microskill questions: closed questions and open questions.

Closed questions typically begin with words like do, did, are, or is and almost always elicit yes, no, or brief answers. They are useful and appropriate to establish specific facts. Open questions are invitations to talk. They generate more information and conversation. Generally, they begin with words like what, could, would, or how. Simply asking the same question in an open-ended fashion has the power to generate more information. To demonstrate this point, please silently respond to the following two questions:

CLOSED QUESTION: Is that Acme proposal in?
OPEN QUESTION: How is that Acme proposal coming along?

The closed question naturally elicits a brief yes or no answer while the open question uncannily encourages us to respond in greater detail. In a multicultural encounter, open questions are useful tools to help access how other individuals see or experience their worlds.

Different open questions generate different types of responses.[5]

Open questions that begin with:	*Generate responses dealing with:*
What	Information and facts

Erving, what's going on with that new account?

How	Process

Joe, how is that new project coming along?

Why	Analysis

Harriet, why did that problem develop?

Could you and Would you	Maximal information

Yolanda, could you give me more feedback on that client?
Jack, would you tell us about what happened in that meeting?

Paraphrasing

Any sign of understanding what another person has told you encourages him or her to say more. Paraphrasing more powerfully encourages continuing the conversation and elaborating thoughts resulting in more details about concerns and issues. One paraphrases by restating, in one's own words, the essence of what a colleague has said. Paraphrasing has three specific components: beginning stem; restatement; and concluding, checking stem.

A beginning stem may be as simple as:
> You're saying that. . . .
> Looks like you see this problem as. . . .
> What I hear you telling me is. . . .

A restatement in your own words of the essence of what your colleague has said:
> Statement: . . . the bureaucratic infighting is stalling my group's progress.
> Restatement: . . . the political battles are impeding your team's performance.

A concluding, checking stem, such as:
> Is that about right?
> Do I have that right?
> Did I hear you correctly?

For example,

HARRIET: Well, that Acme proposal is giving me a headache. I just can't seem to get and keep the people and computers to complete it. As soon as I get them, they're taken away.

DOUG: It sounds like you have a problem just getting the resources to finish the job, is that so?

HARRIET: That's right. And maybe you can help me. This is what I think the bottleneck is.

Paraphrasing conveys to the speaker that you understand and that you are hearing what he or she is saying. Paraphrasing is one of the most powerful microskills that facilitates communication.

Reflection of Feeling

Communication is not just conveying information, and management is not just the bloodless supervision of humans in the machine-like achievement of goals. Human emotions and feelings are involved in many workplace issues, especially in culturally diverse settings. The reflection of feeling captures the emotional aspect of human nature. The purpose of this microskill is to identify and make explicit emotions that are often concealed allowing the listener to tune into the speaker's emotional experience. While nothing seems more ordinary than to empathize with another, the reflection of feeling has a specific structure.

A beginning stem may include your colleague's first name:
> Jackie, you seem to be feeling . . .

A feeling label identifies the emotion expressed:
> Jackie, you seem to be feeling overwhelmed.

A short, present-tense paraphrase of the context of the situation (words like about, because, or when are useful here):

> Jackie, you seem to be feeling overwhelmed because of the amount of work I've given you during the past few days.

A concluding, checking stem:

> Could that be it?
> Is that about it?

In the following dialogue, Doug is attempting to understand and reflect Harriet's feelings:

HARRIET: So the fact that Jim is constantly giving me people and then taking them off the Acme proposal to give to somebody else has me all knotted up inside.

DOUG: Harriet, you seem to be feeling frustrated about Jim's indecisiveness on his unit's priorities. Am I about right on that?

HARRIET: You certainly are. And what's more. . . .

The reflection of feeling informs the speaker that you are aware of his or her emotions. This in turn encourages the speaker to clarify further the issue at hand. The listener needs to be cautious about inaccurately labelling feelings. Adequate time and care must be given to identify the precise feeling correctly. Mislabelling an emotion is a sure sign of misunderstanding the speaker.

Reflection of Meaning

The reflection of meaning may be the microskill that is most relevant to the diverse workplace. It has to do with how different racial, ethnic, gender, or cultural groups organize life and experiences as well as the meaning they draw from those experiences. This microskill may appear to be very much like the preceding ones of the paraphrase (which restates thoughts) or the reflection of feeling (which reflects emotions). Indeed, the reflection of meaning combines thoughts and meanings. The reflection of meaning has a specific structure.

A beginning stem may include your colleague's first name and asks what meaning, sense, or importance your colleague attaches to what was expressed:

> Erving, what sense does this make to you?
> So Miguel, doing business for you means. . . .

A short paraphrase of the essence of the statement just expressed using the speaker's context. (Reflect the central meaning using the speaker's own words, carefully avoiding interpretation or judgment.):

> So Miguel, doing business for you means putting the relationship first,

knowing and trusting the other person. (Note that knowing and trusting are Miguel's own words.)

A concluding, checking stem:
    Do I have that about right?

If one turns "Mike, you seem to feel . . ." into "Mike, you seem to mean . . ." the reflection of meaning appears much like the reflection of feeling.

We should remember that both reflecting skills deal with profound issues — emotions, values, meanings, and the particular sense each one of us makes of the world. Neither skill should be used insincerely or manipulatively. Inappropriate use can cause as much anger and distrust, on the one hand, as understanding and trust, on the other. However, used ethically, with a sincere attitude, no microskill is more useful in helping elicit how a colleague sees a problem, what sense one may make of an office situation, what values may motivate seemingly culturally different behaviors, or why an action or word that is unimportant (or important) to you may be important (or unimportant) to a colleague.

Summarization

Summarization is similar in its impact to paraphrases, but it is much broader in its scope. Summarization allows the listener to attend closely to the facts and feelings as well as to the verbal and nonverbal behaviors of what is being expressed. The response then meaningfully integrates the essential elements of what has been said. Summarization is valuable to both speaker and listener. The speaker gains from the clarification that the listener provides by pulling together the relevant components of what the speaker has said, thereby rendering the situation clearer. For the listener, summarization provides a check on the perceptions and distortions that may have infiltrated the response given. Thus, both individuals become aware of their own personal distortions.

Summarization follows this sequence:

Use every attending skill to listen closely.

Note inconsistencies and polarities between facts and feelings.

Give special attention to major threads of information that are central to the issues.

Summarize what you have heard as accurately as you can.

Check at the end for accuracy.

The following vignette between Phil and his manager, Mary, incorporates each of the microskills discussed in this chapter.

MARY: Phil, I know that you have had a great deal on your mind lately. The last time we met you weren't sure whether you wanted to stay or leave this organization. What would you like to talk about today? (The manager uses the stem "what" to ask open questions to maximize Phil's response.)

PHIL: You know, I've been working hard to get some creative ideas off the ground. But I'm not sure that I have the support I need.

MARY: Well Phil, do you have any doubts about my support? (Mary's closed question starting with "do" is useful because it seeks to establish a specific fact.)

PHIL: No, I'm sure of your support, Mary. What concerns me are the signals I'm getting from others like Tim and Gwen who are more plugged-in and, in a roundabout way, don't seem to think much of my projects.

MARY: Phil, tell me, how did you arrive at this conclusion? (Mary uses an open question starting with "how" to elicit information about the process.)

PHIL: Well, every time I mention my project, they're just not interested in what I'm doing, and, instead, they talk in a positive way about similar products that others are working on and the excitement this is generating. This doesn't feel good.

MARY: Phil, you seem to feel discouraged because your colleagues are not as interested in your work as they are in the work of others. Is that it? (Mary reflects Phil's feelings to let him know that she hears him.)

PHIL: Yes, you're right about that. But I also wonder about my future here. How am I going to get my projects done if there isn't more support and collaboration with my peers somewhere down the road?

MARY: You seem to be concerned about the lack of collegiality with your coworkers and, hence, your future here. Am I hearing you right? (Mary is paraphrasing the essence of what Phil is saying.)

PHIL: Exactly. And more than that, I'm not happy here. I don't know what to do. It is just not working out as I thought it would.

MARY: Phil, you seem sad and at a loss about your peer relationships and your prospects here, is that about right? (Mary seeks to draw out Phil's emotions through a reflection of feeling.)

PHIL: Right. This is not what I expected to happen to me when I joined this group. I thought that there would be more of an esprit de corps and team spirit — that the team would collaborate together on projects and bring them to fruition together. But this is not happening, and I'm disappointed by the whole atmosphere. Frankly, I am thinking that I should be looking elsewhere.

MARY: So far, I have the sense that when you came in you expected to be part of a dynamic team where everyone would welcome your ideas and work collaboratively with one another. Instead, you have been disappointed and discouraged by the attitudes and actions of peers like Gwen and Tim. So given that, you're thinking of leaving and going elsewhere. Does this sum it up? (Mary summarizes the facts and feelings that Phil conveyed to her in their dialogue.

PHIL: Right! That's it exactly. When I came in this afternoon, I wasn't sure how I felt and where to go. All I knew, is that I wasn't helping myself or the company. Gosh, it feels good. This conversation has made things crystal clear. Now I know what to do.

In this dialogue, Mary was able to fully attend to Phil's issues. Through her nonverbal and verbal attending skills she was able to clarify Phil's feelings and position on the problem he is confronting in this organization. Through her use of open and closed questions, Mary was able to understand better the specific facts and processes that led to Phil's discomfort. Then she used the reflection of feeling to tune into his emotional state. By identifying his feelings, Mary helped Phil respond more fully once he felt heard by her.

Subsequently, Mary went on to paraphrase the essence of the conversation, thereby furthering her own understanding of the situation by checking on the accuracy of her perceptions. This gave clarity to Phil as well as the chance to correct any misunderstandings or misperceptions. It further encouraged Phil to disclose his innermost thoughts.

Mary's use of the reflection of feeling deepened her understanding of Phil's emotions and the meanings he attributed to them. As he expressed them, Phil simultaneously clarified his own thoughts and feelings about the situation. The last skill Mary used was summarization. She deftly drew together the central facts of the conversation and the key emotions Phil experienced and helped Phil clarify his thinking about his job. The conversation was probably the catalyst for Phil's decision to leave the company. During the conversation, he came to the clear realization that he could not fulfill his expectations for the job he had taken two years ago.

IMPLEMENTATION OF THE MICROSKILLS

The microskills are specific tools that enhance the communication process. They are relatively easy to learn. The skills are best learned one-at-a-time. Following the presentation and discussion, practice provides a hands-on approach to the mastery of each skill. As one gains proficiency in one skill, another is added and practiced simultaneously. Thus, each remaining skill is added until the complete set of microskills has been acquired.

The key to proficiency with the microskills is practice. While these skills are easy to comprehend and implement individually, making them part of our everyday behavior may not be as easy. Only through continued conscious effort in using and practicing the skills can we successfully make them part of our behavioral repertoire. The more we use the microskills, the more proficient we become in communicating effectively with those around us. Microskills are not limited to use in the workplace. They are skills that can be applied to any life setting to enhance our understanding of one another and, hence, our relationships.

CONCLUSION

According to Paul Watzlawick and his colleagues, "one cannot *not* communicate."[6] Consciously or unconsciously we are always sending messages by way of our verbal or nonverbal behavior. This is particularly true in the workplace where the coordinated achievement of goals depends upon effective communication. It is becoming more difficult to communicate with one another in the increasingly diverse workplace. We need to learn to talk, converse, and transcend the limits of culture. The microskills give us the tools to accomplish this more effectively. Above all, the microskills teach us how to listen and understand one another. Out of the myriad communication possibilities, the microskills provide each one of us with the specific tools to address one of the challenges that diversity brings to the workplace.

NOTES

1.   Allen E. Ivey, Mary Bradford Ivey, & Lynn Simek-Morgan. (1993). *Counseling and psychotherapy: A multicultural perspective* (p. 45). Boston: Allyn and Bacon.

2.   Allen E. Ivey. (1994). *Intentional interviewing and counseling: Facilitating client development in a multicultural society*, 3rd ed. (p. 4). Pacific Grove, CA: Brooks/Cole Publishing Company.

3.   Ray Birdwhistell. (1970). *Kinesics and context: Essays on body motion communication* (pp. 57–58). Philadelphia: University of Pennsylvania Press estimated that no more than 30 to 35 percent of an interpersonal message's social meaning is transmitted verbally while 65 to 70 percent is transmitted nonverbally. In 1987 Edward T. Hall and Mildred Reed Hall estimated, on the basis of research, that 80 to 90 percent of information conveyed between individuals occurs at the nonverbal level. See Edward T. Hall, & Mildred Reed Hall. (1987). *Hidden differences: Doing business with the Japanese* (p. 3). New York: Anchor Books/Doubleday.

4.   Edward T. Hall. (1959). *The silent language* (p. 164). Greenwich, CT: Premier Books/Fawcett Publications; Carmen Judith Nine Curt. (1984). *Non-verbal communication in Puerto Rico*, 2d ed. (p. 21). Cambridge, MA: Evaluation, Dissemination and Assessment Center; Marianne LaFrance, & Clara Mayo. (1976). Racial differences in gaze behavior during conversations: Two systematic observational studies. *Journal of Personality and Social Psychology, 33*(5), pp. 547–552.

5.   Ivey, *Intentional interviewing and counseling*, p. 56.

6.   Paul Watzlawick, Janet Beavin Bavelas, & Don D. Jackson. (1967). *Pragmatics of human communication: A study of interactional patterns, pathologies and paradoxes* (p. 49). New York: W. W. Norton.

5

The White Male Communication Paradigm

> If my reading of American history and understanding of American mores is at all correct, then we may say of a man who aspires to the Presidency: He must be, according to the Constitution: at least 35 years old, a "natural born" citizen. . . . He must be, according to unwritten law: a man, white, a Christian. He almost certainly must be . . . less than sixty-five years old, of Northern European stock. . . . He ought to be . . . of British stock . . . a Protestant. . . . He ought not to be . . . divorced, a bachelor, a Catholic, a former Catholic. . . . He almost certainly cannot be . . . of Polish, Italian, or Slavic stock. . . . He cannot be, according to unwritten law: a Negro, a Jew, an Oriental, a woman.
>
> — Clinton Rossiter[1]

These words were written by Clinton Rossiter, perhaps this century's preeminent scholar of the presidency. They described what once were the constitutionally formal as well as the politically informal qualifications to be elected president of the United States. Generations of students have read these words, which were published a little more than three decades ago.

These words could not be written today. Indeed, they reflect just how far America has come in a few short decades to create a more inclusive and democratic society. And how much the qualifications for our highest office have changed and broadened. Since 1960, the exceptions to Rossiter's criteria have established new and more inclusive rules about who can be elected president.

It is hard to believe how much change has occurred in the United States in a relatively short period of time. In 1960 John F. Kennedy was the first Roman Catholic to be elected president. Ronald Reagan was 69 years old and divorced when he was inaugurated as president in 1981. Geraldine Ferraro, an Italian American, Roman Catholic woman, and Michael Dukakis, a Greek Orthodox congregant whose wife is Jewish, campaigned as the Democratic Party nominees for vice-president and president, respectively. Jessie Jackson, an African American, has twice been a candidate for the Democratic Party's nomination for president.

In 1995, Arlen Spector, a Jewish male, and Allan Keyes, a black male, were contenders for the Republican Party's nomination for president. Colin Powell, the son of Jamaican immigrants, was a leading contender for the presidency as a Republican. In some surveys, he outpolled President Clinton in voter approval. It may be fair to state that if an incumbent president were not seeking reelection, the array of contenders for the Democratic Party's nomination would be even more diverse.

This chapter examines the predominant influence that white, Anglo-Saxon, Protestant (WASP) males have had on America's history, culture, and, in particular, the management of its institutions. For more than 350 years, WASP influence has dominated U.S. society and commerce. Five successive developments changed that preeminence: World War II; the GI Bill of the 1940s; the Civil Rights Movement that gathered momentum in the 1950s; and the Vietnam and women's movements of the 1960s and beyond.

World War II provided the common bond of military service and warfare for millions of American males. World War II also provided the opportunity for countless servicemen to visit ancestral homelands and discover that being "American" was different from being English, Irish, or Italian. At the same time, the horrors of the Holocaust put an end to the public antisemitism that heretofore had been common.

The GI Bill made college, previously a WASP preserve, financially possible for millions of veterans including non-WASPs. It first democratized and then de-ethnicized U.S. colleges. Later, those graduates reshaped America's businesses and corporations — but only for white males.

The Civil Rights Movement and the legislation it brought about also transformed America. It finally made possible the shameful, centuries-delayed entry of African Americans and other minorities into the mainstream of American society and the management of its institutions. The Civil Rights Movement also catalyzed the Women's Liberation Movement, which sought similar equality and opportunity for women.

The involvement of the United States in Vietnam triggered a head-on collision between the largest generation in U.S. history (approximately 78 million baby boomers) and the demand to conform to the dominant WASP values heretofore required in America's institutions. As a result, a dynamic process unfolded that de-ethnicized America's colleges, universities, and then its corporate executive suites. But for white males only. Today that process of unfolding continues for white women and minorities who have the appropriate formal educational credentials and informal management skills.

Every work group demands a common order of talk and common informal values and behaviors — a cultural paradigm — for both admission to and the effectiveness of the group.

Yesterday, it was the WASP cultural paradigm that was operative. Perhaps, today, we can say it is the white male cultural paradigm that is more operative than any other in America's executive suites. The Anglo-Saxon, Protestant component of America's organizations (while diminishing) remains more influential than any other single cultural strand.

Driven by America's democratic and inclusionary values as well as changing demographics, tomorrow's organizations will continue to include new managers of its enterprises and then concomitantly alter its cultural paradigms.

THE WHITE ANGLO-SAXON PROTESTANT
MALE HERITAGE OF AMERICA

We speak their language, read their novels, pledge allegiance to the political institutions they developed, and work in the corporations they founded. From authors Herman Melville and Mark Twain to presidents George Washington and Abraham Lincoln, from the automotive industry's Henry Ford and Walter Chrysler to IBM's Thomas Watson and Microsoft's Bill Gates — there is no end of the contributions that WASPs have made to America.

This is particularly true of our politics and culture. No other society has put together the ideals of individualism, equality, and freedom as has the United States of Thomas Jefferson, James Madison, Thomas Paine, and Benjamin Franklin, all WASPs. It is ironic that those who speak most scathingly of WASPs or most bitterly criticize America as racist, sexist, or oppressive are able to do so by means of the freedoms and institutions that WASPs established. Congress is more diverse than ever. The 104th Congress (1995–97) had more members who are female (57), African American (40), Hispanic (18), Asian American (8), and Native American (1) than ever before in its history. There also are more non-Protestants (5 Greek Orthodox, 33 Jews, and 145 Roman Catholics) than any preceding Congress. Yet, of its 535 members, 87 percent are white, 90 percent are male, and 71 percent are Protestant.[2]

Of the 113 justices appointed to the Supreme Court approximately 90 percent have been WASP males. The few exceptions, primarily in the twentieth century, include Louis Brandeis, Felix Frankfurter, and Abe Fortas (Jewish males); Thurgood Marshall and Clarence Thomas (African American males); Sandra Day O'Connor (Episcopalian female); Ruth Ginsberg (Jewish female); and seven Roman Catholic justices. Reflecting America's more democratic and inclusionary attitudes, the current Supreme Court is more diverse than ever with one black male, two Catholic males, and two females — one of whom is Jewish — among its nine justices.[3]

An astounding 98 percent of our presidents have been WASPs. With the exception of patrician John F. Kennedy (who in many ways fit into the category), all 42 presidents of the United States have been WASPs.[4] Although he was an Irish-Catholic at a time of bitter discrimination against them, Kennedy's father saw to it that he attended Choate, a WASPy New England prep school, as well as Harvard University. The WASP hold on the presidency continues with William Jefferson Clinton.

WASPs also long predominated in industry, commerce, and finance. As late as 1950, 65 percent of top executives in the largest U.S. companies were males of English descent while from 1870 to 1950 an additional 15 to 20 percent were males of Scottish descent.[5] In terms of religion, 85 percent of top executives in 1950 identified themselves as Protestant. Together Episcopalians (30 percent) and Presbyterians (17 percent) accounted for nearly half of all business executives.[6] As late as the 1950s, Episcopalians (who constituted only 3 percent of U.S. population) accounted for approximately 33 percent of the chief executive officers of its 500 largest industrial corporations. This is hardly the case today.[7]

WHITE, ANGLO-SAXON, PROTESTANTS IN AMERICAN SOCIETY AND BUSINESS TODAY

According to 1990 census figures, WASPs comprise the largest ethnic group in U.S. society — 132 million or 53 percent of 249 million Americans. The bulk of the WASP population was of two ancestries: German (58 million or 23 percent of the population) and English (33 million or 13 percent of the population). But the term "WASP," which initially meant only those of English ancestry, has expanded to include not only Germans but also Dutch (2.5 percent), Scotch-Irish (2.3 percent), Scottish (2.2 percent), Scandinavian (4.8 percent), Welsh (0.8 percent), and others. Thirteen million Americans (5 percent) were of such mixed ancestry that they just called themselves "American."[8]

It may be worth noting that the "imprecision" of ethnic identity mentioned earlier applies to majorities as well as minorities. In the 1980 census, 22 percent of respondents identified their ancestry as English to make up the largest ethnic group. In the 1990 census, respondents who self-identified themselves as English dropped to 13 percent, falling from first to third place behind Americans of German and Irish ancestries.[9]

WASP males have continued to predominate in large and small businesses, particularly at the higher decision-making levels. A 1985 *Wall Street Journal* survey found that 68 percent of small business executives, 65 percent of Fortune 500 executives, and 48 percent of entrepreneurs traced their ancestry to "the dominant white Anglo-Saxon or North European nationality groups."[10] Surveying thousands of managers just below chief executive officer rank in 1990 in some of the largest U.S. corporations, Korn/Ferry International found that 96.9 percent were white, 95 percent were male, and 58 percent were Protestant. Carefully note the 10 percent drop from the 1980 Korn/Ferry survey when 68 percent of top executives were Protestant.[11]

Sondra Thiederman obliquely attests to the powerful WASP presence in management:

Obviously if this book is about workers and how to manage them, it also is about managers. You will notice that there are frequent references to mainstream American managers, or to an all-encompassing *us* or *we*. These labels in no way imply that the readers or the managers who will benefit from this book were all born and raised in the United States or that they are of white, Anglo-Saxon extraction. What it does imply, however, is that the manager who needs this material was either raised in the values and perspective of mainstream American culture or has become largely assimilated into that culture. The same distinction applies to any reference to the mainstream American or American worker.[12]

Further, Edward T. Hall and Mildred Reed Hall wrote in their recent study of business and culture:

While the U.S. is a nation of immigrants and there are many people in American business who are not of northern European heritage, for the purposes of our discussion of American culture, it is the American-European culture we refer to and not the many other cultures represented in the American population. This dominant or mainstream business culture is the norm to which people with other cultural backgrounds are expected to conform, particularly in large corporations. Despite its ethnic diversity, the U.S. has managed to absorb bits and pieces of many cultures and weave them into a unique culture that is strikingly consistent and distinct. . . . While the United States has absorbed millions of people from countries around the globe, *the core culture of the United States has its roots in northern European or Anglo-Saxon culture.*[13]

Finally, the view of two scholars who are not necessarily friends of either business or business executives may be instructive. Richard L.

Zweigenhaft and G. William Domhoff have carried on the work of C. Wright Mills, coiner of the term and critic of "the power elite." They conclude by stating their belief that "the Protestant Establishment remains the key reference group in American society."[14]

As recently as 1970, sociologist Charles Anderson wrote that "the English have always enjoyed the enviable advantage of being members of the preferred ethnic group. A person's employment has not always been in a one-to-one correspondence with his ability and talent. Although the technological sophistication of the present makes ethnicity no longer germane to occupational selection, *ethnic status has traditionally been a factor of perhaps equal importance to work history and credentials in the job market.*[15] (emphasis added).

Today it simply is not possible to make such a statement. The progress of the last few decades is evidence of just how inclusive the workplace has become. If anything, the pace toward inclusion has quickened during the 1980s and 1990s. Yet, of all ethnic groups, WASPs remain extraordinarily influential in managing U.S. enterprises. There is a good reason; they were first colonists.

MIGRATION

The first permanent English settlement, Jamestown, was established in 1607. For the next two hundred years, most of the population of what was to become the United States was English or of English descent. In 1690, 90 percent of white inhabitants or their descendants were English. When the fledgling United States conducted its first census in 1790, that number was still 80 percent. In the formative days of the Republic, the English presence was overwhelming in both numbers and cultural precedence and power. Yet, an even greater number of immigrants came to the United States from the British Isles after 1820 than before 1790. If we include Germans and Scandinavians as WASPs — as they came to be considered after decades of WASP exclusion — over 90 percent of all pre-1860 immigrants came from Northern Europe. Nearly 20 percent of immigrants still came from Northern Europe as late as the early twentieth century.

For centuries WASPs capitalized upon their first-comer status and long-term control of key U.S. institutions, which, in many cases, they established. Of all the many, diverse, and valuable ethnic contributions and cultural paradigms in America, that of the WASPs remains the most influential, particularly in managing America's organizations. The obvious question then is Who are the WASPs.

THE WASPS

WASPs have been admired, resented, and, now, ignored as an elite group of long-time status and power in American society. However, there can be confusion about this term. To many, the term "WASP" is: old; usually denotes upper-class, elite Americans who control, if not comprise, what was called the Establishment; and describes individuals of Anglo-Saxon — meaning English — descent who, except for Native Americans, have been here longer than anyone else. None of these statements is entirely correct.

First, WASP is not an old term — at least not in print. While it may have been used previously in conversation, E. Digby Baltzell's 1964 classic, *The Protestant Establishment*, did much to popularize it. Its first printed appearance was in a 1962 scholarly article by E. B. Palmore in which he wrote: "for the sake of brevity, we will use the nickname 'WASP' for this group, from the initial letters of White Anglo-Saxon Protestant."[16]

Second, not all WASPs are members of the elite, upper class. People residing in the Appalachians — among the poorest and most powerless of whites — are quintessential WASPs. In fact, throughout the United States there are Joneses and Smiths found at all levels of society. The last direct male descendant of George Washington, William Augustine Washington, was a retired Bradley, Indiana, tool and die maker — proud and dignified, but hardly representative of a privileged or powerful WASP elite.[17]

Finally, Americans who use the term "WASP" generally may be referring to white Protestants of English origin. In fact, over time WASP has expanded to include several different ethnic groups — first from the British Isles, and later from Germany, Scandinavia, Holland, and other northern European countries. Some readers may be surprised to learn that:

Naval hero John Paul Jones, steel tycoon Andrew Carnegie, and telephone inventor Alexander Graham Bell were Scots.

President Andrew Jackson, Henry Ford, and today's immensely but quietly rich Mellon family of Pennsylvania trace their ancestry to Ireland.

The Heinzs and Rockefellers originally came from Germany as did ill-fated General George Kuester (Custer), World War I General John Pforshing (Pershing), and President Herbert Huever (Hoover).

Economist Thorsten Veblen, poet Carl Sandberg, and aviator Charles Lindberg were all Scandinavians.

Franklin D. Roosevelt, blueblood aristocrat, was educated by private tutor until he finally sat in a classroom with other boys at Groton. Yet, Roosevelt was Dutch, with some Swedish and English ancestry added.[18]

This ethnic fusion did not occur quickly or without discrimination or exclusion. The first-arrival British Americans held stereotypically-negative views of Welsh Americans ("clannish") and Scotch-Irish ("heavy drinkers") and discriminated against them. Benjamin Franklin expressed fears about immigrant Germans who continued to speak and read their own language rather than English. German language newspapers and magazines had a circulation of 300,000 while English language counter-parts had a circulation of 2 million — in 1960. As late as the mid-twentieth century, sociological studies found that 75 to 90 percent of British Americans, Swedish Americans, and Norwegian Americans socialized primarily within their own ethnic groups.[19]

To be a WASP meant to be an ancestrally English, white, Anglo-Saxon Protestant. But the ethnic parenthesis expanded to become more inclusive. The British American WASPs, exclusionary and discriminatory at first, ultimately included and then absorbed the Scots, Welsh, Scotch-Irish, Germans, Scandinavians, and Dutch. Today they, too, are popularly viewed as WASPs or (categorically by some) as "Northern Europeans." Today the parenthesis has expanded again to include yesterday's white male "ethnics," like Chrysler's Lee Iaccoca, leader of one of America's largest industrial era companies. Yesterday's religious and ethnic discriminatory categories have melted so that "white male" is the commonly used term today.

The contrasting leaderships of yesterday's industrial era corporations and today's information era companies are evidence of America's inclusionary dynamic. The "power elite" at the opening of the industrial economy was almost exclusively made up of WASP males — Carnegies and Mellons, Chryslers and Fords. Today's more inclusionary counter-parts of America's informational companies are white males. They include individuals like Irish Catholic John Malone, president and chief executive officer of Tele-Communications, Inc., and Asian American Scott Sassa, president of Turner Entertainment Group, as well as Gerald Levin, Time Warner's chairman and chief executive officer, and Sumner Redstone, chairman of Viacom, both of whom are Jewish. All of them work closely with while competing against WASP males like Berkshire Hathaway's Warren Buffet and Microsoft's Bill Gates. Together they reflect the continual unfolding and quiet transformation of a more inclusionary America.[20]

WASP no longer describes U.S. executive suites as it once did. Even northern European reflects a cultural lag. The ethnic parenthesis has expanded again. U.S. management has been secularized and de-ethnicized by the large-scale entry of Irish Catholic, southern European, eastern European, and Jewish males. The waves of women in the work force have helped us recognize that what had been considered WASP values and behaviors in the workplace actually were WASP *male* attributes. In the past, this recognition was of interest only to women in the work force because they were the first large cohort of newcomers. These women needed to decipher the male business culture in order to understand what prevented them from succeeding, particularly when women were not yet numerous or influential enough to challenge or change the prevailing male paradigm to any great extent.

There are an increasing number of executives in American organizations who are neither ethnically nor religiously WASP but who, in many ways, reflect WASP values and codes of behavior. They include:

Italian American Lee Iaccoca, probably the best-known executive in the United States;

Cuban-born Roberto Goizueta, chief executive officer of one of the most globally-recognized and successful companies in the United States, Coca-Cola;

private investor and entrepreneur Gerald Tsai, former leader of American Can Company and Primarica who is Asian American; and

Thomas Labrecque, a French American Catholic who runs Chase Manhattan, the nation's sixth largest bank.

Today the category of "male" has inclusively grown to include white male managers quite beyond the older Anglo-Saxon, Protestant pool. The WASP or white male cultural paradigm has had a continuing influence upon American business culture. Whether one is an admirer of or contemptuous or indifferent to the WASP or white male influences upon managers, it would be a mistake not to pay attention to them. There are two significant reasons: their continued preponderance in actual numbers, both in society and management and the simple fact that, of the many subcultures that make up mainstream American culture, the WASP or white male cultural paradigm still is the most influential.

One may applaud or criticize those facts, but facts in our best objective judgment they remain. Further, if we accept the principle that all effective human relationships and all effective human learnings are reciprocal, then white female, African American, Hispanic, and Asian American managers have at least as much to learn about white males as white male managers have to learn about them. While trying to avoid chauvinism or doctrinaireness of any persuasion, we simply are trying to address the problem of how individuals can learn to work together effectively in an increasingly diverse America. The workplace has not been as diverse as it will be. This is a new experience for everyone.

WHITE MALE VALUES

What characterizes white male culture in U.S. business? What follows may seem natural and normal to some readers. White males may be struck by seeing their habitual values and behaviors lifted out of context for the first time. This is analogous to traveling abroad and finding ourselves in another culture. Only then do we realize that what is natural and spontaneous to us, in fact, is coded and dictated by our culture. We then become aware of the subtle but powerful impact that culture has upon our behavior.

The values of American organizations are predominantly WASP or white male values. They may seem unconsciously familiar to many, for they are so culturally common that they are taken for granted.[21]

Hyperindividualism

White males are not just individualists, they are hyperindividualists. Americans are taught individualism at an early age:

You can see it in the way Americans treat their children. Even very young children are given opportunities to make their own choices and express their opinions. A parent will ask a one-year old child what color balloon she wants, which candy bar she would prefer, or whether she wants to sit next to mommy or daddy. The child's preference will normally be accommodated. Through this process, Americans come to see themselves as separate human beings who have their own opinions and who are responsible for their own decisions.[22]

Every American knows that their country and government were founded to protect individual rights to life, liberty, and the pursuit of happiness. While valuing team players, white males applaud those who can make tough decisions and amount to something by themselves. Careers are viewed as an individual's trajectory and an individual's responsibility.

The following values, though arranged in a particular order, should not necessarily be prioritized in that fashion. Rather than a prioritized list of ascending or descending significance each is balanced and interdependent upon the others.

Industry and Work

Observers of Americans as early as eighteenth-century French visitor Alexis DeTocqueville have remarked about the willingness of Americans to work extraordinarily long and hard hours. As lax as some Americans may feel their fellow citizens have become, Americans work harder, longer hours than any other people, except possibly the Japanese.[23] To work hard is a virtue. The most revered American sage remains the individual who, by hard work, has risen from rags to riches. Egalitarian Americans have never respected the European gentleman who is wealthy without personal effort or the idle rich of the United States who live well rather than achieve. Inherited wealth is respected, but to have earned or increased it oneself is respected more. In America even those of great inherited wealth should do good works with it. Many U.S. senators who are wealthy from inheritance reflect this value: Rockefeller, Heinz, Chaffee, Danforth, Kennedy. To the white male, work is a pervasive and powerful value. Americans: "talk of 'working' on relationships, love, sex, fulfillment and identity. They even take recreation, hobbies, collections and sports very seriously, with standards of achievement and success in each."[24]

Achievement and Success

From the earliest age, boys generally are encouraged to be aggressive and independent and to pursue the individual achievement of tasks. Traits such as autonomy, self-reliance, and toughness are actively encouraged in males. Americans work hard to succeed. Sociologist Max Weber pointed out that during the Reformation, Protestants believed that earthly success might be a sign of being saved; achievement and success, therefore, could be signs of religious and eternal salvation. Today Americans feel that hard work leads to earthly and secular success. More than that, work leads to higher esteem in the eyes of others and to a sense of self-adequacy for the individual. Industry is the avenue to realize success and self-worth. All individuals should be successful. Life's justification lies in its achievements.

Personal Responsibility, Self-reliance, and Self-sufficiency

According to this white male value, each individual is personally responsible for his or her own fate. Therefore, the responsibility or locus of control for white males is internal. In an era of corporate downsizing, the operation of larger economic and business forces is recognized. Yet, in the United States, failure still carries a personal stigma, while success is the result of personal strength and acumen. Because values empower the individual, there are few limitations upon what the individual is responsible for and should accomplish. One must not only achieve, one must be responsible.

Self-control and Expression of Emotion

White males are renowned for not being able to express their emotions or maintain mutually giving relationships. One should keep a stiff upper lip and take it like a man. According to the WASP ethic: "one denies, carries on, and, above all, takes responsibility for one's problems by not complaining or involving other people. Likewise, one would not risk interfering in another person's business. A man could be an alcoholic for years, and his closest companion or even business partner might not intervene by suggesting treatment. Individuals 'responsibly' keep their problems to themselves and respect the right of others to do the same."[25]

The image of the silent cowboy or the laconic frontiersman who, after months on the trail, says little because there is little to say reflects this value. Men are not supposed to be voluble. Speech serves a utilitarian function. One should not waste words.

Doing over Thinking or Being

In the white male business culture, doing is more valued than being. One should always be active because idle hands do the devil's work. While intelligence is valued, there is something slightly suspect about being overly-intellectual.

Practicality is Preferred over Theorizing

White males are pragmatic problem solvers. Americans generally prefer practice to theory. The only school of philosophy unique to the United States is pragmatism — the practical applications and implications both of theory and behavior. Americans love to solve problems. Frontiers are to be conquered; difficulties are to be surmounted; problems are to be solved. White male values remain the preeminent values of American business.

MANAGEMENT PRACTICES

Impersonal Rules

The behavioral patterns of white males stem from the gender-specific ways they were reared. Boys are socialized to adopt the values of external hierarchy and impersonal principles. Play is a major socializing activity during childhood. Janet Lever found differences in the socializing nature of boys' and girls' games. In studying elementary school age boys and girls, she found that boys tended to play in more age-heterogeneous groups in which older boys hierarchically structured and led these activities. Lever also found that boys played more competitive games than girls. These games had explicit goals, such as runs or touchdowns, which were governed by explicit rules. Ironically, boys quarreled a great deal in their games, yet they seemed to enjoy these disputations and effectively resolved these conflicts. As Lever writes: "During the course of this study, boys were seen quarreling all the time, but not once was a game terminated because of a quarrel." Lever speculates that boys' games "may improve their ability to deal with interpersonal competition in a forthright manner" as well as to "depersonalize" the attack of others. In so doing, they learn to compete with friends and to cooperate with those they may not personally like. She concludes that these boys' games "encourage the development of organizational skills necessary to coordinate the activities of a numerous and diverse group of persons, and offer experience in rule-bounded events and the adjudication of disputes."[26]

Direct Communication

White male business executives tend to be clear, specific, and direct in their verbal communication, even if it means dealing with unpleasant realities. As they like to say: "Let's lay our cards on the table, shall we?" Or, "Let's stop beating around the bush and get to the point."

White male managers generally do not place a high value upon indirection or ambiguity, certainly not as much as some Asian Americans. Even in personal discussion, let alone a more impersonal business conversation, directness frequently is chosen over sensitivity toward feelings. One of the few exceptions is in dealing with women. White males may have great difficulty being direct with women, especially when it involves personal or emotional matters. Generally, little time is taken for small talk. Beyond short and often formalized pleasantries, the thrust is to get right down to business.

The white male manager values the written mode of communication. All important matters should be reduced to written form, the more factual, the more hard data, the better. Written business communication also is direct. Information goes through formal channels. Brief (even one-page) memos are valued.

Silence

White male business executives do not know how to deal with silence. A silence of more than 60 to 90 seconds often generates an array of initiatives ranging from a new topic of conversation to a concession on a negotiating point — a trait of our communication mode of which our foreign friends long have been aware.[27]

Monochronic Sense of Time

Monochronic time means using time to focus upon one task at a time. By contrast, polychronic time means using time to engage in several activities simultaneously. The dominant white male business culture operates on the basis of monochronic time.[28] In a monochronic culture, time is perceived to be finite; it can be segmented, compartmentalized, and scheduled. Time then becomes a resource, which is organized to serve the purposes of present and future-oriented activities — what we call achievement.

Monochronic individuals speak of time in a linear sense. They visualize time as a line that connects one activity to another. This operating conception of time leads individuals to focus upon "one task at a time." Since "time is money" and since money is what business is all about, every activity is controlled by the clock. White male executives feel under constant pressure to meet time commitments.

In the dominant white male business culture, time is carefully scheduled. The monochronic person schedules time with to do lists that rank activities by priority and significance. A statement that an individual has no time for a particular purpose may not be true, literally, but is more likely a statement of its position on a list of priorities.

One always is prompt. It is sinful and almost a taboo to be excessively late. To be five minutes late raises eyebrows, to be 15 minutes late necessitates a profuse apology, and to be 30 minutes late without a reasonable explanation (for example, traffic) is to risk a business relationship. Meetings start on time in the white male business culture. One does not waste time on frivolous conversation but gets right down to business so that the meeting can end on schedule. Only then can one be on time for one's next scheduled meeting.

Low Context

White males tend to be low context in their communication paradigm. That is, they tend to value verbal more than nonverbal communication. "Words mean what they say," as a number of white male executives told us. One pays more attention to verbal communication (or low context) and less attention to nonverbal (or high context) communication.[29]

NONVERBAL COMMUNICATION

White males are not oblivious to nonverbal communication. Some recounted the experience of visiting a customer's or a superior's office to inquire about a proposal made earlier and knowing within seconds without words what the answer would be. In fact, the more successful manager pays attention to nonverbal behavior: "It is probable that the successful businessman does a better job of communicating and understanding communication on this non-verbal plane than the less successful man does. The successful person seems to 'know' when others are ready to understand or cooperate. One of the founders of the American steel industry, Andrew Carnegie, once said: 'As I grow older, I pay less attention to what men say. I just watch what they do.'"[30]

The low context white male communication style places a premium upon words rather than the subtler nonverbal aspects of communication. As in the oratorical style of debate, one concentrates upon the words that one utters and hears to the detriment of other channels of communication, such as eye contact or body posture.

White males tend to be less sensitive to nonverbal communication than individuals from other cultures (for example, higher context Asian Americans) and often miss nonverbal cues.[31] The fact that 65 to 90 percent of face-to-face communication occurs nonverbally often comes as a complete surprise. While certainly aware of body language, the white male business culture does not place a premium upon it.

Jeff and Judith confront a problem in the following interchange. Judith has been asked by her superior, Jeff, to review her team's goals for the next fiscal year. During the past year, her team's performance has lagged. As we listen to the verbal dialogue, let us also focus on Jeff's nonverbal communication.

JEFF: Come in, Judith. Make yourself comfortable. By the way, how did your tennis match go last Saturday?

JUDITH: The match was great! It was loads of fun. And we won.

JEFF: That's great (sitting about three to four feet away, leaning backward, hands clasped behind his neck). Judith, have you given any thought to our conversation last week about your team's performance?

JUDITH (sitting upright and somewhat tense, elbows at her sides and hands on her lap): Oh yes. I have given it a great deal of thought. What would you like to talk about?

JEFF (maintaining eye contact): Well, did you meet with your team? And did you set any goals for the next two quarters?

JUDITH: Well yes . . . we did meet and everyone was full of ideas. But the problem is not a shortage of ideas. It is having the resources to implement them and —

JEFF (sternly and forcefully interrupting while fidgeting with his pen and sitting upright): But what about those goals?

JUDITH: We did meet for about two hours. But the consensus of the team is that if we don't have the necessary support services to do the research and to crunch the numbers, goals do us no good. I think they are right, don't you think so, Jeff?

JEFF (leaning backward again and gesturing expansively): Well Judith, let me tell you what you need to do. You've got to go back and set some goals. Then you make plans to achieve them. Then you achieve them. That's how it works around here. Time is of the essence.

JUDITH (Feeling stymied and unheard, Judith leans back in her chair and breaks eye contact. She becomes less animated.): I will see what I can do, Jeff. But I want you to know that everyone in the group is working very hard, and right now morale is pretty low.

JEFF (unaware of the feelings she has nonverbally communicated, Jeff goes on): But that's not what's at stake here. What I'm talking about is getting that team behind you so you can begin to produce. You know, if the situation doesn't change, and I mean soon, the survival of your team is in question. Do you understand what I'm telling you?

JUDITH: Jeff, you certainly do make yourself clear. But you must try to understand the situation from my team's perspective. I honestly don't know how much more I can get out of them. They are working real hard.

JEFF: Judith, your job is to lead that team and get it going.

JUDITH: I think I am. But what do you exactly mean by "lead that team?"

JEFF (leaning forward in his chair and speaking emphatically): I mean giving them the facts that I've been giving you about the situation you're in. Then telling them, "Okay gang, this is the scoop. We've got to turn this around ourselves. It's up to us. Nobody else can do it." And then taking those ideas, taking their strengths, and moving into new areas. Fast. That's what I mean by leadership. Just tackling the problem head-on, and solving it.

JUDITH: You mean, I should take the ball and run with it regardless of where they are, rather than seeking the team's support and collaboration in this undertaking?

JEFF (beaming and animated): That is it. Exactly, Judith. I will see you next week at the same time, is that O.K.?

JUDITH: Well, O.K. if you say so.

In the preceding conversation, Jeff's behavior was typically white male. In his agonistic style, Jeff was "in charge" in his role as supervisor. He clearly communicated his position of dominance and power through both his nonverbal and his verbal behaviors. As we continue to discuss white male nonverbal and verbal behaviors we might keep in mind Jeff and Judith's dialogue for illustrations of these skills.

Proxemics

Whether we are aware of it or not, our culture determines our proxemics — our customary use of space.[32] Until now, U.S. business executives were aware of differing cultural proxemics only in their international dealings. Because such interactions are occurring increasingly all around us, it is fitting that we begin with the proxemic patterns of the mainstay or white male paradigm.

In the white male business culture, individuals generally stand about an arm's length from one another in normal face-to-face interactions. This means that white males customarily stand farther apart than many Hispanics. When a white male business executive calls a Hispanic pushy he may, in fact, be acknowledging while misinterpreting the impact of cultural proxemics upon us.

White males carry around a number of space bubbles within which they conduct varied activities, depending on the nature of the interaction.

intimate interactions — from skin contact to approximately 18 inches;

personal or business interactions — from about 18 inches to about 30 inches;

general, social interactions — from about 4 feet to 12 feet; and

public space interactions (when making a presentation) — 12 feet or more.

In same-sex groups, males tend to stand or sit farther apart than, for example, white women do. However, white males tend to stand or sit somewhat closer in groups that include women. When white males approach each other, they tend to stop at somewhat greater distances than they do with women.[33]

Eye Contact and Gaze

Patterns of eye contact and gaze also play an underestimated role in interpersonal communication. White males have their own, unique, eye contact patterns. When speaking, a white male looks away from the listener most of the time, making eye contact with the listener to emphasize significant points. While listening, a white male looks at the speaker most of the time. Eye contact indicates that the listener is paying attention to what is being said.[34]

Another pattern of eye contact signals the moment when turn-taking occurs for speaker and listener. Generally, when the speaker is nearing the end of a statement, he briefly looks away from the listener. Then, upon finishing the utterance, he reestablishes eye contact to signal that it is the turn of the other person to speak.[35]

Major communication problems can result if eye contact patterns are not in synchrony. Without either conversant being consciously aware of it, at appropriate times in the white male style a trustworthy person looks you in the eye, while an untrustworthy person does not. If both parties share this pattern, conversation flows smoothly. If the patterns are at odds, one may call the other shifty, while the other may feel uncomfortable. In such a situation, the conversation becomes strained, and the participants are conscious of that fact.

White males do not seem to employ or recognize the value of nonverbal communication, in general, or of eye contact, in particular. Yet, it is evident that eye contact patterns play a significant role in effective interpersonal communication. The general white male pattern is for speakers to gaze less at listeners and for listeners to gaze more at speakers. This is how white male listeners demonstrate their intentional listening or attending behavior.

Kinesics

Kinesic behavior refers to body movement, posture, and gestures. Through kinesics, individuals often send powerful messages of which they are not always aware.

Men tend to have open and relaxed body postures that occupy more space than do women. Men usually swing their arms farther away from their bodies, lean backward more, and stretch their legs farther apart when seated than do women.[36] In addition, men tend to shift their legs and feet frequently.[37]

Men's body postures tend to convey messages of gender power and dominance rather than of affiliation. This was evident in Jeff and Judith's vignette. Often such kinesic behavior discourages rather than invites communication. In contrast, the relaxed attending posture of a forward lean of the upper body invites communication. Such attending nonverbal behavior reflects an individual's openness and willingness to listen and enter into a friendly conversation.

The white male norm is for individuals to gesture with restraint — less than Hispanics but more than Asian Americans or women. Wrists and hands are used much more than arms to gesture. Except at times of great joy or sorrow, elbows generally are not raised above shoulder level. Those who gesture more than this norm may be considered flamboyant; individuals who gesture less than this norm may be considered uptight or cold fish.

Touch

White males generally do not touch or touch very little. They touch less than Hispanics but more than Asians. In one study, psychologist Dean Barnlund reports that, after age 14, the least touched U.S. student was touched more by friends and family than the most touched Japanese student.[38] Generally, in the white male culture, uninvited touching between males and females is viewed as harassing. Similarly, glad-handing or effusive touching between males is viewed as aggressive.

White males try to avoid situations of crowding, such as elevators. If it is unavoidable, they seek to minimize discomfort by momentarily stopping conversation, looking upward, or otherwise trying to pretend they are not there. Otherwise, white males accept contact only with those they have invited in — good friends, family members, and lovers. Even momentary body contact, if not invited, normally is quickly followed by an "Excuse me."

The typical white male kinesic patterns consist of moderate eye contact and gestures with a tendency toward a backward lean of the upper body. Furthermore, whether standing or seated, men tend to use more space than women — nonverbal behaviors characteristic of power, dominance, and hierarchy.[39] On the other hand, such behaviors can inhibit communication. In mainstream white, American culture, one attends and communicates interest in what is being said by maintaining eye contact, a comfortable posture with a forward-leaning upper body, hands at rest, and a facial expression denoting interest.

VERBAL COMMUNICATION

White male verbal communication differs from the other demographic groups we are examining. Walter J. Ong calls it the agonistic style. This agonistic style is deeply rooted in a ritual that captures and describes its evolution. As the story goes,

About 2500 years ago a community of young scholars would gather around their teacher in a grove in Athens, Greece. Their teacher at that time was the philosopher Socrates who was known around that area for his unique way of teaching. He would gather with his pupils every day at sunset to talk about subjects for which his students had no clear answers. The topics ranged from "What is truth?" to "What is justice?" He began each meeting by asking a question, listening to their responses, challenging them, and then going on to encourage others to state their own views and debating their answers with them again. Out of this emerged what we call Classical Rhetoric.

Centuries later, this ritual was renewed elsewhere in Europe. During medieval times, long before universities were founded, students and teachers gathered in churches after worship hours to test those who felt they had completed their studies. The males who gathered spoke Learned Latin, the only written language in Europe at that time, and so the language of upper status and of academic discourse. In the tradition of Classical Rhetoric, one student would rise to proclaim "Thesis" ("I believe . . ."), propound his argument and then defend it against those who criticized it with their "Antitheses." A spirited and combative debate was followed by a decision. Only those candidates who had strenuously and successfully enough defended their theses against all opponents in the combat of intellectual debate were invited to join the ranks of their teachers as equals.[40]

Thus, 2,500 years ago there emerged a communication style that persists today as the white male communication paradigm.

This agonistic style is man's way of communicating. It is a closed, masculine way of expression. Women were denied the opportunity to acquire Learned Latin and so were denied participation in these debates because of the medieval restrictions.

So Classical Rhetoric and Learned Latin were gender-linked public discourses written and spoken by only males. In public settings, males discoursed as individuals on general principles in an objective, detached, and impersonal style. Perhaps the word that captures the essence of this style is agonistic or combative. For millennia, public speaking was a combative male domain.

Thousands of years later, white males perpetuate the agonistic style of communication. In debate the word — the spoken and written channels — predominates. White males tend to emphasize the verbal channel of communication and, therefore, to overly rely on the spoken or written word to convey messages. They often encourage one another to speak up, or to say what's on your mind.[41] Their preference for forthright or even combative face-to-face interaction often leads white males to use the more direct and overt rather than the more subtle or covert levels of communication. Consequently, white males often miss the entire universe of nonverbal communication. And, missing the cues, fail to communicate effectively.[42]

Open and Closed Questions

Research indicates that cultural groups differ in their communication styles and specifically in the use of questions. Some research points out that the white male communication paradigm induces the use of more questions than those of women or American blacks.[43] However, a survey of the literature provides inconclusive and even contradictory findings.

Asking questions is a part of the white male business culture. Questions provide a mechanism for retrieving information and encouraging the flow of conversation. Some interpret this behavior as men's attempt to control the conversation. However, Judith Pearson hypothesizes that men's use of questions may be to secure information.[44] This seems congruent with their orientation toward task achievement. In fact, asking more questions of others is compatible with men's agonistic verbal style. Given their values, white males also find it uncomfortable and even irrelevant to the way they do business to self-disclose and respond to questions. They would rather ask questions. The white males' discomfort with silence may induce them to the rapid use of questions, a behavior that individuals from other cultures can find discomforting and even intrusive.[45]

Reflection of Feeling

White males have a problem expressing emotions. One still should uncomplainingly repress an outward show of emotion. Only recently has it become possible for males to infrequently but openly express emotions to the point of tears. It was not so long ago in a New Hampshire snowstorm that Edmund Muskie lost his primary bid for the presidential nomination because he shed, or at least appeared to shed, tears. In contrast, in 1991, a tearful Norman Schwarzkopf, hero of the Persian Gulf War, was applauded during his address to Congress for no less.

When one expresses emotions in the white male business culture, it is generally with the voice or the face. The voice cracks with emotion, is choked with sorrow, or rises in anger. Even here, the emphasis is upon restraint and control. White males do not freely express their emotions. They even have been accused of "emotional self-containment."[46]

Reflection of Meaning

White male executives pay more attention to the factual than the emotional content of messages. In the business context, they tend to believe that verbal messages should be factual and logical and deal with things or hard facts. Again, this is compatible with the agonistic style of objective evidence and logic. It may be for these reasons that white males whose paradigm embodies objectivity and verbal directness may appear cold to Hispanics or having to say everything to Asians.[47]

White males derive meaning from facts and logic. "Give me the facts," or "What are the numbers?" are constant refrains in white male business conversations. This should come as no surprise because the white male verbal mode of communication is embedded in the heritage of classical rhetoric with its give-and-take of debate and accompanying demand for evidence or proof.

The writings of Walter J. Ong support this notion. Ong has found that the way we communicate affects how we organize our thoughts and express ourselves. Ong writes that the ways we communicate — orally or in writing, agonistically or otherwise — "determine the kind of thinking that can be done, the way experience is intellectually organized."[48]

Unique features dominate the codes and meanings of male conversations. Men, in the public discourse of work, unconsciously encode their language in such a way that others may feel excluded or uncomfortable in participating. For example, compared to women, men are more likely to use language that is more hostile, more profane, uses fewer adjectives or adverbs, and is more likely to be grammatically incorrect.[49] Such encoding by men has an impact on the contexts where meanings are generated. On this basis, Dale Spender concluded: "Inherent in the analysis of dominant/muted groups is the assumption that women and men will generate different meanings, that is, that there is more than one perceptual order, but that only the 'perceptions' of the dominant group, with their inherently partial nature, are encoded and transmitted."[50]

CONCLUSION

This chapter has explored the white male cultural paradigm — the core paradigm for public discourse in the workplace as well as the dominant paradigm of the United States. Its relevance is far-reaching because it is to this paradigm that immigrants have acculturated in the past as they presently are.

The WASP or white male paradigm is rooted in the values and behaviors of the first colonial immigrants to America. They brought with them the puritan values of personal responsibility, hard work, self-control, and practicality that have undergirded the culture, in general, and the workplace, in particular, ever since.

White male values also pervade our interpersonal communications. White males are guarded in their proxemics and always maintain appropriate physical as well as emotional distances. Their kinesic behavior as well as their eye contact patterns convey power and hierarchy. The stiff upper lip attitude of emotional restraint still characterizes interpersonal behavior in the workplace.

White males tend not to express feelings or self-disclose a great deal. They tend to be parsimonious in their verbal behavior by asking direct, specific questions rather than the open-ended ones that invite participation and conversation with others. Their verbal communication is deeply embedded in the 2,500-year heritage of an agonistic style. According to this style, one is combative, direct, objective, and impersonal in both debate and the language one uses.

The white male communication paradigm continues to prevail in America's organizations today. Given that approximately one-third of work force entrants are white males, it is logical to expect that the white male paradigm will continue to be influential in workplaces across the United States well into the twenty-first century.

NOTES

1. Clinton Rossiter. (1960). *The American presidency*, 2d ed. rev., (pp. 193–194). New York: New American Library.

2. Clyde Wilcox. (1995). *The latest American revolution* (pp. 35–36). New York: St. Martin's Press.

3. John R. Schmidhauser. (1959, February). The justices of the supreme court: A collective portrait. *Midwest Journal of Political Science, 3*, pp. 1–57.

4. Richard L. Zweigenhaft, & G. William Domhoff. (1982). *Jews in the Protestant establishment* (p. 110). New York: Praeger.

5. Charles Anderson. (1970). *White protestant Americans: From national origins to religious group* (pp. 18, 36, 143). Englewood Cliffs, NJ: Prentice-Hall.

6. Anderson, *White protestant Americans*, p. 143.

7. Robert Christopher. (1989). *Crashing the gates: The de-wasping of America's power elite* (p. 20). New York: Simon & Schuster.

8. U.S. Bureau of the Census. (1994). No. 56. Population by selected ancestry group and region, 1990. *Statistical abstract of the United States*. Washington, DC: Government Printing Office.

9. U.S. Bureau of the Census. (1985). No. 42. Population by selected ancestry group and region, 1980. *Statistical abstract of the United States*. Washington, DC: Government Printing Office.

10. Ellen Graham. (1985, May 20). The entrepreneurial mystique. *Wall Street Journal*, Sec. 3, p. 4C.

11. Korn/Ferry International. (1990). *Korn/Ferry Inter-national's executive profile: A decade of change in corporate leadership* (pp. 22–23). New York: Korn/Ferry International.

12. Sondra Thiederman. (1991). *Bridging cultural barriers for corporate success: How to manage the multicultural workforce* (p. xix). Lexington, MA: Lexington Books.

13. Edward T. Hall, & Mildred Reed Hall. (1990). *Understanding cultural differences* (pp. 139–140). Yarmouth, ME: Intercultural Press.

14. Zweigenhaft, & Domhoff, *Jews in the Protestant establishment*, p. 110.

15. Anderson, *White protestant Americans*, p. 20.

16. Quoted in Christopher, *Crashing the gates*, p. 23.

17. It's no lie: He's the last of the real Washingtons. (1991, February 18). *Hartford Courant*, p. D2.

18. Christopher, *Crashing the gates*, passim.

19. Anderson, *White protestant Americans*, pp. 21–24. Anderson cites community studies by sociologists that show that as late as the 1940s Anglo-Americans in Connecticut "remained socially aloof from other ethnic groups, with the occasional exception of Scandinavians." And that in Minnesota "fully

three-fourths of the Anglo-Americans belonged to predominantly Anglo-American cliques."

20.   Elise O'Shaughnessy. (1994, October). The new establishment: That was then . . . this is now. *Vanity Fair*, pp. 209–241. See also Suzanna Andrews, Bryan Burrough, Daniel Eisenberg, Bruce Feirstein, Charles Fleming, Emma Gilbey, Phoebe Hoban, Eric Konigsberg, Kim Masters, Deborah Mitchell, Lynn Moloney, Elise O'Shaughnessy, & Mathew Tyrnauer. (1995, October). The new establishment: 50 leaders of the information age. *Vanity Fair*, pp. 269–288.

21.   See Anderson, *White protestant Americans*; Gary Althen. (1988). *American ways: A guide for foreigners in the United States.* Yarmouth, ME: Intercultural Press; Richard Brookhiser. (1991). *The way of the WASP: How it made America, and how it can save it, so to speak.* New York: The Free Press; David McGill, & John Pearce. (1982). British families. In Monica McGoldrick, John Pearce, & Joseph Giordano (Eds.), *Ethnicity and family therapy* (pp. 457–479). New York: Guilford Press; Margaret Mead. (1943). *And keep your powder dry: An anthropologist looks at America.* New York: William Morrow and Company; Edward C. Stewart. (1972). *American cultural patterns: A cross-cultural perspective.* Yarmouth, ME: Intercultural Press.

22.   Althen, *American ways*, pp. 4–5.

23.   Myron Magnet. (1992, May 4). The truth about the American worker. *Fortune, 125*(9), pp. 48–51, 54, 58, 64–65; Gene Koretz. (1995, September 4). Yankees: Nose to the grindstone; their vacations are brutishly short. *Business Week*, p. 28.

24.   McGill, & Pearce, British families, p. 460.

25.   Ibid., p. 458.

26.   Janet Lever. (1976). Sex differences in the games children play. *Social Problems, 23*, pp. 480–485.

27.   Joel P. Bowman, & Tsugihiro Okuda. (1985, December). Japanese-American communication: Mysteries, enigmas and possibilities. *The Bulletin of the Association for Business Communication, 48*(4), p. 19.

28.   Hall, & Hall, *Understanding cultural differences*, pp. 13–22.

29.   Ibid., pp. 6–10.

30.   Hugh G. Russell, & Kenneth Black, Jr. (1972). *Human behavior in business* (pp. 92–94). New York: Appleton-Century-Crofts.

31.   Judee K. Burgoon. (1994). Nonverbal signals. In Mark L. Knapp & Gerald R. Miller (Eds.), *Handbook of interpersonal communication*, 2d ed. (p. 244). Thousand Oaks, CA: Sage Publications; Alice H. Eagly. (1987). *Sex differences in social behavior: A social-role interpretation* (p. 103). Hillsdale, NJ: Lawrence Erlbaum Associates; Judith A. Hall. (1985). Male and female nonverbal behavior. In Aron W. Siegman & Stanley Feldstein (Eds.), *Multichannel integration of nonverbal behavior* (pp. 200–203). Hillsdale, NJ: Lawrence Erlbaum Associates.

32.   Edward T. Hall. (1982). *The hidden dimension* (pp. 114–125). New York: Anchor Books/Doubleday. The term "proxemics" was given currency in Edward T. Hall. (1968, April–June). Proxemics. *Current Anthropology, 9*(2–3), pp. 83–107.

33.   Hall, Male and female nonverbal behavior, p. 214; Anneke Vrugt, & Ada Kerkstra. (1984). Sex differences in nonverbal communication. *Semiotica, 50*(1/2), pp. 2–11.

34.   Ralph V. Exline. (1963). Explorations in the process of person perception: Visual interaction in relation to competition, sex, and need for affiliation. *Journal of Personality*, *31*, pp. 1–20; Michael Argyle. (1979). New developments in the analysis of social skills. In Aaron Wolfgang (Ed.), *Nonverbal behavior: Applications and cultural implications* (p. 139). New York: Academic Press; Adam Kendon. (1967). Some functions of gaze-direction in social interaction. *Acta Psychologica, 26*, pp. 22–63.

35.   Starkey Duncan, Jr. (1972). Some signals and rules for taking speaking turns in conversations. *Journal of Personality and Social Psychology, 23*(2), pp. 283–292.

36.   Elizabeth Aries. (1982). Verbal and nonverbal behavior in single-sex and mixed-sex groups. *Psychological Reports, 51*, pp. 127–134.

37.   Hall, Male and female nonverbal behavior, p. 220.

38.   Dean Barnlund. (1975). Communication styles in two cultures: Japan and the United States. In Adam Kendon, Richard M. Harris, & Mary Ritchie Key (Eds.), *Organization of behavior in face-to-face interaction* (pp. 444–457). The Hague: Mouton.

39.   Hall, Male and female nonverbal behavior, pp. 217–220.

40.   Walter J. Ong. (1981). *Fighting for life: Contest, sexuality and consciousness* (pp. 118–144). Ithaca, NY: Cornell University Press.

41.   Althen, *American ways*, p. 27.

42.   Judith A. Hall. (1984). *Nonverbal sex differences: Communication accuracy and expressive style* (p. 146). Baltimore, MD: Johns Hopkins University Press.

43.   Judith Berman. (1979). Counseling skills used by black and white male and female counselors. *Journal of Counseling Psychology, 26*(1), pp. 81–84.

44.   Judy Cornelia Pearson. (1985). *Gender and communication* (p. 191). Dubuque, IA: William C. Brown Publishers.

45.   Allen E. Ivey. (1994). *Intentional interviewing and counseling: Facilitating client development in a multicultural society*, 3rd ed., (p. 61). Pacific Grove, CA: Brooks/Cole Publishing Co.

46.   McGill, & Pearce, British families, p. 459.

47.   Althen, *American ways*, pp. 27–28.

48.   Walter J. Ong. (1982). *Orality and literacy: The technologizing of the word* (p. 36). London: Methuen.

49.   Robin Lakoff. (1975). *Language and women's place* (passim). New York: Harper & Row.

50.   Dale Spender. (1980). *Man-made language* (p. 77). London: Routledge & Kegan Paul.

6

Women's Communication Paradigm

My biggest problem is that I am simply not taken seriously by my colleagues in this company. I am intelligent, hard-working, experienced, and work well with my colleagues — male and female. But it seems that when I make a point in a meeting, I'm simply not heard. Or I'm interrupted. Or I hear a man acknowledged by name and praised for the exact point I made three comments earlier. It's so frustrating and depressing. And because of this, I feel I am being passed over by males whose contributions *are* recognized and then get the right set of experiences for the next promotion that I don't. When I act like a woman, I feel like I am not even seen. When I try to behave more like a man, trying to assert myself, I am rejected. I am at a complete loss as to what to do.

— Ann, Fortune 500 executive

Ann's contributions are discounted and her voice is not heard. Male managers who joined the company with Ann have no problem being recognized in meetings, getting full credit for suggestions, and securing key assignments for seasoning and then promotion to choice positions. The perceptions and expectations of the workplace still are influenced by gender. During the last few decades more and more women like Ann have entered a male-dominated workplace and encountered similar problems. This chapter addresses women's communication paradigm and its impact on women's position in the workplace.

WOMEN'S CULTURAL HISTORICAL BACKGROUND

To understand Ann's dilemma, we examine the cultural historical background of women. What few of us realize is that how we communicate has historical and cultural roots.

According to Dorothy Smith, throughout history men have dominated language by paying attention only to what other men say. This was particularly true in public discourse. Women were muted, that is, excluded from formulating language in their own voice. "There is a circle effect. Men attend to and treat as significant only what men say. The circle of men whose writing and talk was significant to each other extends backwards in time as far as our records reach. What men were doing was relevant to men, was written by men about men for men. Men listened and listen to what one another said."[1]

Smith describes the historical roots of Ann's problems. She helps us understand why men do not listen to their female colleagues. Women have not been part of the workplace with its public discourse. In patriarchal societies, women generally were not accorded a public place in the counsels of business or a voice in decision making. Thus, consciously or unconsciously, men have not perceived women in the roles of participants or equals in public settings. Therefore, men tend not to pay attention to what women say. Competent women like Ann complain of not being heard. Neither understands why.

Women have been called the muted gender. As is true for men, women's language is gender-linked and rooted in the Western cultural-historical experience. Formally unschooled and denied the chance to speak in public, women learned to express themselves in other settings and in other ways. In the private settings of home, family, and friends, women's manner of expression was more subjective, attached, personal, situational, and relationship oriented. Jesuit scholar, Walter J. Ong, writes, women "normally expressed themselves in a different, far less oratorical voice."[2]

As we saw in the previous chapter, men's agonistic style is rooted in the Western tradition. According to this heritage, opponents take separate positions and then objectively and impersonally attack and debate each other's positions according to the verbal, adversarial style of the Classical and Medieval periods. The agonistic style involves the clash of words instead of swords. Women's voice echoed a more private style of connected relationships. If men's way of communicating is agonistic, then women's way of communication is relational.

These gender communication styles increasingly encounter each other in the workplace, which has been dominated by the male discourse. Dissonance often occurs that neither party knows how to handle, except (as Ann exemplifies) by mutually ignoring the dissonance. The contemporary shift of women from the private domain of home to the public domain of workplace is having an impact on face-to-face communication. It is time to examine the demographics of women in the workplace.

THE DEMOGRAPHICS

Characteristically unheralded, the first white colonist born in what became the United States was female — Virginia Dare in 1603. From that point on, women have played a significant role in building America. Betsy Ross sewed the first American flag. Maria Ludwig, better known by her Anglicized name of Molly Pitcher, helped win the Revolutionary War. During the unquestioned male domination of the nineteenth century, women and men shared the rigors of the frontier equally. Was it by accident that Wyoming's legislature was the first to grant women the right to vote in 1869, and that Colorado was the first state to approve women's suffrage by popular vote in 1893 — frontier states where the reality of equal, shared struggle was strongest and stereotypes weakest. It was female Rosie the Riveters who built the Liberty Ships, B-29 bombers, and Sherman tanks that contributed to the Allied victory of World War II.[3] In fact, the percentage of women in the paid labor force rose by approximately 33 percent between 1940 and 1950.[4] They paved the way for today's pioneers like Esther Dyson, venture capitalist president of EDventure Holdings, editor of the influential information technology publication *Release 1.0*, and organizer of its yearly PC Forum; Heidi Kunz, treasurer of the General Motors Corporation; and Carol Bartz, chief executive officer (CEO) of Autodesk, a cutting-edge computer company with annual sales of a half billion dollars.

Paradoxically, in today's paid labor force, more women are working than ever before in U.S. history — although many are in lower positions and paid less than men in similar positions.

Women comprise 45 percent of the U.S. work force and half of entry-level managers.[5] However, only 2 female CEOs were on *Forbes* 1995 list of the 800 most powerful executives in corporate America.[6] In 1994 *Inc* magazine listed women as CEOs of only 2 of the "100 fastest growing small companies in America."[7] Women own 26 percent of independently-run U.S. businesses, but collect less than 5 percent of the total revenues.[8] Women still predominate in traditional fields — in 1990, 98 percent of secretaries were women as were 94 percent of nurses and 74 percent of teachers.[9]

The average working female still earns 74 percent of what a male earns — up from about 60 percent from 1920 through 1980. However, women's earnings vary by occupation: engineers earn 86 percent, lawyers 75 percent, and physicians 54 percent of their male counterparts. Surprisingly, women managers bring home only 66 percent of their male counterpart's salary.[10]

Women experience every obstacle that men do in their careers plus some others. Among the more pronounced problems are sexual harassment, discriminatory exclusion by members of the old boy network, discrepancy between old and new assumptions about women and behavioral differences between the genders — differences that matter more the higher one goes in the executive hierarchy. In a 1992 survey, 400 senior women managers indicated that women's abilities and contributions are not valued as highly as men's because they do not fit the male model. One of the most commonly voiced observations of these senior woman executives was that the men currently in power "still do not feel comfortable with women as peers" and that "comfort level" remains a decisive factor in selection for top executive positions.[11]

The Glass Ceiling Commission concurs. A central finding of its 1995 report was that women are being discriminated against because they comprise only 3 to 5 percent of top-level executive positions above the rank of vice president.[12] The Commission explained that this discrepancy was caused by a discriminatory "glass ceiling" that prevents women from reaching senior management ranks. Global human resources firm Korn/Ferry International and the women's organization Catalyst concurred, finding that less than 4 percent of America's top executives were women.[13]

In 1991, the Glass Ceiling Commission found that, "Minorities and women have made significant gains at the entry level of employment and into the first levels of management. Yet, they have not experienced similar gains into the mid and senior levels of management." And the reason was a discriminatory "glass ceiling" — "a point beyond which minorities and women have not advanced."[14]

These discriminatory practices are widespread and antithetical to the ethic of the United States. However, there may be good news. Women-owned firms are among the fastest growing segments of the U.S. economy and employ in excess of 11 million persons — more people than Fortune 500 corporations employ around the world.[15]

Most managerial jobs continue to be held by white males, but women have made striking advances since the mid-1980s. According to U.S. Bureau of the Census statistics, women executives, administrators, and managers in the private sector have increased from 32 percent in 1983 to 42 percent in 1993. Women officials and administrators in the public sector have increased from 38 percent in 1983 to 45 percent in 1993.[16] Even more striking, the Glass Ceiling Commission's 1995 report found that 47 percent of America's managers are women (36 percent white,

5 percent black, 5 percent Hispanic, and about 1 percent Asian American).[17] As Peter Kilborn viewed these findings: "Women have found more success in middle management."[18] The same is apparently true in the professions.

According to an article by Sam Roberts citing the U.S. Department of Labor, between 1970 and 1990 the proportion of jobs held by women increased from 3 to 27 percent for industrial engineers, 6 to 27 percent for lawyers and judges, 14 to 44 percent for economists, 13 to 30 percent for stockbrokers, and 24 to 59 percent for public officials.[19] In examining the status of women in the professions, the women's organization Catalyst reported: "According to an analysis of EEOC data conducted by *The Wall Street Journal*, as reported in March 1994, while white men continue to hold a greater share of professional jobs, white women have made substantial gains: In 1982 there were 0.62 white female professionals for every white man; in 1992, there were 0.94."[20]

While studies, methodologies, and results may vary somewhat, they indicate greater inclusion of women managers and professionals in an increasing number of fields. Sexism and discrimination are still prevalent. A national survey of 400 senior women executives found that 59 percent of these women had experienced sexual harassment during their careers but that the number who felt that "being a woman/sexism" was the biggest obstacle they had to overcome to achieve success had decreased from 39 percent in 1982 to 27 percent in 1992 — nearly 33 percent — in just ten years. The survey also found that women executive vice presidents had more than doubled (from 4 percent to 9 percent) while senior vice presidents increased from 13 percent to 23 percent and 60 percent of the female executive respondents expected to be part of their own company's senior management team in the year 2000 while 82 percent of them believed that women will be on that team.[21]

Women managers continue to face more discrimination and difficulties than their male colleagues, yet, they have made progress in breaking the glass ceiling of U.S. corporations. One study found that during the 1980s much larger numbers of women managers began reaching higher posts at a younger age than ever before. Women also began moving into senior ranks (vice president, executive vice president), which are springboards into the even higher CEO positions.[22]

Roy D. Adler and Rebecca M. J. Yates have compared the number of women who earned masters in business administration in 1967 with the number of women in the top 20 management positions of Fortune 500 companies in 1992. The study recognized that 25 years approximates the time required to qualify for these top 20 management positions. The researchers found that women earned 2.6 percent of master of business administration degrees in 1967, but they comprised 7.5 percent (approximately three times their entering number) of top managers among corporations surveyed in 1992. Yates concluded: "We're saying we are starting to break through the glass ceiling, that it's permeable."[23]

This is also the conclusion of Lester Korn. In 1990 he observed that women comprised 50 percent of managers just below the top 20 executives in major U.S. corporations, and, with two to three decades of work experience already behind them, these women will begin breaking through the glass ceiling to top positions by the year 2000.[24] Harvard Business School's Regina Herzlinger was more conservative, forecasting that many Fortune 500 CEOs will be women by 2010.[25] Similarly, U.S. News & World Report published a forecast that 20 percent of Fortune 500 senior executives would be female by the year 2010.[26] And in 1992 the Korn/Ferry study concluded: "There are too few women CEOs and COOs in Corporate America, and too few women accepted as serious contenders for these posts. But there now is a concentration of accomplished, proven senior women executives and it is our view that our next study a decade hence will show them breaking through the 'glass ceiling.'"[27]

Women's climb up the executive and corporate ladders has been arduous and slow. However, the pace is quickening and the top is within sight. It is also obvious that women need to persist in their endeavors to achieve their dreams despite the obstacles they encounter along the way. They should take credit for this encouraging development, particularly the undaunted women who have persisted in their commitment and courage to crack the glass ceiling on behalf of themselves and the many women to come.

Women's status in the business world takes on new importance as more and more of them move from home to office, mother and wife to colleague and boss. In charting the course, we look to the past as well as the future to examine the traditional and new assumptions about women.

ASSUMPTIONS ABOUT WOMEN

Traditional Assumptions

The traditional assumptions about women's identities and roles are deeply embedded in women's unconscious and account for how men have perceived women and some women still perceive themselves.[28] The assumptions are nearly universal in world societies thereby ensuring the rearing of sound children for the next generation. The assumptions are particularly suited to the agricultural and industrial economies where hard physical work is required — a fact that favors the contribution of males over females. These traditional assumptions delineate women as private beings with a private life.

Women are Wives and Mothers

According to this first assumption, a woman's most important roles in life are those of wife and mother. The traditional German proverb "Kinder, Kuche, Kirche" — children, kitchen, church — indicates woman's place in the world. A woman's existence should be centered on her children's care and her family's well-being. Single, unmarried, or childless women cannot develop or be sufficiently fulfilled. Women who focus on their own personal development are considered selfish or narcissistic.

The Primacy of Nurturance

Women are nurturers, caretakers, peacemakers. A woman never says no to her husband's or family's need for nurturance. Women are socialized to be other-centered rather than self-centered. Thus, it is unacceptable for a woman to establish clear boundaries between herself and her family, and to set limits on what she owes to others or may be called upon to sacrifice.

Rigid Differentiation between Women's Roles and Men's Roles

Women cook, clean, and tend home and children. Around the house men do only mechanical or heavy work, never women's work. Until the 1960s, newspaper employment advertisements read "Help Wanted, Male" and (for very different occupations) "Help Wanted, Female." The paid work outside of the home, which is sanctioned for women is primarily in the helping professions of teacher, nurse, or secretary. For some, community volunteer work is always available.

Women as Inferiors and Subordinates

Women are the "second sex," the "weaker sex," the "inferior sex," the "subordinate sex." If assumed to be "inferior" and "subordinate," then women are less well-equipped than men to undertake the full range of human endeavors, especially in the workplace. This assumption especially underlies women's position in organizations.

Some women still hold these assumptions about themselves. Probably, even more men hold these assumptions about women. These traditional assumptions are congruent with the agrarian economy in which so much of women's work is carried out in the private setting of home and farm. But during the nineteenth and twentieth centuries, the U.S. economy was industrialized and is now becoming informationalized. Women's participation in the paid labor force is continually increasing and creating the need for a new set of assumptions about women, this time in the public sphere.

Since the 1960s the feminist movement has provided a political and moral pulpit to address the inequities and injustices that women suffer. Feminist thought has provided a forum to discuss the confluence of economic, behavioral, and psychological shifts that are occurring in America. Furthermore, feminism has brought women together to talk about the need for a new set of assumptions about women not only as wives and mothers but also as public beings with private lives.

New Assumptions

Two emerging realities are compelling women to forge new assumptions about themselves. The first is a new demographic reality: the number of women who work in the paid labor force is increasing (from 19 percent in 1900 to an estimated 63 percent in 2000 and 66 percent in 2005).[29]

The second reality is the global economic shift from the industrial economy to the information economy. More and more educated and credentialed women are entering the work force at a time when brains, not brawn, are the premium. For the first time, large numbers of women are working away from their homes in new roles, in close contact and in positions of equal or greater status and power with men, and in the public sphere. These new realities demand that we forge new assumptions.

Women are Wives, Mothers, and Workers

Whether because of choice or economic necessity, 58 percent of women overall and 46 percent of women of childbearing age were in the paid labor force in 1992.[30] In such circumstances, women cannot be solely responsible for a child's well-being. This new assumption holds that a woman should be career oriented to be sufficiently fulfilled whether single, married, or with children. The development of a woman's independence and self-sufficiency will improve rather than threaten her own and her family's functioning.

Woman as Nurturer of Others and of Herself

Women should not be solely responsible for the emotional well-being of others — especially children. Men can be nurturers and caregivers as well. In today's society, fathers are taking a more active role in the rearing of children and in home responsibilities. Simultaneously, women have realized the necessity to nurture their own personal and professional needs and goals. A new flexibility is emerging in both men's and women's attitudes about their mutual responsibilities for nurturing behavior.

More Diffuse Women's and Men's Roles

Today men's and women's roles have become more diffuse. The division of labor is less rigid and not necessarily gender-linked. Women are astronauts, jet pilots, sportswriters, and have been taken as prisoners of war in Desert Storm combat. Women have proven that they can undertake and discharge the full range of human endeavors in the workplace. As one female journalist put it: "There's been a change in the Zeitgeist — everywhere women have proved they can do it."[31]

Women as the Other but Equal Sex

Women no longer see themselves as inferior, subordinate, or dependent. Women have entered arenas of the labor force that previously had been reserved for males. Women increasingly are the colleagues as well as the superiors of men in the workplace. This trend will continue to unfold as more women enter the work force. The percentage of women who work in the labor force has increased from 38 percent in 1960, to 58 percent in 1990, and is forecast to be 66 percent in 2005.[32]

As the number of working women has changed so have the attitudes supporting the new assumptions. Between 1977 and 1991 the number of Americans who agreed with the statement "It is better for everyone involved if the man is the achiever outside the home and the woman cares for the home and family" dropped from 65 percent to 41 percent. In the same 14-year period, the percentage of Americans who voiced agreement with the statement "It is more important for a wife to help her husband's career than to have one herself" decreased from 55 percent to 29 percent.[33]

The clash between the traditional and new assumptions present profound issues to women. Some managers are career-primary women who, like most men, put their careers first. However, most women choose to be career-and-family women. These women pursue both tracks. Felice Schwartz coined the term "mommy track" career trajectory to describe this emerging reality. She suggests that organizations retain top female managerial talent by creating more flexible career tracks. Thus, women can work part time, or at home, during childrearing years and return to their full-time positions after rearing their children, or they can start paid work in the labor force at mid-life.[34] The task is to forge a new and common set of assumptions that reflect and enrich women's lives as workers, wives, and mothers — as they so choose.

Among the major movements of the twentieth century, feminism has led the dialogue from which the new assumptions have emerged.[35] Feminism also plays a key role in the ongoing debate between the traditional assumptions and the new assumptions about women and addresses the increasing national concern about the growing number of women in the work force and the impact this growth has on private life and family.

The widespread inequity women encounter in the workplace has been a driving force for feminism. Women in the labor force encounter more difficulties than men because they are women. As they reach higher positions, "the normal increase in pressure and responsibility is compounded for women because they are women."[36] The prevailing masculine culture of the workplace intensifies this situation for women but women's characteristic style of relating to others and ways of making meaning are undergirded by a value system that potentially diffuses this intensity. In a stressful situation, women are more likely to talk, network, and form their own support systems. Men are more likely to autonomously retreat from others and deal with the situation independently.[37] Exploring women's values will help us understand how this happens.

WOMEN'S VALUES

> All they cared about was the bottom line, making sure we had the people with the skills and experience necessary to getting that unit's job done. Feelings were secondary. I saw the hurt of the people involved. I knew that we had to downsize. But I concentrated more on trying to minimize the hurt. Not only because these were people I knew, but because of the morale of the people remaining and its impact on working relationships. I wanted to see if there wasn't some way we could save a few more people. I wanted to reach the same goal, but I wanted to do it differently.
> —Jane, Fortune 500 executive

In this interview Jane expressed the complex interplay between women's values and the male culture of the workplace. Jane was the only woman executive on a team charged with corporate downsizing. In order to understand the significance of Jane's statement, one needs to examine the principles that guide her thinking.

Listening attentively to Jane, one hears an empathic voice expressing care for the hurt of the individuals affected by the downsizing. It is also a voice of compassion and connection. At the same time, Jane combines concern and pragmatism when she points to the morale of the people remaining and their working relationships. One might ponder if this is specifically Jane's thinking or typical of women in general.

A substantial body of research indicates that American society socializes males and females differently.[38] From the earliest age, boys generally are encouraged to be aggressive and independent and to pursue the individual mastery and achievement of tasks. Traits, such as autonomy, self-reliance, and toughness, are actively encouraged in males.

Simultaneously, boys are taught to suppress their emotions. All this amplifies men's sense of disconnection with others and lessens their ability to empathize.

Traits that are adaptive for mothering and nurturing are encouraged in females. Dawn-Marie Driscoll and Carol R. Goldberg point out:

From preadolescence on, young girls have an exaggerated notion of the importance of being liked. The behavior of the "good girl" works for them as they bring home rewards from school, summer camp, and church for behaving in deferential and sweet ways. The attributes of caregiver, nurturer and peacemaker are learned early, practiced on dolls and friends, and reinforced in books. Being nice is more important than achieving other goals, especially if the latter requires competition and aggressive behavior. Achievement for girls often means being well-behaved and perfect in everything.[39]

Leading feminist scholars, such as Mary Field Belenky and colleagues, Nancy Chodorow, and Carol Gilligan, agree that the values women cherish most are caring, relationships, and empathy.[40] In his research on children's games, Swiss psychologist Jean Piaget has found that girls tend to be more pragmatic about rules than do boys. In their games, girls tend to discuss rules more, to be tolerant of exceptions, and to collectively arrive at decisions about the validity of rules or the need for changing them.[41] Women tend to be more affiliative and relationship oriented and less focused upon individual autonomy.

Males are guided more by the values of external hierarchy and impersonal principles. Boys are socialized to form groups that operate on the basis of abstract and impersonal rules. Girls are socialized to interact privately and cooperatively in pairs, which takes into account the feelings of others. For girls, the preservation of the relationship is most important.[42] Thus, when boys play softball and the youngest batter strikes out on the third pitch, he is out of the game, but, in the same situation, girls playing softball are more likely to give their youngest batter one more chance.

Women may have a greater capacity for expressing empathy than men. In general, women's experiences may be described best by the characteristics of connection, caring, cooperation, and relationship. According to Jean Baker Miller, girls and women thrive on relationships, because they experience them as empowering.[43]

Why do males experience their own autonomy as empowering while women experience relationships as empowering? Gilligan offers a response. She traces important differences in the formation of gender identity to the ways men and women experience their childhood relationships with their mothers. From about age three onward, girls develop their feminine identities by continuing to be like their mothers while boys develop their masculine identities by becoming unlike their mothers. Girls tend to maintain a deeper emotional connection with their mothers while boys separate and individuate. Attachment and relationships continue to remain important values for women, but men, threatened by intimacy, tend to avoid expressing feelings and become more impersonal in relationships.[44]

WOMEN'S CONNECTED CONVERSATION

Women's style of connected conversation has certain characteristics.

Conversation

Women converse in a world of relational orality. That is, conversation is more central for women than men in such areas as feelings and relationships with family, friends, and colleagues.[45] Women delight in the art of conversing while men's conversation tends to be more purposeful and goal oriented. For women, conversation also means a dialogue rather than a monologue and taking turns rather than competition where listening rather than speaking dominates.

Private Settings

Historically, women have experienced conversation more in the private settings of their home and circle of friends. Denied access to public forums and with their traditional roles and work circumscribed to nurturance and child care, women's speech was not the public speech of facts and disputations but the private speech of caring and feeling. Men's voices prevailed in the public domain of work, although that is changing. Even today, men, both in numbers and in their differing voices, dominate in business, politics, painting, rock and classical music, and even show business comedy.

Close to the Human Lifeworld

Many characteristics of oral cultures identified by Ong are similar to what might be called women's culture. Ong writes that "Oral cultures must conceptualize and verbalize all their knowledge with more or less close reference to the human lifeworld, assimilating the alien, objective world to the more immediate interaction of human beings."[46]

Some of women's speech consists of talking about the actions and events in their own lives and relationships as well as those of others. Yet, there is an even deeper level to women's conversations that stays close to the human lifeworld. Women are likely to see more from their position, and talk more about it, simply because their perceptions are grounded in the happenings of the everyday life around them.

Logic from the Personal Experience Situation

Women tend to approach situations from the perspective of personal experience. People, ideas, problems, and solutions are approached not only from the perspective of objective logic but also from the view of empathetic caring. Women are sensitive to the contexts of situations. They factor in the "practicalities of everyday life."[47] Women express compassion and a sense of reverence for human conditions, such as weakness and vulnerability.

Lawrence Kohlberg's classic moral dilemma — should Heinz steal medicine from a druggist who is charging an outrageous price in order to save his wife's life[48] — elicits different responses from males and females. Gilligan points out that males tend to invoke impersonal and objective principles, such as the right to life over that of property.[49] Women tend to ask such questions as "How perilous is Mrs. Heinz's condition?" "Are there dependent children?" "Who would take care of them if their father was jailed?" These questions illustrate the multiple perspectives that women often seek to clarify and take into account before making a decision. Women consider not only the universal principles involved but also the impact on individuals in context. Jane's experience with the downsizing situation reflects this. In her resolution of that problem she was responding to not only the need to downsize but also the personal needs of the displaced individuals, the remaining coworkers, and the organization as a whole.

DO WOMEN MANAGE DIFFERENTLY?

Evidence suggests that women, as a group, may have the capability for a different managerial approach than men.

In her book, Sally Helgesen identified a feminine leadership style. She found that men operate on the basis of individual achievement and hierarchy while women operate on the basis of caring, helping, connective relationships, and inclusion. She wrote: "We *feel*, many of us that women are more caring and intuitive, better at seeing the human side, quicker to cut through competitive distinctions of hierarchy and ranking, impatient with cumbersome protocols. Our belief in these notions is intuitive rather than articulated."[50]

How do the genders see themselves in organizations? Men see themselves at the top of hierarchies; women see themselves in the middle of "webs." According to Gilligan: "The images of hierarchy and web, drawn from the texts of men's and women's fantasies and thoughts convey different ways of structuring relationships."[51] Being in the middle of webs permits managers to be in the center of vital information flows, to work more closely and acknowledge the individual's role in the organization, and to flatten the pyramid thereby allowing quicker, more spontaneous management functioning — all advantageous qualities in the twenty-first century's informational economy.

Judy Rosenor found that men manage more by hierarchical, command-and-control methods in which success is rewarded and failure punished.[52] Here the power to get things done comes from one's position of authority in the organization. Command and control management worked well in the large-scale military, factory, and office hierarchies of the industrial era.

According to Rosenor, women's interactive or transformational leadership style converts the self-interest of workers into organizational goals by encouraging participation, power sharing, and collaboration. The worker has a greater sense of self-worth and is excited about work. The ways women lead are better suited to the smaller-scale, fluid, if not crises-ridden organizations of the informational era that demand exactly those qualities characteristic of women's transformational leadership. Yet, Rosenor herself cautioned that, although she found these patterns to be gender-linked, women only *tend* toward transformational leadership: "Most men and women describe themselves as having an equal mix of traits that are considered 'feminine' (. . . understanding, compassionate, sensitive, dependent), 'masculine' (. . . aggressive, tough, assertive . . .) and '"gender neutral' (. . . conventional, reliable . . . efficient)."[53]

Rosenor states that when participation does not (or does not have the time to) work women managers have no problem acting unilaterally, that is, in the male management style, and that "Linking interactive leadership directly to being female is a mistake. We know that women are capable of making their way through corporations by adhering to the traditional corporate model and that they can wield power in ways similar to men. Indeed, some women may prefer that style. We also know from the survey findings that some men use the transformational leadership style."[54]

Both genders, then, are capable of acting in a nurturing, supportive, tough, and assertive manner when needed. Both male and female managers have the propensity to act in a way that will accommodate their management needs at the moment. In the sexless realm of achievement or failure, the demands levied upon women are no different than those levied upon men. Gary Powell's research leads him to conclude that male and female managers "differ in some ways and at some times, but, for the most part, they do not differ."[55]

Powell's review of the research literature points out that while some gender differences have been found in laboratory-controlled experiments, this generally has not been the case in studies of how managers actually manage. In working with managers of equal status, Powell found that in each gender's preferred interaction styles all-male groups were more task oriented (problem solving) in their behavior and all-female groups were more relationship oriented (reaching a consensus in problem solving) in theirs. But most important these gender differences tended to disappear in mixed-gender groups whose members had worked together.[56]

A recent study by the National Foundation for Women Business Owners finds both similarities and differences in how men and women entrepreneurs think about and manage their businesses. Reminiscent of their childhood play, women emphasize relationships and intuition whereas men emphasize hierarchy and logical problem solving. Thus, women's thinking can be characterized as being more intuitive and reflective in weighing options during the decision-making process. In such instances, men tend to focus upon facts and structure. Women are more likely to see their businesses as families and perceive their work relationships as supportive networks; men are more likely to perceive their organizations in terms of hierarchies and rules. The study also pointed out that men tend to be more dispassionate about their professional relationships.

It is imperative that we not only dwell on the simplicity of differences between the genders but also recognize the complexity of similarities. A somewhat different picture emerges when we scrutinize the empirical data underlying these findings. For example, the study found that while 53 percent of the women emphasized intuition and relationships so did 30 percent of the men. Yet, while 71 percent of the men emphasized facts and structure, so did 47 percent of the women. In short, while differences exist so do similarities. Both men and women have distinct and different management styles that can overlap simultaneously and be similar. Both styles were found to be equally effective.[57]

WOMEN'S COMMUNICATION STYLE

We submit that the disparity between communication styles is a significant obstacle that women face in organizations, particularly as they climb the corporate ladder to where fit becomes crucial. The following vignette depicts the varying communication styles of men and women.

Harry had come to the meeting confident that he would make the sale. He was proposing a new method to finance the lease of the International Widget

Corporation's personal computers. Harriet, International Widget's assistant vice-president for finance, was on the other side of the table, smiling, nodding her head, and frequently saying "um-hmm."

HARRY (to himself): She's smiling and nodding and saying "um-hmm' — all positive "buy" signals.

HARRIET (to herself): I wish he'd hurry up and finish his presentation. I'm becoming tired of being polite. He has a fairly new approach, but I saw the same idea with much better numbers just a week ago.

HARRY (excitedly to himself): I just may have this sale.

HARRIET (smiling to herself): I wish he'd finish.

HARRY (confidently): Well, that's it. What do you think?

HARRIET: That was an interesting presentation.

HARRY: If you like what I presented, could we talk about doing business?

HARRIET: Well you know, I must bring up your proposal with others. I'm not ready to act on it right now.

HARRY: No, I'm saying if you don't have any questions, can we talk business?

HARRIET: I am sorry, Harry, but I am not ready to do that.

HARRY: But why not? For the last twenty minutes you've seemed so interested — smiling, agreeing, not asking any questions. . . . I thought you liked what you saw.

HARRIET: You presented your material quite well. However, I think that I saw a presentation very similar to yours quite recently. But with different numbers. And I still need to think about it and discuss it further.

HARRY: I don't understand this. If you had any questions, why didn't you say so?

This classic scene is happening all over America. More and more of us are awakening to the fact that men's and women's communication styles differ.

Harry was not aware that women smile more frequently and look longer and more directly into the face and eyes of their conversant. Women also generally attend and listen more intently than men by nodding their heads and uttering verbal encouragers like "um-hmm" that reinforce the speaker to go on. These nonverbal encouragers may have different meanings for men and women. An "um-hmm" for men may mean "I agree" or "I understand your case so far," whereas women may mean "I hear you," or "keep talking." Sometimes the difference in meaning that each gender attributes to minimal encouragers can cause misunderstanding.[58] Harriet did not know that a male like Harry most probably would interpret her female communication style as expressing a buyer's interest rather than simply a woman listening attentively to what was being presented.

Another critical consideration in this interchange is the decision-making process. For Harry, the decision was there to be made one individual to another. For Harriet, a more inclusive and consensual process was necessary. She wanted the input of the team. A female communication style that differs subtly but distinctly from that of males may account for the battle of the sexes. It may also explain some of the miscommunication in the workplace.

The remainder of this chapter will focus on women's communication paradigm using the microskills approach. The first focus will be on the nonverbal attending behaviors. The second focus will be on the verbal attending behaviors. We will address only the microskills that characterize the communication style of women.[59]

NONVERBAL COMMUNICATION

The popular belief that women's intuition makes them better judges of people than men is substantiated by research. Linguists and psychologists find that women tend to be more observant of nonverbal communication and more likely to notice and respond to the nonverbal messages of others. In fact, research documents that women read nonverbal cues more accurately and encode and decode nonverbal messages as well as understand their meanings better than men.[60] In her review of more than 60 studies, Judith Hall found that women were more perceptive interpreters of nonverbal messages than men.[61]

Eye Contact and Gaze

Eye contact in the mainstream business culture signifies interest in what the speaker is saying. It is also a powerful signal of one's attention, a powerful encourager of more communication. In nonverbal communication, eye contact and gaze may be among the most relevant of behaviors.

Women maintain more eye contact than men in conversation. In mixed-gender interactions, women look at their partners for longer periods of time whether they are listening or speaking.[62] In same-gender interactions, women tend to maintain more eye contact when speaking, listening, or gazing at each other.[63]

For women, eye contact is an important nonverbal attending skill that encourages communication. However, eye contact also conveys a host of other signals. In uncomfortable or conflictual situations, women are more likely than men to lower or break eye contact.[64] Thus, it is important to understand the significance of eye contact when communicating with women.

Facial Expression

Women express a great deal through their facial expressions. They are more expressive of their emotions in contrast to men, who generally internalize their emotions. In one laboratory study, men and women were physiologically monitored and their faces photographed as they viewed highly emotional slides. Although their faces remained expressionless, the physiological responses of men were strong. While females also responded physiologically, they more openly expressed their emotions, especially through their facial expressions.[65]

Women smile and return more smiles than men. One study found that while 93 percent of women returned smiles, only 67 percent of men did so.[66] Women, moreso than men, attentively combine greater eye contact, smiles, and conversationally-encouraging nods of the head. In fact, women not only smile more but also laugh more than men.[67] Women, in general, are more animated than men.

Kinesics

What the layman calls body language, the researcher calls kinesics — messages communicated by body movement. Women tend to lean forward more when talking with another person; men tend to recline backward.[68] Leaning forward encourages communication with another person. Research substantiates that leaning forward expresses interest in what is being said; leaning backward generally conveys little interest or even disinterest.

Generally, women's body posture is more constrained, occupies less space, and reflects more constricted arm and leg positions and movements. Men tend to carry and move their bodies in more relaxed and expansive postures. On the surface, women's kinesic behavior appears paradoxical. On the one hand, it may be interpreted as less confident and more tentative than that of men, but, on the other hand, it reflects more attending behavior thereby encouraging conversation. Women's body posture tends to be more responsive to the patterns of their conversants.[69] The synchrony of partners mirroring each others' body movements is a state of ultimate attending and communication.

Proxemics

Proxemics involves the sending and receiving of messages through the use of interpersonal space. What should we know about women's proxemic behavior that can shed light on their communication?

Women tend to take up less space than men whether they sit, stand, or walk. When seated, men tend to occupy more space than women. Men stretch their arms and legs in front of and around themselves. Women occupy less space by maintaining more closed knee and rectangular leg positions and keeping their elbows closer to the sides of their bodies. Men are more likely to walk up to and stand closer to a stationary woman thereby lessening her personal space. When walking and carrying an article, women tend to cross both arms or clasp an article with both arms in front of their chest; men take up more space by freely swinging both arms as they walk while holding an article with one hand at waist level.

In single sex groups, women tend to stand or sit closer together while men tend to sit and stand farther apart. Thus, proxemics plays a very important role in nonverbally cueing communication.[70]

Vocal Qualities

Vocal qualities comprise another set of nonverbal attending skills. Women have higher-pitched voices than men. According to Nancy Henley and Barrie Thorne, women's higher-pitched voices and more variable pitches may be heard as "unsure intonation patterns." They also report that women with lower-pitched voices are more likely to be hired as broadcasters.[71] In another study, both male and female subjects listened more attentively and recalled more information from live speeches by male than female speakers.[72] This may help explain why women often are not listened to as attentively as they would wish to be in the workplace.

Verbal Encouragers

Verbal encouragers or verbal trackers serve as nonverbal attending behaviors. Verbal encouragers are words that encourage the speaker to go on and talk more about a topic. Verbal trackers, such as "um-hmm," "I see," or "okay" reinforce speakers to stay on the topic. Women tend to use more verbal and nonverbal conversational encouragers.[73] The following scenario illustrates the use of verbal encouragers.

ALAN: I have a problem. I just found out that my department is being relocated to the Carolinas, and unless I move I lose my job.

ANDREA (leaning forward and maintaining eye contact): Uh-hmm.

ALAN: And if we move my wife gives up her job, and we're back to one income.

ANDREA: Uh-hmm, I see.

ALAN: You know, this is a difficult decision for me. It's either her job or my job. I don't know what to do here. It has been difficult to talk about this at home. But you know Andrea, I'm glad you understand where I'm coming from. I feel better just being able to talk with you about this.

Through the attending behaviors of eye contact, body posture, and verbal encouragers, listeners can convey their interest in what is being said. When verbal tracking is used congruently with other nonverbal microskills, speakers feel understood. In fact, this is what happened to Alan in the scenario. All that Andrea did was listen to Alan and not drift away from the topic at hand. Andrea neither asked questions nor attempted to shift the conversation in any other direction. She just created the room for Alan to talk about what troubled him. Andrea's simple use of verbal and nonverbal encouragers moved Alan to talk about what he most needed to at that moment.

In summary, women tend to be more sensitive and responsive to nonverbal cues and communications. It may be that their connective and caring values imbue their nonverbal communication style.

VERBAL COMMUNICATION

Attending skills flow from the premise that people communicate more and better with those who attend to them. We have reviewed the nonverbal attending skills of women. Let us now turn to the verbal attending skills of open and closed questions, paraphrasing, reflection of feeling, and reflection of meaning as they are found in women's communication behavior.

Open and Closed Questions

Women tend to ask more questions than men. In analyzing 50 hours of taped conversation among couples in the private setting of their homes, Pamela Fishman found that women ask more closed questions to initiate conversation.[74] Women's communication style also tends to reflect the frequent use of open questions. Even at ages four and five, girls use more "would you's" and "could you's" than boys. Researchers have found that women, reflective of their caring, are more likely than men to use such considerate forms of speech.[75]

Men and women tend to express themselves differently because of their communication paradigms. Men seem to more imperiously order others around. Women seem to make more politely-phrased and complex requests often couched as questions.

MEN: Get that phone.

WOMEN: Would you please see who's on the phone?

Because women's communication style involves more attending, women may seem to pose their requests more in the form of open questions such as "could you?" or "would you?" As stated earlier, open questions are considered maximal invitations to talk. Some may interpret women to be more tentative and men more direct; in fact, women are more attending in their communication behavior.

Women speak less than men but listen more. Contrary to myth, it is not women but men who talk more. Barbara and Gene Eakins taped a university meeting and discovered that, with one exception, the male faculty members exceeded every female faculty member in the number of turns taken to speak. In fact, the male with the fewest turns exceeded, save one, every female professor who spoke.[76]

In another study, men and women were recorded as they described paintings and engravings. Each subject was told to take the time to be thorough and to leave nothing out. According to the results, women took an average of 3.17 minutes to complete their descriptions; men took an average of 13 minutes to complete theirs. Some men spoke until after the audiotape had run out.[77]

Men tend to speak more in a monologue, while women talk more in a turn-taking dialogue. Again, this substantiates women's style as more conversational. Women are more likely to listen and attend to others by asking open questions and listening to what is said. Characteristically, women are more invested in establishing a connective relationship with others.

Paraphrasing

The paraphrase is an essential and powerful microskill for effectively communicating. A paraphrase is an accurate restatement in one's own words of what the speaker has uttered. This indicates to the speaker that he or she has been heard. While the research linking gender with the use of the paraphrase is scanty, there is some substantiation that women tend to be good listeners who thoroughly attend to both verbal and nonverbal communication.[78] Hence, women may be more likely than men to make use of paraphrasing while communicating with others.

The checking stem of the paraphrase ascertains one's understanding of what was just stated. One example of a paraphrase with a checking stem would be: "In yesterday's meeting, you seemed to be asking for more resources. Did I hear you correctly?" In another example, Linda, who has been listening to a presentation by Jim, responds by paraphrasing: "Jim, I heard you talk about your eagerness to submit your project by the deadline of June 1. But you also seem to be concerned about the day-to-day pressure of the office allowing you to meet that deadline, is that about right?"

Linda's paraphrase tells Jim that he has been heard by conveying the essence of what he has said. In her use of the checking stem, "is that about right?" she asks Jim to comment on her understanding of his situation. This allows Jim to feel heard and then gives him the chance to further elaborate on his problems if he chooses. For Linda, the function of the paraphrase is to generate more information to help her understand the situation clearly before acting upon it.

The use of paraphrases with checking stems are indicative of women's tendencies to listen closely to what others are saying. Checking stems help ensure the accurate understanding of the topic being discussed. When used in a paraphrase, checking stems become an asset. The paraphrase is an extraordinarily useful skill that communication experts find critical to effective interpersonal communication. Listeners need to understand clearly what was said, from the speaker's position, if they are to respond effectively. Individuals who understand can not only generate more conversation but also deepen the communication and create more of a common basis for mutual meaning.

Reflection of Feeling

Women tend to use more verbs with an emotional content. According to Eakins and Eakins, women use language with more emotional and lifeworld content than do men.[79] Expressing emotions and reflecting them is very natural for women. In a study of males and females, Ross Buck found that females are more likely to talk about or express their emotions than males.[80] In addition, women tend to be more empathic. They find it natural to be receptive and responsive to the emotional aspects of communication and feel less inhibited to listen, talk, or deal with emotions. Women tend to be more sensitive to the emotional cues in interpersonal interactions.[81]

Reflection of Meaning

Asking males and females to discuss photographs with an audience, one researcher found that males were more factual and objective in their descriptions while females spent more time interpreting the photographs.[82] This should come as no surprise. Women may be more apt to use "experiential logic" than "propositional logic." They seek truths that are not only "objective" but also "personal, particular, and grounded in firsthand experience."[83] That is, in addition to discussing the facts, women are more likely to seek an understanding of the speaker's lifeworld situation that has led to his or her viewpoint. In the following vignette, Joe is angry at the memo he just received from his boss, Martha. He is discussing the memo with his colleague, Debra.

JOE: Look at this memo. It tells me how to do my job. It says: "Prior to responding, please make sure you discuss the content with your division to get their input."

DEBRA: Joe, you sound angry. (reflection of feeling)

JOE: Of course I am. You know I"ve been doing this job for five years, long before Martha came along. What is she doing, telling me how to do my job?

DEBRA: What sense do you make of that, Joe?

JOE: Obviously, she's trying to tell me who's the boss.

DEBRA: You mean she's pulling rank on you?

JOE: You know, come to think of it, this isn't her style . . . hmm.

DEBRA: Then what is the point?

JOE: Could she be telling me to include my team in the decision-making process? I wonder?

DEBRA: Joe, you seem to imply that the meaning of that memo is not so much about doing your job, but more likely about teamwork and inclusiveness. Is that about right? (reflection of meaning)

JOE: Yeah, I guess she does promote collaboration a lot.

DEBRA: Collaboration? (restatement)

JOE: Yeah, that's it, that's it.

Just listening to the words used to describe a situation does not mean that we automatically understand what the speaker intends. The same words can convey different meanings to different people. The reflection of meaning encourages exploration of the different meanings that can be attributed to a statement. In the illustration above, Joe was able to glean a different meaning from the memo when Debra began to search with him for the deeper thoughts and meanings behind Martha's words. The reflection of meaning further helps speaker and listener mutually understand the essence of what is being communicated.

CONCLUSION

Historically, differences between the communication paradigms of the genders have been exaggerated, thus, the traditional assumptions that women are inherently quite different from men. Women were perceived primarily as nurturers — mothers and wives with discrete and sharply differentiated roles.

More recently, differences between the genders have been minimized or ignored. From the feminist movement of the 1960s to the present, the reality and the perception of women have changed. As more and more women have entered the workplace, new assumptions about women have taken hold. Reflecting this new demographic reality, the new assumptions about women overlay the old ones. They include women as workers who are assuming more diffuse and equal roles and who also are self-nurturers.

A review of the communication style of women points to certain significant differences with men. Women's communication paradigm is one of connection in which conversation is embedded more in the private setting of the lifeworld. As women become a significant force in the workplace, in terms of both numbers and influence, their voices will be more clearly heard. There will emerge a circle effect. Men and women's voices will be equally attended to and treated as significant by the other. It is likely that a new communication paradigm will emerge in the twenty-first century, one that embodies both styles of communication.

NOTES

1.   Dorothy E. Smith. (1978). A peculiar eclipsing: Women's exclusion from man's culture. *Woman's Studies International Quarterly*, 1(4), p. 281.

2.   Walter J. Ong. (1982). *Orality and literacy: The technologizing of the word* (p. 112). Ithaca, NY: Cornell University Press.

3.   Sherna B. Gluck. (1987). *Rosie the riveter revisited: Women, the war, and social change*. Boston: Twayne Publishers.

4.   Gary N. Powell. (1993). *Women & men in management*, 2d ed., (p. 19). Newbury Park, CA: Sage Publications.

5.   Howard N. Fullerton, Jr. (1993, November). The American work force, 1992–2005: Another look at the labor force. *Monthly Labor Review*, p. 36; Powell, *Women & men in management*, p. 73.

6.   Eric S. Hardy. (1995, May 22). Payday for America's 800 top chief executives. *Forbes*, pp. 184–232.

7.   Tom Ehrenfeld, & Robert A. Mamis. (1994, May). Growing up in public. *Inc*, pp. 107–123.

8.   Suzanne Caplan. (1994). A piece of the action: How women and minorities can launch their own successful businesses (p. 15). New York: AMACON/American Management Association.

9.   Sam Roberts. (1995, April 27). Women's work: What's new, what isn't. New York *Times*, p. B6.

10.   Powell, *Women & men in management*, p. 74.

11.   Korn/Ferry International. (1992). *Decade of the executive woman* (pp. 3–4). New York: Korn/Ferry International.

12.   U.S. Department of Labor, Glass Ceiling Commission. (1995). *Good for business: Making full use of the nation's human capital* (p. 10). Washington, DC: Government Printing Office.

13.   Ibid., p. 151; Korn/Ferry International. (1990). *Korn/Ferry International's executive profile: A decade of change in corporate leadership* (p. 16). New York:

Korn/Ferry International; Cracking the glass ceiling: Strategies for success. (1994). *Catalyst*, p. 21.

14. U.S. Department of Labor. (1991). *A report on the glass ceiling initiative* (pp. 6, 13). Washington, DC: Government Printing Office.

15. The National Foundation for Women Business Owners. (1994). *Styles of success: The thinking and management styles of women and men entrepreneurs* (p. 1). Washington, DC: The National Foundation for Women Business Owners.

16. U.S. Bureau of the Census. (1994). No. 637. Employed civilians, by occupation, sex, race, and Hispanic origin: 1983 and 1993. *Statistical abstract of the United States*. Washington, DC: Government Printing Office.

17. U.S. Department of Labor, *A report on the glass ceiling initiative*, p. 79.

18. Peter T. Kilborn. (1995, March 16). For many in work force, "glass ceiling" still exists. New York *Times*, p. A22.

19. Sam Roberts. (1995, April 27). Women's work: What's new, what isn't. New York *Times*, p. B6.

20. Cracking the glass ceiling: Strategies for success, p. 20.

21. Korn/Ferry International. (1992). *Decade of the executive woman* (pp. 2–3, 32–33).

22. J. Benjamin Forbes, James E. Piercy, & Thomas L. Hayes. (1988, November–December). Women executives: Breaking down barriers? *Business Horizons*, pp. 7–9.

23. Susana Barciela. (1993, November 26). Female executives cracking the glass ceiling, study indicates. *The Hartford Courant*, p. B1, reporting on Rebecca M. J. Yates' and Roy D. Adler's presentation of their findings at the Fourth Symposium for the Marketing of Higher Education, Orlando, Florida.

24. Patricia Aburdene, & John Naisbitt. (1992). *Megatrends for Women* (p. 62). New York: Villard Books, cites Lester Korn's statements in *Lear's*, March 1990, p. 25 and *USA Today*, June 1, 1990.

25. Patricia Aburdene, & John Naisbitt. (1992). *Megatrends for Women* (p. 62). New York: Villard Books, cites Regina Herzlinger's forecast in *USA Today*, June 1, 1990.

26. Outlook: Database. (1994, July 11). *U.S. News & World Report*, p. 12.

27. Korn/Ferry International, *Decade of the executive woman*, p. 4.

28. The traditional assumptions and the modern assumptions about women are drawn from Cynthia Fuchs Epstein. (1988). *Deceptive distinctions: Sex, gender, and the social order*. New Haven, CT: Yale University Press; Betty Friedan. (1963). *The feminine mystique*. New York: W. W. Norton; Pauline Boss, & J. Pamela Weiner. (1988). Rethinking assumptions about women's development and family therapy. In Celia Jaes Falicov (Ed.), *Family transitions: Continuity and change over the life cycle* (pp. 235–251). New York: Guilford Press; Marianne Walters, Betty Carter, Peggy Papp, & Olga Silverstein. (1988). *The invisible web: Gender patterns in family relationships* (pp. 15–30). New York: Guilford Press.

29. Powell, *Women & men in management*, p. 19.

30. Fullerton, The American work force, 1992–2005, pp. 34, 38.

31. Nardi Reeder Campion. (1995, September–October). Women of the times: Radcliffe rampant at the New York *Times*. *Harvard Magazine*, *98*(1), p. 59.

32. Powell, *Women & men in management*, p. 19.

33.   Jill S. Grigsby. (1992, November). Women change places. *American Demographics*, p. 48.

34.   Felice N. Schwartz. (1989, January–February). Management women and the new facts of life. *Harvard Business Review*, pp. 65–76.

35.   Ginette Castro. (1990). *American feminism: A contemporary history* (Trans. Elizabeth Loverde-Bagwell). New York: New York University Press.

36.   Schwartz, Management women and the new facts of life, p. 70.

37.   Carol Gilligan. (1982). *In a different voice: Psychological theory and women's development* (pp. 151–174). Cambridge, MA: Harvard University Press.

38.   Gilligan, *In a different voice*, passim; Nancy Chodorow. (1978). *The reproduction of mothering: Psychoanalysis and the sociology of gender* (passim). Berkeley: University of California Press; Jean Berko Gleason. (1987). Sex differences in parent-child interaction. In Susan U. Philips, Susan Steele, & Christene Tanz (Eds.), *Language, gender and sex in comparative perspective* (pp. 189–199). New York: Cambridge University Press.

39.   Dawn-Marie Driscoll, & Carol R. Goldberg. (1993). *Members of the club: The coming of age of executive women* (p. 82). New York: Free Press.

40.   Mary Field Belenky, Blythe McVicker Clinchy, Nancy Rule Goldberger, & Jill Mattuck Tarule. (1986). *Women's ways of knowing: The development of self, voice, and mind*. New York: Basic Books; Chodorow, *The reproduction of mothering*; Gilligan, *In a different voice*.

41.   Jean Piaget. (1948). *The moral judgement of the child* (pp. 1–103). Glencoe, IL: Free Press.

42.   Gilligan, *In a different voice*, pp. 8–11.

43.   Jean Baker Miller. (1982). Women and power. In *Work in progress* (No. 82–01), (p. 2). Wellesley, MA: Wellesley College, Stone Center for Developmental Services and Studies.

44.   Gilligan, *In a different voice*, pp. 8–9.

45.   Elizabeth Aries. (1977). Male-female interpersonal styles in all male, all female and all   mixed groups. In Alice G. Sargent (Ed.), *Beyond sex roles* (pp. 295–296). St. Paul, MN: West Publishing Company.

46.   Ong, *Orality and literacy*, p. 42.

47.   Belenky et al., *Women's ways of knowing*, pp. 149–150.

48.   Lawrence Kohlberg. (1984). *The psychology of moral development* (pp. 186–187). San Francisco: Harper & Row.

49.   Gilligan, *In a different voice*, pp. 25–31.

50.   Sally Helgesen. (1990). *The female advantage: Women's ways of leadership* (p. 5). New York: Doubleday Currency.

51.   Gilligan, *In a different voice*, p. 62.

52.   Judy B. Rosenor. (1990, November–December). Ways women lead. *Harvard Business Review*, pp. 119–125.

53.   Ibid., p. 121.

54.   Ibid., p. 125.

55.   Powell, *Women & men in management*, p. 175.

56.   Ibid., pp. 104–109.

57.   The National Foundation for Women Business Owners, *Styles of success*, passim, esp. pp. 3–11.

58. Daniel N. Maltz, & Ruth A. Borker. (1982). A cultural approach to male-female miscommunication. In J. J. Gumperz (Ed.), *Language and social reality* (pp. 201–202). New York: Cambridge University Press.

59. Allen E. Ivey. (1994). *Intentional interviewing and counseling: Facilitating client development in a multicultural society*, 3rd ed. Pacific Grove, CA: Brooks/Cole Publishing Co.

60. Alice H. Eagly. (1987). *Sex differences in social behavior: A social-role interpretation* (p. 103). Hillsdale, NJ: Lawrence Erlbaum Associates; Judee Burgoon. (1994). Nonverbal signals. In Mark L. Knapp & Gerald R. Miller (Eds.), *Handbook of interpersonal communication*, 2d ed., (p. 244). Thousand Oaks, CA: Sage Publications.

61. Judith A. Hall. (1979). Gender, gender roles, and nonverbal communication skills. In Robert Rosenthal (Ed.), *Skill in nonverbal communication: Individual differences* (pp. 35–43). Cambridge, MA: Oelgeschlager, Gunn & Hain.

62. John F. Dovidio, & Steve L. Ellyson. (1985). Patterns of visual dominance behavior in humans. In Steve L. Ellyson & John F. Dovidio (Eds.), *Power, dominance and nonverbal behavior* (p. 140). New York: Springer-Verlag; Burgoon, Nonverbal signals, p. 247.

63. Ralph V. Exline. (1963). Explorations, in the process of person perception: Visual interaction in relation to competition, sex, and need for affiliation. *Journal of Personality, 31*, p. 19; Barbara W. Eakins, & R. Gene Eakins. (1978). *Sex differences in human communication* (p. 150). Boston: Houghton-Mifflin; Judith A. Hall. (1985). Male and female nonverbal behavior. In Aron W. Siegman & Stanley Feldstein (Eds.), *Multichannel integrations of nonverbal behavior* (pp. 210–213). Hillside, NJ: Lawrence Erlbaum Associates.

64. Laurie P. Arliss. (1991). *Gender communication* (p. 84) Englewood Cliffs, NJ: Prentice-Hall.

65. Ross Buck, Robert E. Miller, & William F. Caul. (1974). Sex, personality and the physiological variables in the communication of affect via facial expression. *Journal of Personality and Social Psychology, 30*, pp. 587–596.

66. Nancy M. Henley. (1977). *Body politics: Power, sex and nonverbal communication* (pp. 176–177). Englewood Cliffs, NJ: Prentice-Hall.

67. Eagly, *Sex differences in social behavior*, p. 103; Burgoon, Nonverbal signals, p. 247.

68. Eagly, *Sex differences in social behavior*, p. 104.

69. Burgoon, Nonverbal signals, p. 247.

70. Irene Hanson Frieze, & S. J. Ramsey. (1976). Nonverbal maintenance of traditional sex roles. *Journal of Social Issues, 32*(3), pp. 133–141; Nan M. Sussman, & Howard M. Rosenfeld. (1982). Influence of culture, language, and sex on conversational distance. *Journal of Personality and Social Psychology, 42*(1) pp. 66–74; Frank N. Willis. (1966). Initial speaking distance as a function of the speakers' relationship. *Psychonomic Science, 5*(6), pp. 221–222; Hall, Male and female nonverbal behavior, pp. 213–217, 219–220.

71. Nancy Henley, & Barrie Thorne. (1977). Womanspeak and manspeak: Sex differences and sexism in communication, verbal and nonverbal. In Alice G. Sargent (Ed.), *Beyond sex roles* (p. 207). St. Paul, MN: West Publishing Company.

72. Kenneth J. Gruber, & Jacqueline Gaebelein. (1979). Sex differences in

listening comprehension. *Sex Roles, 5*(3), pp. 299–310.

73. Cited in Eakins, & Eakins, *Sex differences in human communication*, pp. 66–67; Eagly, *Sex differences in social behavior*, p. 104.

74. Pamela M. Fishman. (1978). Interaction: The work women do. *Social Problems, 25*, pp. 397–406; see also Pamela M. Fishman. (1980). Conversational insecurity. In Howard Giles, W. Peter Robinson, & Philip M. Smith (Eds.), *Language: Social psychological perspectives* (pp. 127–142). Oxford: Pergamon; Julie R. McMillan, A. Kay Clifton, Diane McGrath, & Wanda S. Gale. (1977). Women's language: Uncertainty or interpersonal sensitivity and emotionality. *Sex Roles, 3*, pp. 550–559.

75. Arliss, *Gender communication*, pp. 57–58.

76. Barbara W. Eakins, & R. Gene Eakins. (1976). Verbal turn-taking and exchanges in faculty dialogue. In Betty Lou Dubois & Isabel Crouch (Eds.), *Papers in southwest English IV: Proceedings of the conference on the sociology of the language of American women* (pp. 53–62). San Antonio, TX: Trinity University.

77. Marjorie Swacker. (1975). The sex of the speaker as sociolinguistic variable. In Barrie Thorne, & Nancy Henley (Eds.), *Language and sex: Difference and dominance* (pp. 76–83). Rowley, MA: Newbury House.

78. Judith Berman. (1979). Counseling skills used by black and white male and female counselors. *Journal of Counseling Psychology, 26*(1), pp. 81–84.

79. Eakins, & Eakins, *Sex differences in human communication*, p. 28.

80. Ross Buck. (1979). Individual differences in nonverbal sending accuracy and electrodermal responding: The externalizing-internalizing dimension. In Robert Rosenthal (Ed.), *Skill in nonverbal communication: Individual differences* (pp. 140–170). Cambridge, MA: Oelgeschlager, Gunn & Hain.

81. Burgoon. Nonverbal signals, p. 244; Eagly, *Sex differences in social behavior*, pp. 103–106; Catherine Kano Kikoski. (1980). *A study of cross-cultural communication, Arabs and Americans: Paradigms and skills*. Doctoral dissertation, University of Massachusetts, Amherst.

82. Eakins, & Eakins. *Sex differences in human communication*, p. 28.

83. Belenky et al., *Women's ways of knowing*, pp. 112–115.

7

The African American Communication Paradigm

About the last of August, came in a dutch man of warre that sold us twenty Negars.

—John Rolfe, Virginia colonist, 1619[1]

AIDS isn't the heaviest burden I have had to bear . . . being black is the greatest burden I've had to bear.

— Arthur Ashe[2]

These statements, 374 years apart, straddle the continuing story of African Americans. John Rolfe's words record the status of the first African Americans to land on these shores as a commodity to be bought and sold. African Americans are the only people in the history of the United States to be subjected to the legal status of slavery.

Every reader is aware of the great strides made by African Americans since the Civil Rights era. Only blacks might not be surprised by the words of Arthur Ashe. Champion tennis star, highly-esteemed celebrity, director on blue chip company boards like Aetna Insurance, and respected for his decency as a human being Ashe certainly was the last person many might expect to experience the sting of discrimination. Yet, this dying man's words bring home the complex reality of what it means to be black in America.

The life of Ashe embodies a paradox. On the one hand, this man occupied a seat with the innermost power elite of the United States — a position that by any measure marked his acceptance into some of the most exclusive circles of society. Yet, his words resonate with the poorest black in an inner city or the deep South. The contrast between Ashe's achievements and his words should give pause to every American who denies the existence of or extent of racism and discrimination in America today.

WHO ARE THE AFRICAN AMERICANS?

There are, perhaps, two overriding points to consider about the demography of African Americans. First, they are America's largest and most identifiable minority. Second, despite great strides, blacks as a group still rank below whites on almost every socioeconomic measure.

In 1992, approximately 31 million black Americans comprised 12.4 percent of the U.S. population. They are estimated to comprise 15.7 percent of the U.S. population by 2050.[3] As late as 1900, 90 percent of blacks lived in the South. After one of the greatest internal migrations in American history, only 53 percent of blacks remain in the South.[4] Historically a rural minority, today African Americans are more urban. In fact, about one in five blacks lives in only seven cities: New York, Chicago, Los Angeles, Philadelphia, Washington, Detroit, and Atlanta.[5] Perhaps surprising to some, 25 percent of blacks live in suburbs. The number of suburban African Americans grew by 70 percent in the 1970s. During the 1980s, almost 500,000 African Americans became suburbanites in the Atlanta and Washington areas alone. Approximately 75 percent of the black population increase in the late 1980s occurred in the suburbs.[6] Even there, residential segregation remains strong. Blacks still are the most residentially segregated ethnic group in the United States: about one-third of blacks and two-thirds of whites live in racially-isolated neighborhoods. African Americans are much more likely than Hispanics or Asian Americans to live in de facto residentially segregated areas.[7]

One black manager summed up what many African Americans told us in our interviews: "We live in separate suburbs, attend separate churches, belong to separate social clubs and send our kids to separate schools. The only time we meet and talk is at work. Is it any wonder that we sometimes have difficulties relating to one another?"

Since the Civil Rights Movement of the 1960s, African Americans have made great strides in education. Among blacks aged 25 to 29, high school graduation rates have increased from 45 percent in 1964 to 83 percent in 1987 (comparable white figures were 72 percent in 1964 and 86 percent in 1987). While the dropout rate appears high among blacks, when one takes into account background and family as well as risk factors "blacks are no more likely than whites to drop out of high school."[8] In 1960, only

3.1 percent of blacks had completed four years or more of college; in 1993, that number had increased to 12.2 percent.[9]

Greater access to education over the past few decades has had an impact upon the occupational status of African Americans. Before the 1960s, black professionals tended to be lawyers, ministers, teachers, or doctors who served the black community. Today it is no longer unusual for African Americans to supervise whites in the workplace. The number of African American males who were managers increased from 4 percent in 1949 to 13 percent in 1990.[10] This is still only half the rate for whites. For black females, the gains have been even more dramatic. In 1949, 42 percent of African American women in the paid labor force were domestics; in 1990, 19 percent were managers or professionals while 39 percent held administrative or technical positions.[11]

While we never should forget that about six in ten black households still have incomes of $25,000 or less, a growing African American middle class is emerging. If middle class is defined as an annual family income of at least $50,000, the growth of the black middle class has been rapid. In 1967 only 1 of 17 black families qualified as affluent. In 1989, that number was 1 in 7 — a fourfold jump to about 1 million families. These families bore the correlates of the middle class — 33 percent were college graduates and 79 percent were married.[12]

Where comparisons are more precise, the income gap between blacks and whites narrows considerably, particularly for those who have completed more education. In 1989 the average black family earned 56 percent of an average white family's income. However, where both husband and wife worked, the gap narrowed to 82 percent. Married-couple families headed by 25 to 44-year-old, college-educated blacks took home 93 percent ($54,400) of what a comparable white family did ($58,000). Finally, the racial income gap virtually disappeared for single, college-educated females who headed families.[13]

Twice as many white families as African American families had incomes of $50,000 or more, yet, black families had only one-tenth the financial assets of comparable white families.[14] While the racial income gap has narrowed, it is still true that black incomes remain lower than white incomes. Black families with lower financial reserves probably would have more difficulty than a comparable white family weathering a financial crisis, such as unemployment. While a larger African American middle class has emerged during the last 30 years, its grip on that status remains tenuous.

African Americans excel in a wide variety of fields. Many readers are aware of the accomplishments in both entertainment and business of Bill Cosby, Oprah Winfrey, and Quincy Jones. A short list of other achievers includes Dennis Hightower, president of Walt Disney Television and

Telecommunications; Benjamin Carson, chief of pediatric surgery at Johns Hopkins Hospital; Anne Fudge, president of Maxwell House Coffee; Kenneth L. Chenault, vice-chairman of American Express; George C. Wolfe, producer of the New York Shakespeare Festival/Joseph Papp Public Theater; and Richard Parsons, president of media giant Time Warner, Inc.

HISTORICAL AND CULTURAL BACKGROUND

By the millennial year 2000, Americans from Africa will have lived in the United States for 381 years. Blacks were enslaved for almost 250 of those years. From the end of Reconstruction in 1877 until the Civil Rights Era (about nine decades later), blacks were subjected to the legal discrimination of Jim Crow laws. Therefore, for approximately nine-tenths of their time in the United States, African Americans were denied even a chance at the American dream. African Americans have experienced the formal legal equality of most Americans — for example, the right to vote and have access to a career — only during the past three or four decades. Despite their long history and many contributions, in important ways African Americans are among the most recent immigrants and newcomers to access the American dream.

One of the more positive developments in the study and teaching of American history has been the recognition and inclusion of every group whose contributions have built America. Perhaps, no group is more deserving of this than African Americans. One of the first individuals to give his life for the American Revolution was Crispus Attucks in the Boston Massacre of 1770. What is less widely known is that slavery was legal and in some cases practiced in even northern colonies up to the eve of that revolution. By the end of the Revolutionary War only southern states legally sanctioned slavery. In his correspondence with Thomas Jefferson, Benjamin Banneker, one of America's first black intellectuals, queried Jefferson about the contradiction between the ideals of the Declaration of Independence, which Jefferson wrote, and the slavery in which most black American human beings lived at that time.[15] This moral tension — the hypocrisy that Banneker identified between America's ideals of individuality and equality and the immoral reality of slavery — fueled the growth of sentiment to abolish slavery. Their commitment to these American ideals also led countless whites to support the abolition of slavery, with some taking great risks to smuggle slaves to freedom by way of the underground railroad.

Nonetheless, during this era other whites sporadically destroyed the stores of free black shopkeepers, vandalized the tools of black mechanics, and took the lives of blacks in riots — even in the North. Overt racial prejudice ran so deep that, in a few instances, free African American women complained of discrimination when they sought to join pre–Civil War white women's abolitionist societies.[16] Despite slavery, their commitment to freedom was so strong that 186,000 black Americans served so valiantly in Lincoln's Union armies that one-third of them were listed as dead or missing in action.[17]

At the time of the Civil War, approximately 10 percent of blacks in the United States were free. The descendants of these free blacks (who carried a somewhat lighter legacy of slavery) have heavily contributed to the leadership of the black community and to black achievement in America. Examples include author W.E.B. DuBois; Supreme Court Justice Thurgood Marshall; UN Ambassador Andrew Young; former secretary of the army and Teachers Insurance and Annuity Association President Clifford Alexander; and U.S. Representative Julian Bond. However, African Americans from every background and ancestry have risen to positions of leadership and prominence against great odds.[18]

We also should be aware of another group of black Americans — those who have immigrated from the West Indies. Largely English-speaking, these voluntary and more recent immigrants have had a somewhat different historical and cultural experience than many U.S.-born blacks. West Indian blacks were freed from slavery decades before U.S. blacks. Most have lived in island societies where rigorous education was more accessible to them than was generally true in the United States. West Indian blacks also lived in societies where they almost totally predominated in numbers, and so became accustomed to seeing other blacks achieve positions of prominence in commerce or education. One result has been a disproportionate number of Caribbean Americans and their descendants contributing to American life. They include Shirley Chisholm, first black woman to run for president; civil rights activist Stokley Carmichael; two Congress of Racial Equality executive directors, Roy Innis and James Farmer; professional basketball star Patrick Ewing; and the son of Jamaican immigrants, retired chief-of-staff Colin Powell.[19] The legacy and burden of slavery may weigh somewhat less heavily upon some blacks than others. However, we can only note these historical differences that are not generally recognized in American society. In the public perception, blacks fall into only one category regardless of their historical heritage.

Compared to other ethnic groups in the United States especially the newcomers — not only the more recently arrived Hispanics or Asian Americans but also the southern Europeans, Slavs, and Jews whose ancestors arrived only a century or less ago — blacks have experienced a length and depth of discrimination that is true of no other American ethnic group. The voices of blacks who were free prior to the Civil War resonate with the reality of their experiences. One wrote of his "disheartening consciousness that while our existence was tolerated, we were powerless to appeal to law for the protection of life or property when assailed." A black woman returning to Boston from Europe wrote: "The weight of prejudice has again oppressed me, and were it not for the promises of God one's heart would fail."[20] It is difficult for those who have not suffered this experience to comprehend the depth of suppressed pain, rage, and powerlessness this entails. In an essay on the legacy of slavery, respected social work educator Elaine Pinderhughes movingly depicts the meaning of these experiences and their impact: "The stress of the ongoing economic, social, and political powerlessness that has characterized reality for Afro-Americans has been magnified by its systemic nature: denial of access to resources reduces the opportunity for acquisition of skills and employment and threatens the opportunity to develop self-esteem."[21] For those who have not known it, this insight illuminates the profound impact that such experiences of pain and powerlessness have had on Americans of black ancestry. It is inevitable that experiences of such magnitude will shape attitudes, thoughts, values, and behaviors both verbal and nonverbal.

AFRICAN AMERICAN VALUES

Three cultural-historical forces have shaped the African American value system: a residual African heritage; the internalization of the mainstream U.S. value system; and, most important, an experience with slavery and discrimination that has existed for nearly four centuries.[22]

The residual African heritage is illustrated by the values of collectivism, community, and kinship. These values were crucial to survival in Africa and later to surmount the trials of slavery in America. Blacks also strongly share the core middle class values of work, education, and achievement. As we discussed earlier, the African American experience with enslavement and discrimination reinforced and strengthened the character of those who survived. Religion and the church became significant factors in helping blacks overcome the despair created by racism and poverty.

Collective Kinship

This value emanates from shared loyalty to group and bonds of kinship with family. These relationships are common in traditional societies, such as those of seventeenth-century through nineteenth-century Africa. For example, it is not blood alone that makes one family or kin. The African American family often is an extended one that includes individuals who are aunts or uncles as much by bonds of affection as by ties of blood. The much-quoted proverb, "It takes a village to raise a child" reflects this value. So does the greater frequency with which blacks, even in the workplace, refer to and value their community. The collective kinship value provides a major resource for coping with the discrimination and pressures that blacks experience in an often discriminatory American society. One scholar found that strong nuclear and extended family support continues to be a major factor in upward black mobility.[23] As scholar John Mbiti points out, this black value has African roots. He writes: "Whatever happens to the individual happens to the whole group, and whatever happens to the whole group happens to the individual. The individual can only say: *'I am because we are, and since we are, therefore I am'*"[24] (emphasis added).

In addition to being an individual unto himself or herself, in keeping with the individualistic premise "I think, therefore I am," many African Americans value relationships and tend to see themselves as part of a set of human networks.

Work, Education, and Achievement

Robert B. Hill wrote "Contrary to popular conception, black families place a strong emphasis on work and ambition."[25] In fact, according to 1993 statistics, 62.4 percent of blacks were in the civilian labor force (compared to 66.7 percent of whites), 54.4 percent were employed (compared to 62.7 percent of whites), 8 percent were unemployed (compared to 4 percent of whites), and 37.6 percent were not in the labor force (compared to 33.3 percent of whites).[26] Prior to and after the Civil War, free blacks passionately desired education.[27] Following the Civil War and the abolition of slavery, two of the greatest desires by newly-freed blacks were for land to work self-reliantly and for schools to educate their children and themselves. During the decade following the Civil War there was a virtual explosion of black schools and learning in the South by adults as well as children.[28] Today black parents place a high premium on education and have high expectations for achievement by their children. If one holds factors of socioeconomic status constant, blacks compare favorably in educational aspirations and attainment with other ethnic groups.[29]

Role Flexibility

In the African American family, gender roles are quite often flexible and fluid. Historically, black males and females worked equally in the fields as slaves. Following Emancipation, black women were more apt to find paying jobs as household help than were black men. In such circumstances, role reversal often occurred. This role flexibility between the genders could be an asset in the fluid organizations of the informational era.

Religion

The black church was one of the few institutions owned and managed by blacks throughout their American experience. Religion helped provide the faith and strength to survive a discriminatory and often painful society. Around the world Negro spirituals and gospel music that helped African Americans survive deep pain and sorrow provide the same solace and strength to others. For centuries these churches were one of the few institutions that African Americans could control and where they could acquire the necessary experience to manage and lead institutions well. The twentieth-century leadership of men of the cloth like Martin Luther King, Jr., Malcolm X, and Jessie Jackson is no accident. They are just one measure of the influence that religion and the black church have had on African Americans.[30]

Humanism

African Americans place a high value on human relationships. They tend to have fewer reservations (than many whites, for example) about demonstrating their care for another. Blacks express their humanism in open, affiliative, and sharing behaviors. In the organizational setting this often translates into an informality and genuine concern for maintaining relationships, particularly with others in need of help.

Locus of Control

The "locus of control" is a psychological term. It indicates whether individuals believe they have the inner ability to control the events in their lives (internal locus of control) or if they believe that events outside of or beyond their power are responsible for controlling their lives (external locus of control). Because of the experience of slavery as well as disproportionate discrimination and poverty, some research indicates that blacks are more likely to have an external locus of control.[31] However, a review of 39 research studies arrived at very different conclusions, and only one yielded evidence of external locus of control among blacks.[32] Furthermore, psychologist Derald Wing Sue cautions us against imposing one culture's worldview upon another in evaluating and interpreting the dimension of locus of control.[33] In the interviews conducted for this book, it was consistently evident that goal-achieving individuals see themselves in charge of their lives and destinies. This was no less true of African American individuals than individuals of any other ethnic group.

CULTURE AND COMMUNICATION

The African American community is diverse. Blacks live in the North as well as the South, in urban as well as rural areas, and reflect socio-economic backgrounds that range from some who are poorly educated to others who have earned Ivy League degrees. African Americans range from those who are unemployed to others who hold what many would consider power elite positions. There are some families that have been part of what is called the black bourgeoisie for generations. But many middle-class African Americans are no more than one or two generations removed from grinding poverty and often have close relatives still enmeshed in those circumstances. Yet, for all their diversity — a healthy sign of movement into more segments of American society — most African Americans, to greater or lesser degrees, are still members of a common speech community.

Some African Americans speak an identifiable black English. Others speak English in a manner virtually unidentifiable from any other American of their region and educational or economic circumstance. In this context, scholars point out that there are at least three somewhat differing though overlapping groupings within the black speech community:

the less-formally educated inner-city or rural blacks who would tend to be more identifiably fluent in what is called black English than in the mainstream standard English with which they might have some problems;

the well-educated and formally educated African Americans who, while tending to be fluent in mainstream standard English, might have some identifiable problems when speaking black English; and

those who are proficient in both language genres.[34]

As is true of every American, blacks differ by education, residence, and region as well as class, gender, religion, and personality. Despite these differences, some common patterns within the African American communication paradigm are evident in their nonverbal and verbal communication styles.

NONVERBAL COMMUNICATION

Nonverbal communication is particularly significant to African Americans. The heritage of humanism and person-oriented behavior as well as the tendency to express emotions freely inclines some blacks to be more reliant upon nonverbal communication. On the basis of her review of the literature, black educator Janice Hale-Benson states that blacks are more proficient than are whites in expressing and detecting emotions.[35]

Eye Contact and Gaze

Subject to the usual qualifiers of education, income, class, occupation, gender, and region, research indicates that some blacks exhibit different patterns of eye contact than some other ethnic groups.

A number of studies indicate that both gender and race influence gaze behavior. They have found that females engage in more eye contact than males. Further, that black females gaze less than white females. And that black males tend to engage in less gaze behavior than white males.[36] Other research focusing upon race found that black interviewers tended to elicit less eye contact and white interviewers more eye contact when they interviewed subjects of both races.[37]

In reviewing the research on gaze behavior, Amy Halberstadt concluded that African Americans gaze less frequently during conversation than whites.[38] Marianne LaFrance and Clara Mayo detected significant differences between the gaze patterns of blacks and whites.[39]

The comparative eye contact patterns of blacks and whites when speaking and listening are:

Speaking
Blacks look at the listener when speaking
Whites look away from the listener except when initiating conversation, emphasizing points, or signaling the listener's turn to speak

Listening
Blacks look away from the speaker when listening
Whites look at the speaker when listening.

However, these findings apply more to same sex than to mixed sex conversants.[40] Yet, other research indicates that black gaze behavior corresponds more closely to the white pattern than LaFrance and Mayo indicate.[41] While these may be viewed as characteristics of both black and white paradigms, it is always best to hold such generalities lightly, keeping always in mind the uniqueness of each individual.

Some scholars speculate that this black gaze pattern originated during the time of slavery when it was inadvisable for a slave to gaze directly at a white who bore authority. Others have found that blacks tend to engage in less gaze behavior while talking to elders as well as authority figures. Still others have attributed this pattern of gaze behavior to African cultural practices.[42]

Another explanation for differences in gaze behavior can be attributed to patterns of childrearing and socialization. Whites are likely to remember their parents saying, "You'd better look me in the eye!" (a sign of respect by the listener). Blacks may remember their parents saying: "You'd better *not* look me in the eye!" (a sign of insolence by the listener).[43] Each set of parents was trying equally hard to teach its child how to show attention and respect for the speaker.

These differing patterns of gaze behavior could produce erroneous attributions in the workplace.[44] A white manager may feel that a black colleague is not paying attention or is even untrustworthy because he is "not looking me in the eye." By the same measure, a black manager may feel a colleague is either rude or aggressive because he is "staring at me." Cultures, not individuals, are speaking to one another in such situations.

One researcher found that whites who are more eager to communicate with blacks tend to engage in more and longer eye contact than whites who are less eager to communicate with blacks. Ironically, because of these whites' heightened gaze behavior, those who were more eager to communicate with blacks sometimes elicited the most negative responses. Unfortunately, neither was aware of the gaze pattern of the other.[45]

In another experiment, black subjects looked away from white speakers during conversation. At the same time, white speakers looked at the black listeners, expecting to signal nonverbally the end of their conversational turn. In more than one study, whites could not make the eye contact that was necessary to signal that it was the turn of the black listener to speak. In these studies, the white speakers found it necessary to verbally cue the black person that it was their turn to speak by asking, for example, "Am I being clear?"[46] Any manager reading about these nonverbal behaviors might ask "So what if there are differences in eye contact behaviors? What does that have to do with me doing my job?"

Misinterpreting the meanings of such seemingly simple situations can unintentionally create conflict, particularly when both parties are unaware of each other's culturally-based nonverbal and verbal behaviors. Each individual attributes a different meaning to the verbal communication, "Am I being clear?" The white manager's verbal cue could be perceived as seeking to be in charge. In this case, he or she may be seen as assuming a higher hierarchical position and dictating the terms of conversation. The black manager could be perceived as being inattentive.

Charles, a brand new black management trainee and Jim, his white supervisor, provide a good example of misinterpretation.

JIM (gazing at Charles then looking away): Glad to have you on board, Charles. I want to take time this morning to orient you to how we do things around here.

CHARLES (looking away): I am glad to be here too, Mr. Harris. That will help me get things done here.

JIM (continuing to look away with occasional gazes toward Charles): Let me begin by going over your responsibilities in this position. (now seeking eye contact)

CHARLES (continuing to look away): That's fine.

JIM (continuing to seek eye contact): I want to use your expertise in dealing with high-tech start-up portfolios by developing a business plan for dealing with them.

CHARLES (still looking away): That's kind of the challenge I came here for.

JIM (increasing his gaze behavior): Would you need any resources for this project?

CHARLES (still looking away): I sure will.

JIM (pauses, continuing to seek eye contact): Charles, I'm not sure I'm reading you on this. Am I being clear?

CHARLES (shocked, makes eye contact): I've been with you all the way. I appreciate your offer to provide resources for this project. That way I can give you a better product sooner.

JIM (more relaxed): That's great Charles. Now we're in synch.

Seemingly innocuous eye contact patterns can be very important in cueing conversational turn-taking and promoting synchrony. In this vignette, Jim and Charles's gaze behavior reflects their communication paradigms. Whites tend to look away from their partner when speaking, making eye contact primarily at points of emphasis or to signal the moment of turn-taking. White listeners tend to look at the speaker. In contrast, blacks tend to look at their partner when speaking and away when listening. So while whites tend to rely more on the nonverbal, visual channel for cueing conversational turn-taking, blacks often rely more on verbal or vocal channels. In particular, some blacks may utilize certain rhythmic pitch and intonational patterns in their speech whose intent and meaning may elude whites.[47] Jim might have had a different experience with a black female management trainee. Gender seems to mediate race or ethnic gaze behavior. In same-sex dyads, black females and black males have been found to engage in less eye contact than white females — although these differences disappear with the degree of the acquaintanceship.[48]

Proxemics

Whether we stand close together or far apart can make us feel more or less comfortable in dealing with one another. Some research indicates that, while conversing, black children tend to stand closer together.[49] In her analysis of research on proxemics, Halberstadt found that blacks tend to stand closer to one another when young but farther apart when older — black primary school children stand closer together than black junior high or high school students. Distances increased still more for black adults.[50]

Additional research indicates that African American adults tend to greet each other and stand somewhat further apart than other ethnic groups. Studies have found evidence that black Americans greet each other (and Caucasians) at greater distances than white Americans greet each other.[51] A comparative study showed that black Americans interact at the greatest distances, Mexican Americans interact at the closest distances, and white Americans interact at intermediate distances.[52] Another study concluded that during interviews whites tend to sit farther away from blacks than they do from other whites.[53] While seated, black females tend to lean forward synchronously (or attend) more frequently than black males or even white females.[54]

In her analysis of the literature, Halberstadt found that in three-fourths of the studies reviewed "adolescent and adult black males interacted at further distances than did adolescent and adult whites." However, she found that the small number of available research studies that controlled for social and economic status suggested that "SES may well be influencing the spatial relations" of blacks and whites.[55] While some general guidelines may be deduced from this review of research, it is always useful to keep in mind that the best understanding is the one we arrive at on the basis of our mutual experience with one another.

Kinesics

African Americans tend to touch more than whites.[56] Research substantiates that many African Americans appear to be members of a high-contact rather than a low-contact subculture. As members of high-contact subcultures, African Americans and especially Hispanics (whose rate of touch generally exceeds blacks) touch more than do low-contact subcultures, white males, and Asian Americans.

Hand movements appear to be particularly important nonverbal cues to blacks. Among some blacks, "giving skin" is an in-group behavior of acceptance and solidarity. Such behaviors may be adopted by members of other ethnic groups, particularly youths, and, thus, may not remain exclusively black. These and other nonverbal behaviors may be less likely to be exhibited by African Americans of higher socioeconomic and educational status to whom understatement applies.

Synchronous body alignment is another nonverbal behavior. Conversants who reflect each other's body alignment attend to each other, and, by so doing, encourage the other to talk. Blacks are less likely than whites to face each other directly. That is, they are less likely to stand or sit directly facing one another with shoulders parallel to those with whom they are interacting.[57] Typically, blacks attend by standing or sitting with their body at an angle to their conversant; whites attend by standing or sitting directly facing their conversant. The variance in preferred posture may cause misinterpretations and misattributions. Neither party acts as the other expects; neither party reciprocates the nonverbal code of the other. The result is possible bewilderment, causing a negative impact on the flow of conversation without either party knowing why.

The influence of nonverbal communication upon our lives cannot be overestimated. Three decades ago anthropologist Edward T. Hall, who studied black and white communication patterns, wrote:

The voice, the feet, hands, eyes, body, and space are all handled differently, which often causes even highly motivated Negroes to fail to get jobs for which they apply. These failures are not always because of prejudice, but can be traced to instances where both parties misread the other's behavior. . . . The Negro is well aware of the fact that his white interlocutor is not "reading him." What he doesn't know is that while he may be more aware of the nuances of white-Negro interaction than the white man, there are many, many points at which he too is being miscued.[58]

VERBAL COMMUNICATION

One of the most significant characteristics of the African American verbal communication style is its oral tradition. Africans were forcibly transported from traditional societies that were oral. During slavery most were purposely kept illiterate by their owners as a means of control. Since then, many African Americans persistently have been discriminated against in education. The heritage of orality may be most evident in two areas of the African verbal communication style: the mode of listening, and the importance of expressing feeling during interpersonal interaction.

Comparative studies have found that blacks and whites have different verbal communication styles. Whites tend to make more use of the attending or listening skills in their face-to-face communication by using a forward lean of the upper body or asking open-ended questions. Blacks tend to be more directive by giving advice or confronting.[59]

Other research points out that blacks are more likely to openly express their thoughts and emotions. The African American communication paradigm tends to be characterized by a more direct conversational style. Some blacks' conversational style may seem direct in a conversation because they do not use the attending behaviors that whites expect of them. Unintentionally, a conflict may develop. A better understanding of the verbal communication style of African Americans could defuse such a situation.

Open and Closed Questions

An earlier discussion of microskills noted that open questions are less direct and invite a conversational partner to provide more information on a topic while closed questions tend to retrieve specific pieces of information and limit dialogue. Depending upon the circumstances, each type of question is equally valid. However, a dialogue with predominantly closed questions can take on the tone of an interrogation. Similarly, a conversation replete with open questions lends a less tenuous tone by giving respondents more room to provide information at their own pace. Therefore, the type of question sets the tone of a conversation.

Berman examined the use of questions by over 80 black and white male and female counselors. She found that white males and females asked more open questions and that black males and females were significantly more directive in their use of questions. In fact, while white females and males asked open questions 37 and 42 percent of the time, respectively, black females asked open questions 12 percent of the time. In addition, whites attended and listened 84 percent of the time while blacks did so only 27 percent of the time.[60] A study of white collar employees found that blacks ask more questions and talk longer with females. In contrast, whites ask more questions and talk longer with males. Blacks also tended to rely on the use of leading statements when gathering interpersonal data from same gender partners.[61]

Research indicates some cultural differences in the use of questions. Blacks tend to ask fewer questions, but, when they do so, their questions may tend to be more direct. Two African American researchers stated that blacks in organizational settings are more likely to ask direct and confrontational questions like "Do you have a problem with me?"[62] What these researchers identified as direct questions, we call closed questions according to the microskills. While using closed questions may help identify issues by eliciting a specific response, such a communication style may also contribute to a dissonance with those who are not familiar with the black communication paradigm.

Encouragers

The listening modes of some blacks can very from other ethnic groups. In the mainstream business culture, individuals use nonverbal cues to indicate that they are listening and understand what is being said. Examples include such nonverbal cues as leaning forward, maintaining eye contact, and physically moving closer to the speaker. About the only verbal encouragers used by whites are the occasional utterances of "uh-mm," "I see," or "go on." Thus, whites mainly convey their attentive listening nonverbally. The opposite is often true in the black communication paradigm. Attentive listening is more verbally active. When blacks talk with one another, their listening style is more likely to involve verbal as well as nonverbal behaviors.[63]

Readers may be familiar with the "call-response" process by which preacher and congregation interact during black church services but may not know that this is an African-rooted practice that has been carried down to the present. "Not only is call-response necessary in the Traditional Black Church, it is also a basic communication strategy permeating black secular life."[64] Rap is just another example of the call-response mode. This mode of interaction can be a part of the everyday communication repertoire of some African Americans and indicates that the speaker and the listener are in synch with what is being verbally communicated.

Varying expectations of how one listens attentively can complicate face-to-face communication between blacks and nonblacks in the workplace. African Americans tend to encourage conversational partners by means of vocal cues; whites do so by means of eye contact. The difference between these two modes of attending can create dissonance. This was the case in the vignette involving Jim and Charles. Jim expected to cue Charles to respond to him through eye contact but was unable to do so. Charles did not respond to such signals because he expected to be cued verbally. Thus, both Jim and Charles were unaware of each other's style of communication.

Black management trainees speaking to white colleagues might find them attending nonverbally by a forward body lean, direct eye contact, and with only an occasional "uh-hmm." The whites are indicating that they are paying attention to what is being said according to their own principally nonverbal attending mode. In frustration, the black trainees might misunderstand the white nonverbal way of encouraging more face-to-face communication.

An African American executive may ask "Do you understand?" or "Do you hear me?" Over a period of time, the repetition of such verbal signals might become disconcerting to colleagues of other ethnicities whose communication paradigms simply may not contain such verbal expressions. When whites talk, they expect nonverbal attending behavior. When the African American executive begins to verbally attend by responding

"I hear you," or "go on," whites may process this black style of encouraging as interruptive and even harassing.

In neither case is the problem what is being said. Rather, it is understanding how what is said is meant by the speaker and interpreted by the listener. Therefore, it is essential to be familiar with each other's communication paradigm. What goes awry is that each individual's expectation of listening behavior is not fulfilled. What is attending behavior to a white manager may communicate inattentiveness to a black trainee; what is active listening to a black trainee may be interruptive behavior to the white manager. The regret is that both want only to attend to and communicate with each other.

Expression of Feeling

The African American's expression of feeling may also contrast with white expression of feeling. Whereas emotions may be more openly expressed according to the African American communication paradigm, they are more repressed by the mainstream white paradigm. According to the African American communication paradigm, one is more congruent when one expresses emotions. According to the norm of the white male communication paradigm, one expresses one's reason and logic dispassionately. For many blacks, the expression of feeling is crucial to genuine communication between individuals. Therefore, in the black paradigm one is credible when one expresses emotions; one is more credible when emotions are expressed resolutely. Thomas Kochman, scholar of African American linguistics, holds that one achieves ultimate credibility when logic and affect harmoniously intertwine. Only then can there be congruence between one's thoughts and verbal communication. When one represses thoughts and feelings and expresses only logical thoughts, the discrepancy is likely to emerge through nonverbal behavior, such as moving away or breaking eye contact. The meanings that may be attributed to such incongruencies according to the African American communication paradigm may range from deceit or hypocrisy to weakness.[65]

The black style of greater and more open expression of feeling can result in behaviors that may seem overly assertive and even confrontational to many whites. In conflictual situations, black nonverbals tend to include loud tones of voice, intense eye contact, and sweeping gestures. Verbally, blacks may freely express their emotions and, according to Kochman, directly challenge not only facts or ideas but also the individuals who present them. Many may interpret such behaviors as not only confrontational but also preludes to aggression. However, for blacks the expression of one's mind and spirit only mean being true to oneself.[66]

MANAGEMENT PRACTICES

Ben is an African American executive. He grew up in an inner city and earned a masters in business administration from an Ivy League school. Ben was responding to his fellow executives about the need to continue promoting more minorities within the company because of the government policy on affirmative action. A number of problems were raised by the white male managers who made up a majority of those present. The last of the critics was another white male manager, Harry.

HARRY: There are a number of points to consider. Do candidates for this position have the right "mix" of experiences? It's difficult to find a suitable number of qualified minority candidates. We also have to look at this from a bottom-line perspective: where is the dividing line between promoting a possibly less-qualified minority employee because it's in society's or our own company's best long-term interest. Or promoting instead one of a larger number of possibly more qualified white candidates to the same position?

BEN (leaning forward, making direct eye contact): And what is wrong with that? It wasn't so long ago that people around here were promoted more because they were someone's good golfing partner than because they were the best qualified. And what do you mean by your words "lesser qualified" — someone who actually is less capable, or just less experienced?

HARRY: We need to be objective here and take into account many, not just a few, factors. I've stated my points as clearly as I can. I agree with Ben. I want to promote more minority managers, too. But they need to have had the right experience to prepare them for the job.

BEN (raising his voice): How do you expect minority employees to get the experience you say they need to have if you don't promote them? (drumming the table with his fingers) And how do they get promoted if managers at lower levels quietly keep them off the projects where they'll get both the experience and the visibility they need to get ahead?

WHITE COLLEAGUE: Now, Ben, take it easy. Don't get emotional. We've got to be rational about this situation.

BEN (angrily and loudly): Are you implying that I'm not rational? I certainly am. Dammit, all I hear is that we can't promote minorities for one reason or another. In the meantime, our company is both losing good people now as well as the ability to attract minorities in the future. Do you know what that will mean in just a few years with the demographics that are happening?

(Managers on either side of Ben are wide-eyed and leaning away from him)

BEN (suddenly noticing their nonverbals): What are you all worried about? I'm O.K.

SECOND WHITE MALE MANAGER: I'm not sure we can accomplish anything if we can't control our emotions here.

HARRY: Perhaps it would be better to take up this discussion sometime later. The time is not right for it today given the feelings in this room.

BEN: What are you trying to do? I'm only expressing what I really feel about something that's important to me and this company. All I want to know is where you all are on this issue. And what this company is going to do.

HARRY: I've said all I'm going to say. I think this meeting has gotten off the tracks.

THIRD WHITE MANAGER: I think that we should adjourn the meeting and pick this up later when everyone is calmer.

It is evident from this interchange that Ben's communication style and that of his colleagues is different. On one level, it might appear that what occurred was the simple misunderstanding between nonverbal and verbal communication styles. On another level, it might be that no single aspect of behavior contributed to this communication breakdown. Rather, the dissonance between two different communication paradigms, their cultural-historical backgrounds and values as well as their nonverbal and verbal behaviors, and the way they interacted accounts for this communication failure.[67]

Ben's behavior was perceived by his white colleagues as emotional, so he was asked to address the problem more rationally. His body language contributed to that perception. For Ben, this is more than an impersonal business item, as it may be for his white colleagues also. For Ben it may epitomize not only the cultural-historical experience of the black struggle in America; it could possibly epitomize his own struggle.

Such meetings are generally characterized by a reserved, rational, task-oriented manner of communication. However, the black communication style can be more emotional and personal and so may appear confrontational to nonblacks. In the black communication style, Ben was asking Harry to give his honest opinion on this matter not just to conceal it behind ostensibly objective arguments.

The history of slavery and discrimination has at times induced African Americans to mask their true feelings and beliefs.[68] Thus, blacks learned to withhold rather than voice their passionate feelings and convictions. The meaning of whites' dispassionate and rational verbal behavior may be perceived by some blacks as deceitful and an attempt to mask true motivation and intent. Even today, this projection of meaning by some blacks onto whites may be all too often true. It should be kept in mind, however, that the communication style of many mainstream whites tends to involve negotiating in a dispassionate, rational, low-key mode. Thus, such behavior is not necessarily devious. Indeed, the interchange between Ben and his colleagues could be one of fundamental misunderstanding and misattribution of each other's culturally determined behaviors.

According to Kochman blacks are more likely to express their emotions in tandem with their beliefs.[69] "Whites react to this anger and hostility in negotiating sessions in much the same way that white students react to emotional expression in the classroom: they consider it disabling to what they regard as a rational process. Consequently they feel that passion, prejudice, fear, and hatred should be set aside before negotiations even begin. Blacks do not believe that emotions interfere with their capacity to reason."[70] For blacks, persuasion may mean including one's own emotions as well as the emotions of others in what one says. One cannot otherwise persuade.

For whites, the process of negotiation means excluding one's own feelings as well as the feelings of others. One cannot otherwise negotiate. We should not forget that to negotiate effectively, all issues relevant to the negotiation should be addressed. What transpired in the interchange among Harry, Ben, and the others was exclusive of this point. At no time did anyone try to understand what Ben felt. One wonders where such an interchange would have led had it continued in that direction. The outcome would have been different had the participants engaged in the reflection of feeling rather than ignoring it. Reflection of feeling would have rendered the implicit emotions explicit and clear. In fact, all parties would have benefited had they attempted to see each other's perspective. Operating within these respective paradigms neither furthers our common cause nor promotes understanding of one another. We need to find a common ground.

CONCLUSION

African Americans are, perhaps, the most American of all ethnic groups. In Africa, they were a mosaic of tribes and cultures who spoke many different languages. There they plowed fields and erected cities, traded goods and made art, celebrated and mourned the passage points of birth, adulthood, marriage, and death, and warred and made peace with each other.

African Americans became one in a cultural sense. Among their great and unique gifts to America and the world — gospel music, blues, and jazz — one can hear the roots of Africa suffused and enveloped by their American experience. The music is a testament to the African American triumph by sheer commitment of soul and strength of human spirit over slavery, discrimination, and degradation. The same can be said of the African American communication paradigm. It has African roots and an American body, and is, in many ways, the same as yet different from the mainstream. In addition to the legacy and experience of blacks, this chapter has addressed the verbal and nonverbal communication modes that can create subtle but powerful barriers to the full participation of

those who, more than any other ethnic group, have earned the right to the
fruits of America.

NOTES

1. Quoted in Ronald Takaki. (1993). *A different mirror: A history of
multicultural America.* Boston: Little Brown and Company, p. 53.

2. Arthur Ashe. (1993). *Days of grace* (p. 126). New York: Alfred A. Knopf.

3. U.S. Bureau of the Census. (1994). No. 12. Resident population
characteristics — Percent distribution and median age, 1850–1992, and projections, 1995 to 2050. *Statistical abstract of the United States.* Washington, DC:
Government Printing Office.

4. Nicolas Leman. (1991). *The promised land: The great black migration and
how it changed America.* New York: Alfred A. Knopf; see also William P. O'Hare,
Kevin M. Pollard, Taynia L. Mann, & Mary M. Kent. (1991, July). African
Americans in the 1990s. *Population Bulletin, 46*(1), p. 5.

5. O'Hare et al., African Americans in the 1990s, p. 6.

6. Ibid., p. 6; William P. O'Hare, & William H. Frey. (1992, September).
Booming, suburban and black. *American Demographics,* p. 33.

7. O'Hare et al., African Americans in the 1990s, p. 7; Dan Gilmore, &
Stephen K. Doig. (1992, January). Segregation forever? *American Demographics,* pp.
48–51; see also Douglas S. Massey, & Brendan P. Mullan. (1984). Process of
Hispanic and black spatial assimilation. *American Journal of Sociology, 89*(4), pp.
836–871.

8. O'Hare et al., African Americans in the 1990s, pp. 18–21.

9. U.S. Bureau of the Census. (1994). No. 232. Educational attainment by
race and ethnicity: 1960–1993. *Statistical abstract of the United States.* Washington,
DC: Government Printing Office.

10. O'Hare et al., African Americans in the 1990s, p. 22.

11. Ibid., pp. 22–23.

12. Ibid., pp. 25–29.

13. Ibid., pp. 25–26.

14. Ibid., pp. 27–28.

15. On these and other points, see Mary Francis Berry, & John W.
Blassingame. (1982). *Long memory: The black experience in America.* New York:
Oxford University Press; John Hope Franklin. (1974). *From slavery to freedom: A
history of negro Americans,* 4th ed., (pp. 181–182). New York: Alfred A. Knopf;
Cynthia Greggs Fleming. (1992). African Americans. In John D. Buenker &
Lorman A. Ratner (Eds.), *Multiculturalism in the United States: A comparative guide
to acculturation and ethnicity.* Westport, CT: Greenwood Press; Thomas Sowell.
(1981). *Ethnic America: A history* (pp. 183–224). New York: Basic Books; Takaki. *A
different mirror: A history of multicultural America,* (passim but esp. pp. 24–76,
106–136, 340–369).

16. Roslyn Terborg-Penn. (1978). Discrimination against Afro-American
women in the women's movement, 1830–1920. In Sharon Harley & Rosalyn
Terborg-Penn (Eds.), *The Afro-American woman: Struggles and images* (pp. 17–27,
esp. 18–19). Port Washington, NY: National University Publications.

17. Sowell, *Ethnic America: A history*, p. 196.

18. Ibid., pp. 195–224; Berry, & Blassingame, *Long memory: The black experience in America*, pp. 33–69.

19. Sowell, *Ethnic America: A history*, pp. 216–24; Sharon-Ann Gopaul-McNicol. (1993). *Working with West Indian families* (passim but esp. pp. 52–54). New York: Guilford Press.

20. Berry, & Blassingame, *Long memory: The black experience in America*, pp. 49–50.

21. Elaine Pinderhughes. (1990). Legacy of slavery: The experience of black families in America. In Marsha Pravser Mirkin (Ed.), *The social and political contexts of family therapy* (p. 292). Boston: Allyn and Bacon.

22. Nancy Boyd-Franklin. (1989). *Black families in therapy*. New York: Guilford Press; Franklin, *From slavery to freedom*; Robert Hill. (1971). *The strengths of black families*. New York: Emerson Hall Publishers, Inc.; Paulette Moore Hines, & Nancy Boyd-Franklin. (1982). Black families. In Monica McGoldrick, John K. Pearce, & Joseph Giordano (Eds.), *Ethnicity and family therapy* (pp. 84–107). New York: Guilford Press; Elaine Pinderhughes. (1982). Afro-American families and the victim system. In Monica McGoldrick, John K. Pearce, & Joseph Giordano (Eds.), *Ethnicity and family therapy* pp. 108–122. New York: Guilford Press; Janet Brice. (1982). West Indian families. In Monica McGoldrick, John K. Pearce, & Joseph Giordano (Eds.), *Ethnicity and family therapy* (pp. 123–133). New York: Guilford Press; Harriet Pipes McAdoo. (1978, November). Factors relating to stability in upwardly mobile black families. *Journal of Marriage and the Family*, 40(4), pp. 761–776; Joseph White, & Thomas Parham. (1990). *The psychology of blacks*, 2d ed. Englewood Cliffs, NJ: Prentice-Hall.

23. McAdoo, Factors relating to stability, pp. 761–776.

24. John S. Mbiti. (1969). *African religions and philosophy* (pp. 108–109). New York: Praeger Publishers.

25. Hill, *The strengths of black families*, p. 9.

26. U.S. Bureau of the Census. (1994). No. 49. Social and economic characteristics of the white and black populations: 1980 to 1993. *Statistical abstract of the United States*. Washington, DC: Government Printing Office.

27. Berry, & Blassingame, *Long memory: The black experience in America*, pp. 44–48.

28. Sowell, *Ethnic America: A history*, pp. 202–205.

29. Hill, *The strengths of black families*, pp. 29–32.

30. Berry, & Blassingame, *Long memory: The black experience in America*, pp. 70–113.

31. Janet E. Helms, & Tedia W. Giorgis. (1980, November). A comparison of the locus of control and anxiety level of African, black American, and white American college students. *Journal of College Student Personnel*, 21(6), pp. 503–509; James E. Savage, Jr., Annita D. Sterns, & Philip Friedman. (1979). Relationship of internal-external locus of control, self-concept, and masculinity-femininity to fear of success in black freshman and senior college women. *Sex Roles*, 5(3), pp. 373–383.

32. W. Curtis Banks, Wanda E. Ward, Gregrory V. McQuater, & Ann Marie Debritto. (1991). Are blacks external: On the status of locus of control in black

populations. In Reginald L. Jones (Ed.), *Black Psychology*, 3rd ed. (pp. 181–192). Berkeley, CA: Cobb & Henry.

33. Derald Wing Sue. (1978). Eliminating cultural oppression in counseling: Toward a general theory. *Journal of Counseling Psychology*, 25(5), pp. 419–428.

34. Harry N. Seymour, & Charlena M. Seymour. (1979, June). The symbolism of ebonics: I'd rather switch than fight. *Journal of Black Studies*, 9(4), pp. 408–409.

35. Janice E. Hale-Benson. (1982). *Black children: Their roots, culture and learning styles*, rev. ed. (pp. 69–75). Baltimore: Johns Hopkins University Press.

36. Marianne LaFrance, & Clara Mayo. (1976). Racial differences in gaze behavior during conversations: Two systematic observational studies. *Journal of Personality and Social Psychology*, 33(5), pp. 550–551; Robert Shuter. (1979, December). Gaze behavior in interracial and intraracial interactions. *International and Intercultural Communication Annual*, 5, pp. 53–54; Althea Smith. (1983). Nonverbal communication among black female dyads: An assessment of intimacy, gender, and race. *Journal of Social Issues*, 39(3), pp. 55–67.

37. Stephen S. Fugita, Kenneth N. Wexley, & Joseph M. Hillery. (1974). Black-white differences in nonverbal behavior in an interview setting. *Journal of Applied Social Psychology*, 4(4), pp. 343–350, esp. pp. 348–349.

38. Amy G. Halberstadt. (1985). Race, socioeconomic status, and nonverbal behavior. In Aron W. Seigman & Stanley Feldstein (Eds.), *Multichannel integration of nonverbal behavior* (p. 251). Hillsdale, NJ: Lawrence Erlbaum.

39. LaFrance, & Mayo, Racial differences in gaze behavior during conversation, pp. 547–552.

40. Halberstadt, Race, socioeconomic status, and nonverbal behavior, p. 252.

41. Shuter, Gaze behavior in interracial and intraracial interactions, p. 53.

42. Kenneth R. Johnson. (1972, Spring/Fall). Black kinesics — Some non-verbal communication patterns in the black culture. *The Florida FL Reporter*, 9, p. 18; Hale-Benson, *Black children: Their roots, culture and learning styles*, pp. 15–16.

43. Norman Ashcraft, & Albert E. Scheflen. (1976). *People space: The making and breaking of human boundaries* (pp. 15–16). Garden City, NY: Anchor Press; Johnson, Black kinesics — Some non-verbal communication patterns in the black culture, p. 18.

44. Halberstadt, Race, socioeconomic status, and nonverbal behavior, p. 261.

45. William Ickes. (1984). Compositions in black and white: Determinants of interaction in interracial dyads. *Journal of Personality and Social Psychology*, 47(2), pp. 330–341.

46. LaFrance, & Mayo, Racial differences in gaze behavior during conversation, p. 551; Shuter, Gaze behavior in interracial and intraracial interactions, p. 53.

47. Mark Hansell, & Cheryl Seabrook Ajirotutu. (1982). Negotiating interpretations in interethnic settings. In J. J. Gumperz (Ed.), *Language and social identity* (pp. 85–94). New York: Cambridge University Press.

48. Smith, Nonverbal communication among black female dyads, pp. 62–64.

49. John R. Aiello, & Stanley E. Jones. (1971). Field study of the proxemic behavior of young school children in three subcultural groups. *Journal of Personality and Social Psychology*, 9(3), pp. 351–356; Stanley E. Jones, & John

Aiello. (1973). Proxemic behavior of black and white first-, third-, and fifth-grade children. *Journal of Personality and Social Psychology*, 25(1), pp. 21–27.

50. Halberstadt, Race, socioeconomic status, and nonverbal behavior, p. 241.

51. Frank N. Willis, Jr. (1966). Initial speaking distance as a function of the speaker's relationship. *Psychonomic Science*, 5(6), pp. 221–222; James C. Baxter. (1970). Interpersonal spacing in natural settings. *Sociometry*, 33(4), pp. 444–456.

52. Baxter, Interpersonal spacing in natural settings, pp. 444–456; Daniel J. Thompson, & James C. Baxter. (1973, March). Interpersonal spacing in two-person cross-cultural interactions. *Man-Environment Systems*, 3, pp. 115–117.

53. Carl O. Word, Mark P. Zanna, & Joel Cooper. (1974). The nonverbal mediation of self-fulfilling prophecies in interracial interaction. *Journal of Experimental Social Psychology*, 10, pp. 114–115.

54. Smith, Nonverbal communication among black female dyads, pp. 62–63.

55. Halberstadt, Race, socioeconomic status, and nonverbal behavior, pp. 240–242.

56. Ibid., p. 247; Richard Majors. (1991). Nonverbal behaviors and communication styles among African Americans. In Reginald L. Jones (Ed.), *Black psychology*, 3rd ed. (p. 283). Berkeley, CA: Cobb & Henry.

57. Halberstadt, Race, socioeconomic status, and nonverbal behavior, pp. 242–246.

58. Hall. *The hidden dimension*, pp. 182–183.

59. Judith Berman. (1978). Counseling skills used by black and white male and female counselors. *Journal of Counseling Psychology*, 25(1), pp. 81–84; Robert Shuter. (1982). Initial interaction of American blacks and whites in interracial and intraracial dyads. *The Journal of Social Psychology*, 117, pp. 45–52.

60. Berman, Counseling skills used by black and white male and female counselors, pp. 82–83.

61. Shuter. Initial interaction of American blacks and whites in interracial and intraracial dyads, pp. 45–52.

62. Anita K. Foeman, & Gary Pressley. (1987). Ethnic culture and corporate culture: Using black styles in organizations. *Communication Quarterly*, 15(4), pp. 297, 303.

63. Frederick Erickson. (1979). Talking down: Some cultural sources of miscommunication in interracial interviews. In Aaron Wolfgang (Ed.), *Nonverbal behavior: Applications and cultural implications* (pp. 99–125). New York: Academic Press.

64. Jack L. Daniel, & Geneva Smitherman. (1976, February). How I got over: Communication dynamics in the black community. *Quarterly Journal of Speech*, 62, p. 37.

65. Thomas Kochman. (1981). *Black and white styles in conflict* (pp. 16–42). Chicago: University of Chicago Press.

66. Ibid., pp. 24–25; Thomas Kochman. (1974). Orality and literacy as factors of "black" and "white" communicative behavior. *Linguistics*, 3, pp. 102–105.

67. Kochman, Orality and literacy as factors of "black" and "white" communicative behavior, pp. 101–102.

68. Ibid., pp. 101–103; see also Marsha Houston Stanback, & W. Barnett Pearce. (1981). Talking to "the man": Some communication strategies used by

members of "subordinate" social groups. *The Quarterly Journal of Speech, 67*, pp. 21–30.

69.   Kochman, Orality and literacy as factors of "black" and "white" communicative behavior, pp. 104–108.

70.   Kochman, *Black and white styles in conflict*, p. 38.

8

The Hispanic
Communication Paradigm

Hispanics have immigrated from different countries at different times, for different reasons, and have settled in various parts of the United States. . . . Persons of Hispanic origins make up one of the fastest growing worker groups in the United States. Their number . . . has increased 65 percent since 1980, a rate of growth 4 times that for the non-Hispanic work force. A heterogeneous population, Hispanics represent many nationalities and ethnicities.[1]

WHO ARE THE HISPANICS?

The nation's second largest minority ethnic group is comprised of 27 million Hispanics, 10 percent of all the people in the United States. In just 15 years, the number of Hispanics has nearly doubled from 14.6 million in 1980 to nearly 27 million in 1995. According to Bureau of Census forecasts, the further we peer into this country's future the greater the percentage of Americans who will be Hispanic (Table 8.1). As this table indicates, at the mid-point of the twenty-first century more than one in five (and almost one in four) Americans are forecast to be Hispanic.[2] Latinos already are making their numbers felt in today's labor force: during the 1990s, approximately one in four net new entrants to the labor force will be Hispanic.[3] So, who are the Hispanics?

The term "Hispanic" is itself the result of a U.S. government action. In 1978, a decision by the U.S. Office of Management and Budget categorized as Hispanic those who lived in the United States and were

TABLE 8.1
Past and Forecasted Hispanic Population of the United States

	Total U.S. Population	Total Hispanic Population	Percent Hispanic Population
1980	227 million	14.6 million	6.4
1990	249	22.4	9.0
2000	276	31.2	11.3
2025	338	56.9	16.8
2050	392	88.0	22.5

Source: U.S. Bureau of the Census. (1994). No. 11. Resident population — Selected characteristics, 1790 to 1992, and projections, 1995 to 2050, and No. 12. Resident population characteristics — Percent distribution and median age, 1850 to 1992, and projections, 1995 to 2050. *Statistical abstract of the United States*. Washington, DC: Government Printing Office.

born in or can trace their ancestry to Mexico, Puerto Rico, Cuba, any 1 of 17 other Spanish-speaking Latin American countries, or to Spain itself.[4] In so doing, the U.S. government created a new racio-ethnic category found nowhere else in the world.

Elsewhere, individuals identify themselves and each other as Argentinian, Cuban, Dominican, Ecuadoran, Honduran, Mexican, Puerto Rican, Spanish, and others and recognize one another as such — individuals who, while sharing a common language and cultural heritage, come from distinctly different national and ethnic communities. Given the imprecision of ethnic groups, it is in some ways anomalous that Hispanic excludes individuals from Portugal, Brazil, and even the Philippines (whose heritage and culture is heavily influenced by its 500-year experience with Spanish colonial rule).

There is no single type of Hispanic. Beyond the standard variables — gender, educational attainment, occupation, income, class, and region — Hispanics may also differ by migratory experience, degree of acculturation, and English language fluency. Some Hispanics can trace their family tree to ancestors who lived in what is now the United States before the Pilgrims set foot on Plymouth Rock. These individuals became citizens not by immigration but by treaty or annexation.[5] In 1990 after much immigration, 59 percent of Hispanics were native born.[6]

The Hispanic community is comprised of diverse groups that have been known by a number of different names over the years. Like other U.S. minorities, individuals from these groups have alternatively called or identified themselves as Spanish American, Spanish-speaking American, Hispano, Hispanic, Hispanic American, or more lately as Chicano, Latino, or Latino American. One authoritative survey found that two-thirds to three-fourths of Hispanics self-identify according to national or ethnic categories, such as Mexican, Puerto Rican, or Cuban.[7] Today, the most inclusive of the widely-used terms are "Chicano," "Latino," and "Hispanic." Each denotes a slightly different connotation that may change.

Chicano (feminine, Chicana) refers primarily to those of Mexican ancestry and, in the past, has denoted a sense of militancy. Survey research indicates that while Latino or Hispanic have been equally popular self-descriptive terms, Hispanic is preferred by respondents who are more acculturated and Latino (feminine, Latina) by those who are somewhat less acculturated to the United States. Seventh and eighth generation Hispanics in southwestern states like New Mexico have used this term to identify themselves as a subculture in the U.S. mosaic for a long time. While Latino or Latino American often are preferred by some individuals of higher educational or income status, the authors of one major study confessed their surprise "that more respondents prefer to be called 'American' than 'Latino.'"[8]

Among Hispanic cultures there is little mistaking the often more open and friendly Puerto Rican from the more formal Peruvian, or the sometimes more stoic Mexican from the more assertive Cuban. The sometimes haughty Argentinian or individual from Spain might feel there are reasons to distinguish herself or himself from all other Latin Americans or Hispanics.[9] Mexican culture reflects a blend of the Spanish and Aztec, Mayan, and other Indian civilizations. Because the indigenous Indians of Puerto Rico and Cuba were virtually wiped out by conquest, slavery, or disease these two cultures in many ways reflect a blend of Spanish and African influences.

Within each culture (often within a family) there are individuals whose physical appearance reflects the full range of Spanish, Indian, African, or mixed features. A contemporary Latino family may consist of a mother who is fair, a father who is dark, and children who reflect the shades of color in between. Their cultural ancestry may be a mixture of Spanish, Indian, African, and, often, other European ancestors. However, their ethnic identification will be Hispanic — for example, Mexican American, Cuban American, or Puerto Rican American. In these cultures, color does not count for as much as it may in the minds of some Anglo Americans. Historically, individuals in the middle and upper classes have tended to have lighter skin color, although the importance of this factor is fading. What unites all of these groups is their rich Spanish heritage and their common migratory experience. This book will chiefly use the Bureau of Census appellation, Hispanic.

HISPANIC DEMOGRAPHIC CHARACTERISTICS

In 1990, the Hispanic community included individuals from various demographic categories (Table 8.2).

TABLE 8.2
Hispanic Population of the United States in 1990

	Millions	Percent
Hispanic origin	22.4	100
Mexican Americans	13.5	61
Puerto Ricans	2.8	12
Cubans	1.0	5
Other Hispanics*	5.1	22

*Hispanics from other Latin American countries and Spain or individuals who call themselves Spanish American.

Source: U.S. Bureau of the Census. (1992). No. 16. Resident population, by race and Hispanic origin: 1980 and 1990. *Statistical abstract of the United States*. Washington, DC: Government Printing Office.

These are conservative figures because individuals with Spanish surnames who do not speak English, are poor, or may be illegal aliens generally are undercounted in a census. The following demographic characteristics further describe the Hispanic community in the United States.

States

Hispanics reside in all 50 states, but 75 percent live in just five states: California, Texas, New York, Illinois, and Florida.[10]

Region

Almost 50 percent of Mexican Americans live in California and more than 25 percent in Texas. About 60 percent of mainland Puerto Ricans live in the mid-Atlantic region with 40 percent found in New York state alone. About 66 percent of Cuban Americans live in Florida.[11]

Urbanization and Suburbanization

Approximately 63 percent of Hispanics reside in only 25 metropolitan areas. The concentration of Hispanics in cities ranges from Laredo

(94 percent) and El Paso, Texas (69 percent) to Los Angeles (40 percent), Miami (63 percent), and New York (24 percent). It may be less well-known that approximately 43 percent of Hispanics live in suburbs, some of which are poor while others are affluent. During the 1980s Hispanics accounted for about 25 percent of the gain in suburban population.[12]

Educational Achievement

The educational achievement of Hispanics has improved but still lags behind national averages. In 1993, approximately 80 percent of males and females of all races had completed four years of high school or more; for Hispanics the figure was 53 percent. In 1993, about 25 percent of all males and 19 percent of all females in the United States had completed four years of college or more; about 10 percent of Hispanic males and 9 percent of Hispanic females had completed four years of college or more. About 31 percent of Hispanics had attended only the eighth grade or less. Approximately 3.3 percent of Hispanics earned graduate or professional degrees, while the national average was 7.2 percent.[13]

Income

In 1992, the Hispanic household median income was $22,846, with 33 percent of Hispanic households having incomes below $15,000. The median household income for all U.S. families was $30,786 with 24 percent having incomes below $15,000. Suburban Hispanic households had a median income of $26,811 in 1991.[14]

Occupational Status

In 1990, only 3.5 percent of Hispanic males and 3.1 percent of Hispanic females worked at executive, administrative, or managerial occupations in the private sector. This compares with 49.4 percent of white males and 35.9 percent of white females who worked at the same occupations.[15]

HISTORICAL AND CULTURAL BACKGROUND

Both the oldest and newest migrants to the United States are Hispanic. Spanish conquistadores were actively exploring parts of the present United States as early as 1513. Latino Americans lived in what is now the United States prior to the early English settlements of Jamestown and Plymouth. Their ancestors founded St. Augustine, Florida, in 1586. By the Revolutionary War, they also had founded what are today Santa Fe, New Mexico; El Paso, Texas, Albuquerque, New Mexico; San Antonio, Texas;

and San Francisco, California.[16] The United States established its sovereignty over these territories during the nineteenth century by purchase (all or part of Florida, Arizona, and New Mexico), annexation (Texas), and war (all or part of Arizona, California, Colorado, Kansas, Nevada, New Mexico, Oklahoma, Utah, and Wyoming). Following each expansion, old Mexican families found that their titles to their often vast land and property holdings had been nullified by devices ranging from new laws of questionable legality to outright fraud by gringo officials and newcomers.[17]

Most Hispanics have migrated to the United States more recently, having been propelled by the push of poverty in their own country and attracted by the pull of opportunity in the United States. The difficulty of policing a long, common border and the recent lack of effective sanctions have resulted in a substantial increase of legal immigrants and illegal border crossers. Immigrants from Puerto Rico greatly increased when the cost of commercial air travel came down. Between 1945 and 1950, a net average of 8,500 Puerto Ricans came to the U.S. mainland each year. Between 1960 and 1965, immigration from Puerto Rico had increased to 85,000 annually.[18]

Immigration from Cuba was largely a political phenomenon generated by Fidel Castro's imposition of a Marxist regime upon the people of Cuba. The first migratory wave in the early 1960s was largely comprised of educated, middle class, mainly white professionals who tended to settle in southern Florida near Miami. Their educational attainment and professional skills enabled them to do remarkably well in the U.S. work force. Later waves were comprised of individuals who sometimes were less well-educated and often did not possess equivalent professional status.

Since 1965 increasing numbers of Hispanics from Latin America have immigrated legally and illegally to the United States. They too were pushed by the poverty and civil wars in El Salvador and Nicaragua, as well as pulled by greater opportunity and freedom in the United States. So many have come from Colombia, the Dominican Republic, Ecuador, Guatemala, Honduras, Panama, and Peru that the diverse group of Other Hispanics now comprises nearly one-fourth of all Hispanics.[19]

The proximity of the United States to Latin America, the ease of travel, and the strength of the Hispanic family have helped perpetuate the Spanish language and Hispanic cultures moreso than has been true, for example, for French Canadians who emigrated to the northeastern United States from nearby Canada.

HISPANIC ACCOMPLISHMENTS AND ACHIEVEMENTS

Given the recent newcomer status of many, Hispanics are only begin-ning to contribute to life in the United States. Among the many talented Hispanics are singers Placido Domingo, Gloria Estefan, Joan Baez, Linda Ronstadt, and Mariah Carey; actors Charlie Sheen, Edward James Olmos, and now-deceased Rita (Margarita Carmen Casino) Hayworth; baseball greats Orlando Cepeda and Roberto Clemente; and legendary football quarterbacks Joe Kapp and Jim Plunkett.

Ellen Ochea was the first Hispanic astronaut to enter space. Linda Chavez is a respected social commentator. The film "Stand and Deliver" portrayed the inspiring mathematics teacher Jaime Escalante. The writing of Piri Thomas, Sandra Cisneros, and Pulitzer Prize-winner Oscar Hijuelos is renowned. In labor, Cesar Chavez commanded respect. In politics, two Hispanics presently serve in the White House cabinet — Secretary of Transportation Federico Pena and Secretary of Housing and Urban Development Henry Cisneros. Fashion designers Adolfo and Oscar de la Renta set trends while Yale-educated Cuban American Roberto Goizueta heads the company that produces the most globally-renowned American product — Coca-Cola.

HISPANIC VALUES

Mainstream U.S. values stress individualism, self-realization, a future orientation, achievement, and optimism. The education and training of managers is implicitly permeated by these values. Such values uncon-sciously establish expectations about the correct behavior of colleagues, what constitutes good management procedures, and implicit approaches to problem solving and leadership. In contrast, Hispanic values tend to emphasize collective interdependence (especially for and within the family), personal dignity, greater acceptance of age or gender hierarchy, collectivism, affiliation, and cooperation. The Hispanic worker may want his or her manager to be flexible in keeping appointments, to take the initiative for change, to give advice, or to educate him or her about the solution to problems.

The differences between the more task-oriented white male cultural paradigm and the more person-oriented Hispanic cultural paradigm are laden with positive potential if handled knowledgeably. It is not that one cultural style is superior or another is deficient but rather that mutual expectations are not met in their interaction. Both the challenge and the promise lie therein.

Collectivism

Perhaps the central Hispanic value is collectivism characterized by interdependence, sensitivity, and empathic sacrifice — all in the name of maintaining personal relationships. Here individuals act in conformity with and sensitivity to the needs of their in-group before they act to satisfy themselves. In contrast, individuals who are guided by the value of individualism (as are Americans, in general, and white males, in particular) emphasize achieving individual goals and satisfying individual needs, sometimes at the cost of damaging personal relationships.

In his survey of multinational managers from 40 countries, Geert Hofstede ranked Hispanic executives high in collectivism.[20] So have Gerardo Marin and Harry Triandis, who studied Hispanic youths and adults in the United States and Latin America.[21] Collectivistic Hispanics tend to be more sensitive and respectful in their interpersonal relationships while individualistic white males are likely to be more confrontational in theirs.[22]

Family

The family (*familism*) is an extraordinarily important Hispanic value. The strong ties of loyalty, unity, and reciprocity between members of nuclear and extended families define and provide strength and support to large numbers of Hispanics. Hispanic families frequently are extended families and include numerous aunts, uncles, cousins, and close friends. Visiting is a constant affair and strong family loyalty supersedes differences in education, occupation, or income. A geographic job change, although accepted at the same rate as blacks or non-Hispanic whites, may take longer to decide, especially if the new area does not have a high concentration of Hispanics.[23]

Although much of what follows changes with acculturation to the United States, decision-making power usually is vested in the male whose patriarchal authority is unquestioned. A stern disciplinarian, aloof but approachable (particularly by the mother), the husband publicly makes all major decisions. The female's role is to tend to her husband and rear her children. She should be submissive and tolerant (of alcohol and mistresses) and a devoted mother who is respected by her husband and revered by her children. For the Hispanic male the strongest bond often is between mother and son. Great care should be taken never to cast the slightest shadow upon a Hispanic's mother. While this stereotype may be prevalent, it is not the only model for the locus of authority and its exercise.

Parental authority (particularly patriarchal) is unquestioned. Children are told what to do. "Unlike WASP or Jewish families, Puerto Ricans do not see their children as individuals with minds of their own."[24] Fathers discipline and mothers protect the children. They are taught to lower their heads and eyes when being given advice or disciplined — behaviors school teachers often see in the same circumstance. Caught in this vise, children often learn to repress their questions, be outwardly obedient, and seek their wishes through their mother's intercession.

As a result of such an upbringing, Hispanics may not be as likely to question a superior's decision. They may appear deferential to a superior and accept instruction unquestionably (even if they do not understand clearly). The autocratic and hierarchical nature of authority in Hispanic society does not encourage individual initiative or problem solving without consultation with a superior.[25]

For Hispanics work and personal lives are closely connected, with family taking a much higher priority than among whites. To whites professional and personal lives are separate with work taking priority. Except with a few very good friends in the office, one simply does not poke or pry into the personal life or family of a colleague unless the colleague first broaches the topic.

HISPANIC (with consternation): How can I get to know him if I don't inquire about his family?

WHITE (uneasily): How can I ask about his family? I don't know him well enough.

For Hispanics, family comes first. Managers who deal with Hispanics and wish to do so effectively are advised to take this cultural value into consideration. Without being insincere or manipulative, managers might make an effort to learn something about their Hispanic colleagues' families, inquire of them periodically, and, particularly with recent immigrants, expect occasional absences. As one consultant put it, managers "should be alert to the possibility of finding in family ties and concerns an explanation for behavior they don't understand."[26]

Self-worth

Self-worth (*personalismo*) involves the recognition of the importance of each individual on the basis of one's inherent worth. Each person is judged worthy according to those intrinsic inner qualities that make a human being worthy of proper respect. Hispanics assess themselves by inner qualities that bestow self-worth and elicit respect from others. In traditional societies where status was fixed, focusing on inner qualities allowed one to experience self-worth regardless of social status, worldly success, or failure. It stands in contrast to the paramount significance accorded the white male value of individual achievement.[27]

Dignity and Respect

Roughly translated, dignity (*dignidad*) and respect (*respeto*) also are central values for Hispanics. One Hispanic professional wrote: "Not to show the proper respect to the Puerto Rican male assaults the very core of his manliness and the integrity of his family and puts in question his self-esteem as a human being."[28] Given the tremendous gaps between rich and poor, educated and uneducated, the powerful and the powerless in traditional Latin American societies, dignity and respect pervaded these societies because no one could grant or take away these qualities. They truly belonged to the individual.

Dignity and respect have different meanings in the white and Hispanic cultures. To the Hispanic, respect is accorded to the individual for courage, fearlessness of death, intellectual achievement, and sexual attractiveness to women. It is also accorded to those philosophical inner qualities that whites often feel uncomfortable even talking about but that Hispanics can discuss for hours. As one Hispanic academic expressed it: "Respeto is acquired by virtue of being, not by virtue of doing."[29] To the white, respect resonates with democratic equality, fair play, and impersonal admiration of personal qualities exhibited in performance.

Respect also can be granted on the basis of the hierarchical position one occupies. One need not epitomize any values to earn the respect of his subordinates; one possesses respect in an organization simply by virtue of the position he occupies. One's dignity and the respect shown one by others are linked. Failure to show a Hispanic proper respect violates his dignity and is a direct blow to his manliness. Personalismo also can be defined as a preference for face-to-face contact. In many instances, Hispanics may prefer such face-to-face or personal contact to the more impersonal norms that are dominant in mainstream organizational behavior.[30]

Manliness

To Hispanics, manliness (*machismo*) implies a spectrum that ranges from dignity and fearlessness in the face of death to distinguished, intellectual accomplishment, for example, in poetry or philosophy — all of which serve to elicit the proper respect.[31] Manliness also involves a sensitivity that may be at the base of the Hispanic psyche. One should be aware not to intentionally or unintentionally attack an Hispanic's manhood; appear to engage in a public humiliation or insult; or engage in a joking pretense of disrespect for any member of his family, especially a female. The organizational implications of manliness may be less understood. In this domain, manliness may involve an element of authoritarianism that has an impact on leadership and the relationship between superior and subordinate.

The authoritarian element of manliness carries with it an element of dominance and direction. In contrast, the mainstream U.S. management style is characterized by egalitarianism and participation. Where an Hispanic is the superior, direction may stifle participation; competence may be seen as a threat to dominance. As one observer put it: "The father . . . wants his son to be macho, but not so much as he."[32] The Hispanic subordinate may have an expectation of strong, somewhat distant, and even directive behavior by a superior. But the line is fine. While strength of leadership may be expected arrogance is not. If the employee is treated with respect, a tremendous amount of loyalty can accrue toward the superior.

Womanliness

Some Hispanic women may feel as bound by womanliness (*marianismo*) as Hispanic males feel compelled to live up to manliness. However, many Hispanic women who have become acculturated to the mainstream American culture are seeking new roles and identities.[33]

According to the value of womanliness, marriage, home, and children are the chief domains of women. Self-sacrifice in these areas accords greater respect from the community and greater self-respect. According to womanliness, women defer to men, particularly in decision making, while work outside of the home can be a source of conflict.[34] Research indicates that, in actuality, egalitarian decision making between Hispanic husbands and wives is far more the norm than may be expected, although the process may be more covert than overt to save the respect of the husband or father.[35]

Womanliness may be among the first casualties of acculturation into the United States. Many Hispanic women, particularly among the well-educated and immigrants, appreciate and value the greater freedom and choice that U.S. culture offers them.

Sensitivity

For all the reasons cited above, Hispanics tend to be emotionally expressive and sensitive.[36] In their interpersonal relationships Hispanics may attend more to the feelings of others. In fact, Hispanics tend to be very sensitive to people and to their relationships with them. Given the importance of dignity, subtle face-saving strategies generally are preferred to open conflict, as is a consensus to confrontation. Open and direct criticism is intolerable and can cause one to lose face. In contrast, the white male norm holds that one should repress emotions, and that direct criticism of performance should be taken in the spirit of impartial improvement.

Honesty

Hispanics respect and value honesty. However, there are times when one recognizes the very tender sensitivities of others. One, therefore, may tell a white lie to avoid criticizing another's error or avoid embarrassing one's boss by not admitting that he does not fully understand the directions given. To so confess might highlight one's own inadequacies in listening as well as to bring into question the boss's explanation. In either case:

Any given statement may appear completely ethical to a Mexican, whereas to an American it would appear to be a lie. It must be remembered, however, that because of their high degree of interpersonal sensitivity, the first concern of Mexicans is to avoid hurt feelings and confrontation. Therefore, one cannot always get a direct or a completely honest answer to a direct question. In general Mexicans feel that, in the long run, diplomacy and an indirect, discreet response lead to better understanding and achieve more than do blunt truth and direct confrontation.[37]

Mexican psychologist Rogelio Diaz-Guerrero speculates that each culture may possess two differing "realities" which govern the "truth."[38] Diaz-Guerrero sees U.S. culture as characterized by objective reality according to which objective and empirical principle prevails. One not only tells it straight but usually is asked to do so. One conveys this objective truth even if it is grim and painful. In contrast, Hispanic, and especially Mexican, culture is governed by interpersonal reality. Accordingly, one should make another happy, should not upset another, or embarrass another's dignity. That is why a Hispanic may be more likely to put down the pen and listen to another person despite the rush of a deadline. One should be grand and always put people first because they have sensitivities.

Hierarchy

Hofstede's cross-cultural research indicates that Hispanic executives are high in power distance or hierarchy. This means that they tend to be outwardly deferential and respectful as well as obedient and conformist toward those who hold greater power. This tends to breed a more authoritarian and autocratic exercise of power on the part of superiors, and to foster agreeable behaviors for fear of violating respect on the part of subordinates. Care should be taken here because respect for hierarchy may be truer of more recent immigrants than of acculturated Hispanics who have lived and worked in the United States for even a few years.

Religiosity

Hispanics tend to revere the soul and spirituality over the temporal or material aspects of life. "Being is more important than doing or having."[39] The individual is surrounded by strong forces and invisible spirits of good and evil. Good behavior and deeds strengthen one in the face of these powerful forces or spirits. One also seeks their appeasement or protection through the intercession of mediating agents. For example, one prays to saints to intercede on one's behalf for the grace of Jesus. One lights candles, makes promises, and undertakes pilgrimages to express one's faith in the intercessor. This fatalism is also part of the secular life of the Hispanic. The invocation of God's will and the proverb popularized in the song "Que Sera, Sera" (Whatever Will Be, Will Be), reflect the secular belief in tragic inevitability as well as the religious belief in divine predestination characteristic of so many Hispanics. Hispanics struggle and work mightily against these forces and powers; ultimately, they accept their fate.

CULTURE AND COMMUNICATION

Linda had come to visit Juan in his office but was becoming more and more disconcerted. He was late returning to his office to meet with her to discuss the strategy for her new sales campaign. During their meeting, Juan took a few quick telephone calls and signed some papers that his secretary brought in. To Linda, Juan's behavior was impolite, inattentive, and bordered on rudeness.

Juan had hurried back from his meeting. He knew he had spent more time than his schedule allotted with Jack. But as Juan said to himself: "Jack is my good friend and a subordinate. He had a problem. And I had to listen to him until he was finished." As soon as he arrived, his secretary started to let through a few calls and bring in some important papers because she knew his way of working.

Polychronic Time

Hispanic culture is characterized by polychronic time. It is customary for Hispanics to see time not as a line but as a web and to do many things at once. Hispanics typically place less emphasis on their time schedule than on the importance of the person they are with at the moment. Polychronic time individuals tend to be more present oriented and less likely to be punctual for unimportant business occasions. Researchers report that Hispanics are more relaxed about time. They are less likely to estimate accurately how long a task takes to complete or to be on time for an appointment.[40]

Mainstream U.S. culture operates on the basis of monochronic time.[41] This means that executives generally like to do one thing at a time. They see time as linear, segment and schedule it, and become quite upset at tardiness, delays, or missing deadlines. Completing tasks is primary while developing relationships is secondary. Given their differing concepts of time, whites tend to be more optimistic and future oriented while Hispanics may be more fatalistically present based. Some Hispanics feel that whites are so concerned with planning for the future that they do not enjoy the pleasures of the present. Hispanics do not think less of time; they think more of their relationships with people and value them.

High Context Culture

Hispanic culture is a high context culture.[42] In high context cultures, nonverbal behaviors are expected to convey as much if not more of the message than words alone. Accordingly, unless one is familiar with the culture-specific cues, high context (or nonverbal) communication often is more ambiguous and indirect.

In low context societies, such as the United States, words are considered the primary channel for communication. Words ought to be specific and concise — words mean what they say. In summary, the low context white culture relies more upon verbal communication while the high context Hispanic culture relies more on nonverbals in face-to-face communication.

Simpatia Cultural Script

According to cross-cultural psychologist Harry Triandis and his colleagues who coined the phrase, a "cultural script" involves a pattern of communication that is shared by a particular ethnic group. It embodies the key values of an ethnic group with the behaviors that are characteristic of them. For example, the "Simpatia" cultural script links the Hispanic values of respect and dignity with their avoidance of conflict in face-to-face interaction. To criticize or slight a person may be to infringe upon their self-respect and dignity. Consequently, according to Triandis, social behaviors of courtesy and indirection, which lead to social harmony, are emphasized among Hispanics while direct argumentation, public disagreement, and open competition are avoided. The simpatia script helps account for the greater value that Hispanics place upon relationships than the more singular focus upon task achievement, which is so characteristics of whites.[43]

The following vignette illustrates some of the issues embedded in the Hispanic and white communication scripts as individuals from each subculture encounter one another in the work place. Here Luis, a fifteen-year veteran of his company, is meeting his new colleague, Robert.

LUIS (approaches Robert to within 10–12 inches and shakes his hand while tapping his bicep): Welcome to the company, Robert. I am glad you've joined us. We're happy to have you on board.

ROBERT (moving backward, seemingly uncomfortable): Thanks, Luis. I'm really looking forward to working here. This place offers a lot of advancement and career growth. I'm happy to be here.

LUIS (advancing a step toward Robert, gazing but not looking directly at him): You know, Robert, what you'll like most about this place is the friendly atmosphere. People are not strangers; it's like a family.

ROBERT (Body rigid hand in pocket, Robert seeks eye contact. Luis listens and looks intently at Robert.): That's great. But I've come here looking for advancement in the next few years. I didn't get any at my last job. That's why I left.

LUIS: You know, Robert, Pedro, the boss, is a good man. I'm sure that he will realize your value soon enough and will treat you well. More than that, he cares a lot for his workers. Last year he was very kind to me when my son was sick in the hospital. He makes it his business to know our problems. I think you'll like it here because it's not all business. You'll never want to leave this place.

ROBERT (thinking to himself, I don't like people knowing about my personal life): Well, I've always looked upon work as a place to do my job and leave when I finish.

LUIS: Well, you know, this place grows on you. In a year you'll feel differently, you'll feel part of this family. By the way, at the next break stop by and we'll have a coffee together.

What appears like a normal, introductory conversation between Luis and Robert in actuality reflects the difference between their communication paradigms. Luis was more person-oriented in his behavior while Robert was more task-oriented. This was evident in Luis' welcoming words as well as in his nonverbal touching gestures. Furthermore, Luis' verbal comments typified the value of collectivism in his reference to the work setting as family. Robert's words underlined the value he places on individualism and task achievement when he spoke of advancement and his own career trajectory as the justification for his efforts. One can surmise that the simpatia script pervaded Luis' interchange with Robert. In it, Luis joined the values of the collective family as well as respect and dignity. Luis also conveyed a positive social situation in which the personal relationships depicted by Luis' affability and Pedro's caring overshadowed Robert's task achievement and the advancement he was aiming for.

NONVERBAL COMMUNICATION

It was evident in the vignette that individuals in a high context culture tend to utilize more nonverbal cues in their face-to-face communication. Because nonverbal behaviors are out of consciousness, they are particularly likely to cause discomfort between individuals who are communicating across cultural lines without either party quite knowing why. Therefore, it is particularly important to be aware of culturally differing nonverbal behaviors.

Eye Contact and Gaze

Direct eye contact — a stare — is likely to be perceived among Hispanics as lacking in respect or even as confrontational. Given the hierarchical nature of the traditional Hispanic culture, listeners tend to avoid eye contact with higher status speakers. What non-Hispanic individuals may interpret as disregard ("Jose, why aren't you looking me in the eye when I talk to you?") may actually be an expression of respect. Remember, Hispanic children are taught to avoid direct eye contact when they are being disciplined or advised by their parents. Hispanics tend to avoid eye contact whenever possible, using peripheral gaze instead. Thus, high context Hispanics engage in more gaze, though of an indirect sort. This was evident in Luis' pattern of eye contact while speaking with Robert. However, when Luis was listening to Robert, he maintained direct eye contact with him. Generally prolonged and direct eye contact conveys confrontation between males and possible sexual overtures when it occurs between males and females.[44]

Proxemics

Body distances tend to be much closer for Hispanics than what is either normal or comfortable for whites.[45] For whites, intimate space is skin contact to about 18 inches; one interacts with a business colleague or friend from about 18 to 30 inches. A general rule of thumb is that Hispanics interact at closer proxemic distances than mainstream U.S. personal and business cultures. It is not uncommon to see Hispanics speaking with one another, standing just a few inches apart, heads bent, bodies at a slight angle, and engrossed in conversation.

Unless both parties are aware of the other's cultural proxemic behavior, an interaction between a white and an Hispanic may resemble an interaction of distance and pursuit with one uncomfortably back-pedaling while the other exasperatedly pursues. This was the case between Luis and Robert. Robert's backpedaling response was a nonverbal indication that Luis' proxemic behavior was intrusive to him. While one individual may call the other pushy, the other person may call such behavior aloof. Carmen Judith Nine Curt points out that some Hispanics may perceive such behavior as cold and even racially prejudiced.[46] In fact, all of these judgments are erroneous. Here cultures, not people, are being judged. One culture is not better or worse than the other; the success of the interaction is what counts — in other words, how well Luis and Robert understand one another as they walk away from their conversation.

However, care should be taken not to overgeneralize about the proxemic distances at which Hispanics stand and interact with one another. One study found that proxemic distances among Latin Americans varied as much and more than among North Americans.[47] Another study concluded that South Americans tend to stand farther from each other than Central Americans.[48] As is always the case, one should be careful about the shared behavioral pattern of any ethnic group.

Touch

Hispanics tend to be a higher touch subculture than whites.

Initial meetings between Hispanics generally involve reserved polite-ness, the use of formal names, and a handshake. Research indicates that even everyday meetings between Hispanics in the workplace entail some kind of physical contact: males at least shake hands.[49] As the vignette indicates, Luis not only shakes hands with Robert but also touches his arm in a friendly gesture. Hispanic females are more likely to kiss each other on the cheek and are much more likely than white women to walk arm-in-arm. Hispanic males are likely to grasp the arm or touch another with the tip of their finger when making a point, a behavior that can make whites quite uncomfortable.[50]

However, here too caution is urged about overgeneralization. According to a cross-cultural study of the nonverbal behavior of Central Americans and South Americans: "The results indicate that . . . the frequency of contact diminishes, and fewer touch and hold as one travels from Central to South America."[51] Here again, although common cultural patterns exist, it is always better to see the person before you as an individual.

The mainstream U.S. behavior is generally to shake hands upon being introduced or concluding a deal. Women tend to hug each other during greetings, and to exchange cheek pecks with each other and with men who are close to them. Generally for whites a "Hello, how are you?" suffices for a first or an everyday encounter.

Kinesics

Hispanics tend to use their bodies, heads, and hands in free, relatively unrestrained body movements or rhythms. In the white workplace culture, one tends to move the trunk as one unit and use the neck and head to emphasize points. Hispanics move their entire trunk.[52] A researcher notes that while whites move their necks and heads for emphasis, "The Latin will move all parts of the body separately, but flowingly. The Anglo, on the other hand, will be more rigid, carrying the body as if it is one unit. This can be illustrated in the dance."[53] As one Hispanic manager was told by his white male boss: "Don't wave your hands so much. It's distracting."

VERBAL COMMUNICATION

In this scenario, Allen conducts a 6-month performance appraisal with his new Hispanic employee, Oscar.

ALLEN: Well, Oscar, it's been six months since you joined us. As you know it's time for your first performance appraisal. I've scheduled an hour to do this. Here we deal with the positive and negative aspects of your performance as objectively as possible to help you do your job better.

OSCAR: That's fine, I'm ready for it.

ALLEN: Let me begin by asking you how you like being here?

OSCAR: Well, I've been very happy here. I like working with everyone in this office. I also like this line of work.

ALLEN: It seems to be reciprocal. Here in the office everyone seems to like you and finds you very friendly. You're a good addition to the team.

OSCAR: I'm happy to hear this.

ALLEN: However, I'd like to see you do better with your sales. From my observations and these numbers, you're just spending too much time on too few customers. Look Oscar, ten customer contacts per week averages out to three sales. What do you think is happening here?

OSCAR: I do see close to ten customers a week, but I don't always make three sales. I guess I have to try harder.

ALLEN: Well, Oscar, if you're seeing ten people, why aren't you closing at least three sales?

OSCAR: I guess these are high quality prospects. But they're not yet ready to buy.

ALLEN: Why not?

OSCAR: You see, Allen, I spend time with these people. I take time to know them, they get to trust me. And when they're ready, they'll come back and buy from me.

ALLEN: Oscar, you have to understand that the sales need to be closed when you're with the customer, otherwise you lose.

OSCAR: In my last job, it took me a while to get started, but after a year I was among the top five salesmen in the company. The way it works for me is to give people the time they need to shop around and when they're ready, they come back and buy from me. The reason they come back is that they find out that they can trust me.

ALLEN: O.K. But just keep in mind that a bird in the hand is worth two in the bush. Let's check in again in six months.

Cultural differences can be responsible for problems in verbal communication. Culture helps determine how we respond to every communication interaction. As is typical of every culture, Hispanics generally have two verbal communication styles — one that is formal and public for new acquaintances and business associates and the other that is informal and private for family and friends.

In their formal communication style, Hispanics tend to be polite and restrained and possessed of impeccable manners and etiquette. Their language is indirect, allusionary, and sometimes florid. Being aware of the centrality and personal sensitivities engendered by respect and dignity, Hispanics tend to be more indirect and tactful than direct and specific in their statements. As one long-time observer and scholar put it, "Mexicans have a hundred ways of saying 'No' without every saying it."[54] This aspect of the Hispanic communication style may create dissonance for others, particularly in the mainstream U.S. culture. Writing on this subject, John Condon states that Hispanics tend to convey pleasant rather than negative information although it may be critical.[55] The single most important motive for this action is the high value placed upon establishing and maintaining a personal relationship.

What a white hears as an inquiry, the Hispanic hears as a dictate. What one may perceive as the normal interplay of points of view, the other may interpret as conflictual. Once one has passed through the formal phase, established a relationship of trust, and become accepted as a close friend, the Hispanic communication style changes. It becomes more relaxed, informal, and jovial although always conscious of the other's dignity. Hispanics are always careful not to embarrass, demean, or cause their close friend to lose face. Hispanics also tend to express their innermost emotions more freely and to engage in philosophical and even mystical discussions about intellectual topics as well as themselves. Once a deep and meaningful relationship has been established, Hispanics are more likely to share their innermost feelings and self-disclose. A white male may find this a much deeper relationship than ever before encountered and become bewildered by it.

Hispanics are more likely than whites to utilize silence when dealing with others. As a sign of respect for age or position, out of politeness, or just to ponder Hispanics tend to feel more comfortable with long pauses than do whites. Silence should not necessarily be interpreted as an unfriendly, discomforting, or negative message. This is more true of some Hispanic groups than of others. Verbal communication styles vary among the different Hispanic subcultures. For example, Mexican Americans have more of a reputation for quietness and silence than Cuban Americans, who are reputed to be more rapid and loquacious in their speech.

MANAGEMENT PRACTICES

Hispanic managers are more likely than whites to take the time to develop and nurture personal relationships on and off the job. Typically, Hispanic managers take more time than whites to address the concerns and needs of their colleagues and subordinates. No matter how busy they are, their sensitivity to relationships obliges them to attend to the feelings and accommodate the needs of others regardless of the demands of their personal schedule. One study found that Hispanic managers prefer a collaborative style of leadership with an open door policy for subordinates and colleagues.[56]

Out of the Hispanic sensitivity and desire for harmonious relationships, their verbal style may appear more indirect and even allusionary to others. Their sense of polychronic time reflects their relational culture because it places more importance upon personal relationships than the simple use of time to achieve results. As a high contact culture, Hispanic nonverbals include closer proxemic distances, more touch, more indirect gaze, less direct eye contact, and more gesturing than the mainstream white business cultural paradigm. As a high context culture, Hispanics are more sensitive to subtle nonverbal cues. They, thereby, derive and expect others to derive information less from words and more from subtle nonverbal or contextual cues. Hispanic managers tend to prefer face-to-face communication to the more impersonal mediums of memos or telephones. These managers report themselves as being at their best when they interact in a face-to-face setting.

In their organizational life, Hispanics tend to operate initially at a more formal level with others. This allows them to be as task oriented and goal achieving as any manager. Their politeness and relationship orientation often make Hispanics more sensitive in their interactions than individuals from some other ethnic groups.

CONCLUSION

Hispanics are among the oldest and newest U.S. immigrants. Some come from families that lived in this country before the pilgrims landed at Plymouth Rock. Yet, about four in ten were born outside the United States. As is true of every culture, Hispanic values have a deep impact on their communication behavior. The importance Hispanics place upon the value of relationships is reflected in their attempt to balance task achievement with their sensitivity to relationships in their dealings with others. Perhaps, more than the mainstream white business culture, Hispanics place greater emphasis upon relationships.

Hispanics differ by region, education, class, income, and length of residency in the United States. Thus, their rate of acculturation into the mainstream culture will vary accordingly. It is always best to come to know the individual.

NOTES

1. Peter Cattan. (1993, August). The diversity of Hispanics in the U.S. work force. *Monthly Labor Review*, p. 3.

2. U.S. Bureau of the Census. (1994). *Current population reports: Population projections of the United States, by age, sex, race, and Hispanic origin: 1993–2050*, P-25-1104. Washington, DC: Government Printing office. Tables I and J on page xxii forecast that the U.S. Hispanic population in 2050 may vary from 20.2 percent in the lowest series to 24.6 percent in the highest series.

3. Howard N. Fullerton. (1993, November). Another look at the labor force: The American work force, 1992–2005. *Monthly Labor Review*, pp. 36–37.

4. Gerardo Marin, & Barbara VanOss Marin. (1991). *Research with Hispanic populations* (pp. 20–21). Newbury Park, CA: Sage Publications.

5. See Walker Connor. (1985). Who are the Mexican-Americans? A note on comparability. In Walker Connor (Ed.), *Mexican-Americans in comparative perspective* (p. 16). Washington, DC: The Urban Institute.

6.   Thomas G. Exter. (1993, February). The largest minority. *American Demographics*, p. 59. There is wide variation on this point. See, for example, Patricia Braus. (1993, June). What does Hispanic mean? *American Demographics*, p. 47, who cites a Yankelovich Partners survey that found that 72 percent of Hispanic respondents had been born outside of the United States while 40 percent of nonnative Latinos have lived in the United States for ten years or less.

7.   Rodolfo O. de la Garza, Louis Desipio, F. Chris Garcia, John Garcia, & Angelo Falcon. (1992). *Latino voices: Mexican, Puerto Rican, and Cuban perspectives on American politics* (pp. 62–63). Boulder, CO: Westview Press.

8.   Marin, & Marin, *Research with Hispanic populations*, pp. 18–24; de la Garza et al., *Latino voices*, p. 13.

9.   Calvin Sims. (1995, July 30). The South American art of name-calling. New York *Times*, Sec. IV, p. 4.

10.   Kathy Bodovitz. (1991, July). Hispanic America. *American Demographics*, p. 14.

11.   Cattan, The diversity of Hispanics in the U.S. work force, p. 5.

12.   U.S. Bureau of the Census. (1994). No. 46. Cities with 100,000 or more inhabitants in 1992, and land area, 1990. *Statistical abstract of the United States*. Washington, DC: Government Printing Office; William H. Frey, & William P. O'Hare. (1993, April). Vivan los Suburbios. *American Demographics*, p. 32; Bodovitz, Hispanic America, p. 27.

13.   U.S. Bureau of the Census. (1994). No. 233. Educational attainment, by race, ethnicity, and sex: 1960 to 1993. *Statistical abstract of the United States*. Washington, DC: Government Printing Office; Educational attainment of the U.S. population by racial and ethnic group, 1990. (1994, September 1). *The Chronicle of Higher Education*, p. 16.

14.   U.S. Bureau of the Census. (1994). No. 712. Money income of household — percent distribution, by income level, race, and Hispanic origin: 1992. *Statistical abstract of the United States*. Washington, DC: Government Printing Office; Frey, & O'Hare, Vivan los Suburbios, p. 32.

15.   U.S. Department of Labor, The Glass Ceiling Commission. (1995). *Good for business: Making full use of the nation's human capital* (p. 79). Washington, DC: Government Printing Office.

16.   Ford Foundation. (1984). *Hispanics: Challenges and opportunities* (p. 5). Ford Foundation Working Paper. New York: Ford Foundation.

17.   For sources on Hispanics, see Leo Grebler, Joan W. Moore, Ralph C. Guzman. (1970). *The Mexican-American people: The nation's second largest minority*. New York: The Free Press; Joan W. Moore. (1970). *Mexican Americans*. Englewood Cliffs, NJ: Prentice-Hall; Thomas Sowell. (1981). *Ethnic America: A history* (esp. pp. 227–270). New York: Basic Books; Earl Shorris. (1992). *The Latinos: A biography of the people*. New York: W. W. Norton & Co.; Ronald Takaki. (1993). *From a different shore: A history of multicultural America* (esp. pp. 160–190, 311–339). Boston, MA: Little, Brown and Company.

18.   Sowell, *Ethnic America: A history*, p. 231.

19.   Morton Winsberg. (1994, February). Specific Hispanics. *American Demographics*, pp. 44–53.

20. Geert Hofstede. (1980). *Culture's consequences: International differences in work-related values* (pp. 92–152). Beverly Hills, CA: Sage Publications.

21. Gerardo Marin, & Harry C. Triandis. (1985). Allocentrism as an important characteristic of the behavior of Latin Americans and Hispanics. In Rogelio Diaz-Guerrero (Ed.), *Cross-cultural and national studies in social psychology* (pp. 85–104). North Holland: Elsevier Science Publishers B.V.

22. Harry C. Triandis, Gerado Marin, C. Harry Hui, Judith Lisansky, & Victor Ottati. (1984, September). Role perceptions of Hispanic young adults. *Journal of Cross-Cultural Psychology, 15*(3), pp. 297–320.

23. Jack E. Edwards, Paul Rosenfeld, Patricia J. Thomas, & Marie D. Thomas. (1993, February). Willingness to relocate for employment: A survey of Hispanics, non-Hispanic whites, and blacks. *Hispanic Journal of Behavioral Sciences, 15*(1), pp. 121–133.

24. Nydia Garcia-Preto. (1982). Puerto Rican families. In Monica McGoldrick, John K. Pearce, & Joseph Giordano (Eds.), *Ethnicity and family therapy* (p. 172). New York: Guilford Press.

25. Eva S. Kras. (1989). *Management in two cultures: Bridging the gap between U.S. and Mexican managers* (pp. 34–36, 47–48, 52). Yarmouth, ME: Intercultural Press.

26. Ibid., p. 64.

27. Garcia-Preto, Puerto Rican families, p. 169.

28. Ibid.

29. Orlando Isaza, personal communication, October 1995.

30. Sally Innis Klitz. (1980). *Crosscultural communication: The Hispanic community of Connecticut* (p. 15). Storrs: The University of Connecticut; Sidney W. Mintz. (1973). Puerto Rico: An essay in the definition of a natural culture. In Francesco Cordasco & Eugene Bucchioni (Eds.), *The Puerto Rican experience: A sociological sourcebook* (p. 68). Totowa, NJ: Rowan and Littlefield.

31. Alfredo Mirande. (1988). Que Gacho Es Ser Macho: It's a drag to be a macho man. *AZTLAN, 17*(2), pp. 78–87.

32. John C. Condon. (1985). *Good neighbors: Communicating with the Mexicans* (p. 32). Yarmouth, ME: Intercultural Press.

33. Melba J. T. Vasquez. (1994). Latinas. In Lillian Comas-Diaz and Beverly Greene (Eds.), *Women of color: Integrating ethnic and gender identities in psychotherapy* (pp. 114–138). New York: Guilford Press.

34. Maria Nieto Senour. (1977). Psychology of the Chicana. In Joe L. Martinez, Jr. (Ed.), *Chicano psychology* (p. 333). New York: Academic Press.

35. Vicky L. Cromwell, & Ronald E. Cromwell. (1978, November). Perceived dominance in decision-making and conflict resolution among Anglo, black, and Chicano couples. *Journal of Marriage and the Family*, pp. 754–758.

36. Edward T. Hall. (1977). *Beyond culture* (pp. 156–158). Garden City, NY: Anchor Books.

37. Kras, *Management in two cultures*, pp. 44–45.

38. Rogelio Diaz-Guerrero. (1967). *Psychology of the Mexican: Culture and personality* (pp. 17–20). Austin: University of Texas Press.

39. Garcia-Preto, Puerto Rican families, pp. 168–169; Man Keung Ho. (1987). *Family therapy with ethnic minorities* (pp. 126–127). Newbury Park, CA: Sage

Publications.

40.   Marin, & Marin, *Research with Hispanic populations*, p. 16.

41.   Edward T. Hall, & Mildred Reed Hall. (1990). *Understanding cultural differences* (pp. 13–22). Yarmouth, ME: Intercultural Press.

42.   Ibid., pp. 6–10.

43.   Harry Triandis, Gerado Marin, Judith Lisansky, & Hector Betancourt. (1984). Simpatia as a cultural script of Hispanics. *Journal of Personality and Social Psychology, 47*(6), pp. 1363–1375.

44.   Carmen Judith Nine Curt. (1984). *Non-verbal communication in Puerto Rico*, 2d ed. (pp. 30–31). Cambridge, MA: Evaluation, Dissemination and Assessment Center.

45.   Edward T. Hall. (1959). *The silent language* (p. 164). Greenwich, CT: Fawcett Publications; Curt, *Non-verbal communication in Puerto Rico*, p. 21; James C. Baxter. (1970). Interpersonal spacing in natural settings. *Sociometry, 33*(4), pp. 444–456; Daniel J. Thompson, & James C. Baxter. (1973, March). Interpersonal spacing in two-person cross-cultural interactions. *Man-Environment Systems, 3*(2), pp. 115–117.

46.   Curt, *Non-verbal communication in Puerto Rico*, p. 21.

47.   Robert F. Forston, & Charles Urban Larson. (1968, June). The dynamics of space: An experimental study in proxemic behavior among Latin Americans and North Americans. *Journal of Communication, 18*, pp. 109–116.

48.   Robert Shuter. (1976). Proxemics and tactility in Latin America. *Journal of Communication, 26*, pp. 46–52.

49.   Bernardo M. Ferdman, & Angelica C. Cortes. (1992). Culture and identity among Hispanic managers in an Anglo business. In Stephen B. Knouse, Paul Rosenfeld, & Amy L. Culbertson (Eds.), *Hispanics in the Workplace* (pp. 256–257). Newbury Park, CA: Sage Publications.

50.   Baxter, Interpersonal spacing in natural settings, pp. 444–456; Gary P. Ferraro. (1990). *The cultural dimension of international business* (pp. 84–87). Englewood Cliffs, NJ: Prentice-Hall; Shuter, Proxemics and tactility in Latin America, pp. 46–52.

51.   Shuter, Proxemics and tactility in Latin America, p. 52.

52.   Condon, *Good neighbors: Communicating with the Mexicans*, p. 60.

53.   Klitz, *Crosscultural communication*, p. 22.

54.   Celia Jaes Falicov. (1982). Mexican families. In Monica McGoldrick, John K. Pearce, & Joseph Giordano (Eds.), *Ethnicity and family therapy* (p. 153). New York: Guilford Press.

55.   Condon, *Good neighbors: Communicating with the Mexicans*, p. 45.

56.   Ferdman, & Cortes, Culture and identity among Hispanic managers in an Anglo business, pp. 256–265.

9

The Asian American Communication Paradigm

I would like in spirit to share this award with my grandfather, Shuichi Ujifusa, also known as Sam. He's been dead now for 25 years. In 1904, he arrived in Wyoming to work as a railroad laborer. In 1910, he broke farmland out of sagebrush to grow sugarbeets. Later he raised cattle and toward the end, dabbled in oil and natural gas.

I loved grandpa. One day when I was about 12, I asked him why he left Japan for America. He said, "because in Japan life is complicated, but in this country, life is simple. You see, in Japan, you have to know your place. You bow so low to a person one station above you, and bow lower for someone two stations above you, and lower still for a real big shot. It gets hard to remember who and where you are and keep things straight.

"But in America," grandpa said, "life is simple. Right away, it's easy for anybody: work hard, study hard, love your family, be a good neighbor."

Then he said in Japanese-accented farmer-rancher English, "Know your place? Grant Masashi, in our house, we don't put no stock in that proposition."

So because of my grandfather, I am very proud of my Asian heritage. And because of my grandfather, I am prouder still to be an American.

— Grant Ujifusa[1]

The four major elements to the story of Asian Americans in the United States are the discrimination they have experienced, the distance Asian

Americans have traveled, the diversity they embody, and their promise to America. "From pariah to paragon" is the way one sociologist described the socioeconomic distance Asian Americans have traveled.[2] Few Americans are aware of the depth of discrimination that marked the Asian Americans' starting point or their journey.

From 1854 to 1874 Chinese were precluded by law from testifying in court against a white man.[3] In 1871 approximately 20 Chinese were hanged or shot in Los Angeles during a single night of mob violence.[4] The 1879 Constitution of the State of California denied them entrance to certain professional occupations as well as the right to own land.[5] In 1885 and 1886 all Chinese were expelled from Seattle and Tacoma, Washington.[6] At varying times, Asian Americans were restricted from swimming at beaches or even attending theaters.

For decades federal law excluded Asian Americans from immigrating to the United States and Asian Americans who already lived here from becoming citizens. By World War II's Executive Order 9066, Japanese Americans who lived in western states were unjustly incarcerated in remote and barren internment camps.[7] This intensely discriminatory and painful experience contributed to our language the once commonly-used but now, perhaps, more tragically meaningful phrase "Not a Chinaman's chance."[8]

Yet, by 1959, a higher proportion of Chinese Americans than Caucasians were working in professional occupations.[9] By 1969, Japanese American personal income was 111 percent of the national average.[10] In 1990, Asian Americans were graduating from college at almost twice the rate as all races.[11] In fact, some select universities have acknowledged using subtle means to reduce the number of able Asian American students being admitted. For example, Brown University confirmed that it treated Asian American applicants "unfairly," Stanford University acknowledged "unconscious bias" in its admissions process, and Berkeley's chancellor apologized for "disadvantaging" Asian Americans.[12] In 1992, the nation's median household income was $30,786; for whites it was $32,368 and for Asian Americans it was $38,153. In the same year 4.9 percent of U.S. households had incomes above $100,000; for whites the figure was 5.3 percent and for Asian Americans it was 8.3 percent.[13]

Few ethnic groups are as demographically diverse as Asian Americans. The category "Asian American" covers 25 groups so different that even we are not using the full title of the Bureau of the Census category: "Asian American and Pacific Islanders." Listing only the Asian ethnicities includes Americans who are Asian Indian, Cambodian, Chinese, Chinese Taiwanese, Filipino, Hmong, Indian, Indonesian, Japanese, Korean, Laotian, Pakistani, Thai, and Vietnamese.[14]

Because of their diversity and this book's focus, when we use the term "Asian American" we shall mean only Americans of Chinese, Japanese, Korean, or Vietnamese ancestry. These groups make up the numerical majority of Asian Americans, and they commonly share Confucian and Buddhist roots and influences upon their values and behaviors.

Asian Americans already have made substantial contributions to America. A partial list would include architect I. M. Pei; industrialist and financier Gerald Tsai; computer pioneer Charles Wang; Citicorp vice chairman Pei Yuan Chia; congressmen Hiram Fong, Daniel Inouye, Minoru Yamasaki, Masayuki Matsunaga, S. I. Hayakawa, and Robert Matsui. In sports and the arts, tennis star Robert Chang is joined by cellist Yo-Yo Ma, violinist Sarah Chang, and actor Noriyuki "Pat" Morita of "Karate Kid" fame.

In the discrimination they have experienced, the socioeconomic distance they have traveled, their ethnic diversity, and their dramatic population growth, few groups can rival the Asian Americans. The ethnic history of Asian Americans in the United States may be divided into two eras: prior to World War II and after the passage of the Immigration and Naturalization Act of 1965.

CHINESE AND JAPANESE IN THE UNITED STATES BEFORE 1965

Prior to 1965, the Asian American community was largely made up of Chinese Americans and Japanese Americans whose forebears had immigrated to the United States during the nineteenth century. Today many are largely acculturated as third-generation, fourth-generation, and even later Americans.

Chinese Americans

Drawn by the news that gold had been discovered in California, large numbers of Chinese Americans first came to the United States in 1849.[15] Leaving a China wracked by famine and revolt, 25,000 Chinese had emigrated to California by 1851. First murder and then legal discrimination forced the Chinese out of the lucrative field of gold mining that had attracted them. Many were recruited to build the transcontinental railways and to labor in the fields. They were denied membership in labor unions because of intense discrimination and their willingness to work long hours for low wages. Consequently, many worked in employment that did not threaten whites, for example, laundries and restaurants. In the 1920s in excess of 50 percent of working Chinese Americans labored in laundries and restaurants.[16] As late as 1970,

24 percent of Chinese American males were employed in laundries and restaurants.[17]

The Chinese Exclusion Act of 1882 closed the door on not only emigration but also citizenship for Chinese who resided in but had not been born in the United States. The Exclusion Act also made it impossible for the male Chinese immigrants to establish or reunite families by bringing their wives and children to the United States. The intentional disruption of normal family life caused a reduction by half of the Chinese American population from about 125,000 in 1882 to 62,000 in 1920.[18] As late as 1960, there were only about 236,000 Chinese Americans in the United States.[19]

Japanese Americans

Japanese Americans first came to Hawaii in 1868 as contract laborers for sugar plantations. Ambitious and hard-working immigrants drawn by the higher wages in the United States, their numbers approximated 70,000 when their immigration too was limited. According to the Gentlemen's Agreement of 1908, the Japanese government restricted emigration to the United States except for the wives and children of the Japanese already here. Consequently, family life was possible for Japanese Americans, although discrimination remained intense. In 1924, legal emigration from Japan to the United States was ended.

As immigrants who were legally ineligible for citizenship, Japanese Americans were unable to purchase land and property or to marry Caucasians. Nonetheless, many became successful farmers by renting or owning land through sympathetic white intermediaries or their U.S.-born children.[20]

The Japanese American population grew to approximately 125,000 by 1940 as the immigrant generation reared the generation who were born in the United States. Despite intense discrimination and immigrant parents who generally possessed little formal education or ability to speak English, by 1940 the average Japanese American already was more educated than the average Caucasian.[21]

The surprise attack on Pearl Harbor stunned the Japanese American community. An even greater shock was the forced movement to internment camps of more than 100,000 Japanese American men, women, and children from California and other western states. According to Federal Reserve Bank estimates, the forced liquidation of furniture, homes, businesses, real estate, land, and other assets cost Japanese Americans $400 million at 1942 prices.[22] Curiously, a similar measure was not imposed upon the even larger community of 150,000 Japanese Americans in Hawaii, many of whom worked at military bases. In 1944, the Supreme

Court declared the internment of Japanese who were U.S. citizens to be unconstitutional. In 1988, the federal government officially apologized and paid $20,000 in reparations to each survivor of the internment camps.

Given these circumstances, few would have expected 33,000 Japanese Americans to volunteer for service in the armed forces of the United States. U.S.-born Japanese Americans played a critical role in the Pacific theater as translators of Japanese military communications. In the European theater, the 442nd Regimental Combat Team suffered 9,000 casualties to become the most decorated military unit in U.S. history. After the war, President Truman honored the "Fighting 442nd" by bringing the entire unit to the White House to receive a Presidential Unit Citation.[23]

Respect for such sacrifice shamed and eroded what had been normal discriminatory laws and practices before World War II. Antimiscegenation laws, which made it illegal for Japanese Americans to marry Caucasians, were repealed in 1948.[24] Another milestone was Hawaii's admission to statehood in 1959. Daniel Inouye and Masayuki Matsunaga, both World War II veterans and Japanese Americans, were elected to Congress.

ASIAN AMERICANS AFTER 1965

The passage of the Immigration Act of 1965 dramatically changed both the size and composition of the Asian American community. Each year since then from one-third to one-half of legal immigrants to the United States have come from Asian countries. Currently, this means approximately 1 million new immigrants from Asia every three years.[25]

In 1960 fewer than 1 million mainly U.S.-born Chinese and Japanese Americans made up 0.5 percent of the nation's population. In 1990 nearly 7.5 million mainly foreign-born Asian Americans comprised 3 percent of the nation's population. Between 1960 and 2000, the Asian American population will have increased ten times — from under 1 million to over 10 million individuals and from 0.5 percent to nearly 5 percent of the total population.[26] These immigration and demographic changes have changed the composition of the Asian American community.

Before 1965 Japanese Americans and Chinese Americans comprised the two largest Asian ethnic groups in the United States. Table 9.1 shows ranking by size of Asian American ethnic groups and the percent native-born.

The second wave of post-1965 immigrants from Asia is much more diverse. Some are university educated and cosmopolitan in the most modern sense of the word. Others are not literate in their native language and are the products of traditional societies.

TABLE 9.1
Asian American Ethnic Groups In 1990:
Population And Percent Native Born

Ethnic Group	U.S. Population (in millions)	Native Born (in percent)
Chinese American	1,645	30.7
Filipino	1,407	35.6
Japanese American	848	67.7
Asian Indian	815	24.6
Korean American	799	27.3
Vietnamese American	615	20.1

Source: U.S. Bureau of the Census. (1994). No. 11. Resident population — selected characteristics, 1790 to 1992, and projections, 1995 to 2050. *Statistical abstract of the United States*. Washington, DC: Government Printing Office; U.S. Bureau of the Census. (1994). No. 12. Resident population characteristics — percent distribution and median age, 1850 to 1992, and projections, 1995 to 2050. *Statistical abstract of the United States*. Washington, DC: Government Printing Office; Pyong Gap Min. (1995). An overview of Asian Americans. In Pyong Gap Min (Ed.), *Asian Americans: Contemporary trends and issues* (p. 29). Thousand Oaks, CA: Sage Publications.

Chinese Americans

The immigration of Chinese, particularly from Hong Kong, has been explosive. There were approximately 117,000 Chinese Americans in 1950; 236,000 in 1960; 431,000 in 1970; 812,000 in 1980; and 1,650,000 by 1990.[27]

Decades ago, earlier European immigrants to America spoke of the newer "greenhorn" immigrants from their mother country. Today, Chinese Americans talk of the differences between the ABCs (American-born Chinese) and the FOBs (those fresh off the boat or more likely the airplane). Because many of the earlier Chinese immigrants came from the Toishan district of Kwantung province and the post-1965 wave mainly from Hong Kong, dialectical differences often exist between them — that is, if third or fourth generation Chinese Americans speak Chinese at all.[28] Chinese Americans run the gamut of diversity. Some set foot in the United States only yesterday, speak no English, and work in inner city sweatshops. Others are middle-class suburbanites who, while "usually assimilated Americans . . . also tend to preserve ancestral customs."[29]

In 1990, 22 percent of Chinese Americans over age 25 were college graduates (compared to 14 percent of whites) and 19 percent held post-graduate or professional degrees (compared to 8 percent of whites). This translates into 43 percent of native-born Chinese Americans holding managerial or professional positions (compared to 27 percent of whites) and a median Chinese American family income of $41,316 (compared to $37,152 for whites).[30]

These are impressive figures for an ethnic group that is approximately 70 percent foreign-born immigrants. However, it does not exclude the bipolar distribution of occupations and incomes. Some Chinese Americans operate their own businesses or are high-income managers or professionals. Others work at such lower-paying jobs as waiters, maids, and even sweatshop seamstresses. The incomes of 11 percent of Chinese American families are at or below the poverty level. Chinese Americans generally have been absent from the higher reaches of corporations, law firms, banks, and other institutions of major decision-making power.

The rate of Chinese Americans who marry exogamously has risen from a negligible level just a few decades ago. Intermarriage between Chinese Americans, Japanese Americans, and Korean Americans is increasingly common. Currently, about 22 percent of Chinese Americans marry Caucasian partners. While this is low in comparison to the 50 to 80 percent rate of exogamous marriage among whites of European ancestry, one should keep in mind that almost 70 percent of Chinese Americans are foreign-born.[31]

Japanese Americans

Since 1965 only a few thousand Japanese have immigrated to the United States each year. The generation born between 1924 and 1940 who served in World War II are retiring after much success. The third generation, born between 1940 and 1965, follows behind them, having reared the fourth generation, born after 1965. Today, second through fourth generation Japanese Americans are, perhaps, the most acculturated and successful of all Asian Americans.

According to the 1990 census, the $51,550 median income of Japanese American households was significantly higher than even the white household income of $37,152. Solid education made this possible. According to the 1990 census, 88 percent of Japanese Americans graduated from high school and 35 percent completed four or more years of college compared to 75 percent of all races who graduated from high school and 20 percent from college.[32] People who attend school together also are more likely to marry. During the 1970s, 60 percent of Japanese Americans in Los Angeles exogamously married non-Japanese, half of them non-Asians. By 1980, the national outmarriage rate was close to 50 percent.[33]

The 1990 census also reported that 37 percent of Japanese Americans were managers or professionals, compared to 27 percent of the total population.[34]

Korean Americans

The first sizable group of Koreans came to labor on Hawaiian sugar and pineapple plantations during the early years of the twentieth century. Legal immigration ended in 1924.[35] By 1970, 70,000 Koreans were in the United States, principally descendants of the early immigrants who had been joined by post–Korean War brides of U.S. soldiers as well as some war orphans.[36]

After the Immigration Act of 1965 and its family reunification provision, the Korean American population skyrocketed from approximately 70,000 in 1970 to 355,000 in 1980 to close to 800,000 in 1990, making them the third-largest Asian American group we are considering.[37]

While most live and work in urban areas like Los Angeles–Long Beach or New York City, Korean Americans are, perhaps, more likely than other Asian immigrants to disperse to smaller cities and towns and even rural areas.[38] Because Christian missionaries had been active in Korea since the late nineteenth century, many Koreans and Korean Americans are more likely to be Christian (especially Protestant) than other Asian American ethnic groups. As was true of earlier immigrants from Europe, the ethnic church strengthens and supports the Korean American community.[39]

Koreans also have demonstrated an entrepreneurial bent by opening tens of thousands of small businesses across America, mostly grocery stores, convenience or liquor stores, gas stations, restaurants, or laundromats, where long hours of inexpensive family help translate into profits. One study in Los Angeles found that of Korean Americans, 53 percent of males and 36 percent of females were self-employed.[40]

Given their comparatively brief experience in the United States, many Korean Americans are less acculturated than some other Asian ethnic groups, yet, the past is instructive. One study conducted in Hawaii during the 1960s found that 80 percent of Korean Americans married outside their ethnic group. Another study found that exogamous marriages rose to 90 percent in 1980 with Korean females preferring more egalitarian Caucasian husbands and Korean males preferring more traditional Asian American wives. Another study of Korean American immigrants, in 1986, found that while only 3 percent of males married exogamously, 14 percent of females did, 66 percent of them to Caucasian males. The study also found that marriages between a Korean American and a spouse from Korea involved more conflict because of cultural differences than one between Korean Americans and that marriages between Korean American women (who wish to live according to America's more egalitarian values) and males from Korea (who tend to embody the more traditional chauvinistic values of Korea) are particularly problematic.[41]

Korean Americans have a reputation within the Asian American community for hard work, a direct communication style, competitiveness, patience, and perseverance.

Vietnamese Americans

Vietnamese Americans have a recent and tragic past. The first eight legally documented Vietnamese immigrated to the United States in 1952.[42] The vast majority have come since the 1975 fall of Saigon and end of the Indochina War. They came in waves, each with its own characteristics. They also came not as immigrants but as tragic and often traumatized war refugees.

The first wave of approximately 141,000 Vietnamese reached the United States between 1975 and 1978 following the fall of Saigon to communist forces. They tended to be well-educated, English-speaking officials and military officers and their families who had cooperated with the Americans during the war. These refugees were helicoptered, sea-lifted, or otherwise escaped Vietnam, often with U.S. government help.

Approximately 158,000 Vietnamese (joined by another 139,000 Laotians and Cambodians) arrived in the second wave between 1978 and 1980. Increasing communist oppression and genocide throughout Indochina triggered their departure. They were the "boat people" who had been driven out of their homes by oppression and genocide so severe that they knowingly risked not only an unforgiving sea but also attacks by plunderous and murderous pirates to seek freedom.[43] They also were the "jungle people," those who, without food or weapons, risked wild animals, communist patrols, and minefields in hopes of reaching a free land. Since then, at least 18,000 Vietnamese have immigrated to the United States annually, along with smaller numbers of Cambodians and Laotians.[44]

Initially Southeast Asian refugees were dispersed to many parts of the United States. They remain more dispersed than some Asian American ethnic groups. California is home to 46 percent of all Vietnamese Americans as well as similar percentages of Cambodians, Laotians, and Hmong. Substantial Vietnamese communities also are found in Texas and along the Gulf Coast.[45] This more diverse wave ranged from urban professionals to the traditional Hmong, some of whom were not literate in their own language, and from Vietnamese who often were Confucian or Roman Catholic to Laotians and Cambodians who tended to be Buddhist. Yet, their strides, too, have been remarkable. Although half of the Vietnamese have come to the United States since 1980, 61 percent have graduated from high school and another 17 percent from college. The figures translated into 47 percent holding white collar jobs, and a median family income of $30,550 compared to $35,225 for all U.S. families in 1990.[46]

THE ASIAN AMERICAN VALUE
SYSTEM OF CONFUCIANISM

Confucianism has had a major impact on many Asian societies, particularly in China, Japan, Korea, and Vietnam.[47] Immigrants from these four countries comprised 54 percent of the Asian American population in 1990.[48] Hence, while we acknowledge the great variation among Asian American cultures as well as the diversity among Asian Americans of the same culture, we suggest that Confucianism is a common unifying element among these ethnic groups and that knowledge of Confucian values will help managers understand common patterns of behavior among Asian American employees.

The teachings of Confucius (551–479 B.C.) have left a powerful and enduring legacy for most Asian societies. The influence of Confucianism has been partly philosophical, partly religious, partly political, partly a body of precepts for daily living, and partly a map for social life. Confucianism performs much the same central organizing role for Asian societies that Christianity does for Europe. Although time and acculturation naturally weaken ties with ancestral homelands, one can understand many Asian Americans and their behavior better through an awareness of Confucianism.

The teachings of Confucius provide a way of life that spells out the values as well as the social conduct of followers. Confucianism influenced the governing behavior of Asian rulers and bureaucrats for thousands of years. Today, it continues to guide the conduct of believers in almost every area of daily life. Confucianism's code of ethics mandates loyalty between ruler and ruled, bonding between fathers and sons, differential duties between husband and wife, obedience by youth to elders, and reciprocal faith among friends.[49]

Confucianism proposes four central principles from which flow not only right conduct for individuals but also prescriptions for ethical human behavior. Benevolent humanism is the first basic principle — the ability to put oneself in another person's place and see the world from his or her position. The second principle is the practice of reciprocity in one's dealing with others, which also implies empathy with others. Confucius' version of the Golden Rule would read, "Do not do unto others what you would not have them do to you." The third basic principle refers to allegiance and devotion to the long-term common good. Again, this principle is most relevant to social relationships. The fourth principle is the process by which harmonious social relationships are brought about through discretion and deference in human interaction.[50] A number of values flow from these central Confucian principles.

Confucian values stress the importance of the group or a collectivist approach to human relations. The first characteristic of a collectivist orientation to human behavior is that the interest of the group supersedes that of the individual. Accordingly, it is the group that endures, whose harmonious equilibrium is paramount, and to which individual needs always are subordinated. Individuals, therefore, are dependent upon the group. Among one's weighty obligations and duties to the group are one's selfless suppression of individuality and expression in the name of group harmony. As one U.S. resident of Japan stated: "If Descartes had been Japanese, he would have said 'we think, therefore we are.'"[51]

A second characteristic of a collectivist society is its hierarchical nature. Cooperativeness is crucial to the harmonious operation of a society structured by group and hierarchical relationships. One should defer to one's superior, be circumlocutous in one's speech, and indirect in one's behavior to perpetuate an ordered society. Communication becomes a vehicle for promoting group harmony as well as individual expression.[52]

Harmony, for example, is reflected in a Japanese concept that involves caring for others, which, in turn, engenders trust and cooperation. The Japanese conception of leadership relies on caring and requires attentive listening as well as patiently working to build the necessary consensus and solidarity for true group harmony.[53]

In Asian culture conformity to the norm of proper behavior is the value through which the social harmony of the group is realized. To verbally express how one feels is less important than expressing oneself in accordance with expected role behavior. In addition, one tends to be more quiet, understated, indirect, and deferential in one's behavior and communication with others.

The Asian American value system emphasizes self-discipline rather than external punishment as a means of control. Shame and guilt are internalized as a mechanism to control one's behavior. Failing to act morally brings about feelings of shame.[54] Asian Americans who are less acculturated tend to have more of an external locus of control. Asian Americans who are more acculturated tend to have more of an internal locus of control. Certain Buddhist and Taoist precepts teach that life is inherently difficult and fateful. Consequently, some less acculturated Asian Americans tend to feel that they have limited control over the environment. Instead, fate, chance, or other factors help determine the unfolding and consequences of their actions. This is in contrast to the white belief in an internal locus of control. With an internal locus of control, self-reliant individuals feel that they can responsibly determine the outcome of their actions through their own efforts. A number of studies indicate that Asian Americans who are more acculturated to U.S. society and values possess a more internal locus of control.[55]

Collectivism stands in sharp contrast to the individualism that is characteristic of U.S. society. The value of the individual has been paramount in the United States from its inception.[56] Robert Bellah and his associates also found this to be true in their 1987 study of the United States, *Habitats of the Heart: Individuals and Commitment in American Life*.[57] The individual has been and remains the central value of the U.S. pantheon. As such, the individual is free to join and leave groups since Americans believe that it is the individual who endures. From the trappers of the frontier to the high-tech entrepreneurs building the twenty-first century economy, the self-reliant individual is the central building block of American society.

Another characteristic of an individualistic society is its profound commitment to equality among individuals. In short, because all men are created equal all men should be treated equally. To Americans, different treatment on the basis of particular status or rank is undemocratic if not un-American. Because human relationships in the United States tend to be horizontal (egalitarian), people feel most comfortable in non-hierarchical relationships. A third characteristic of individualism is competitiveness. Competition between individuals is healthy and good. It is seen as essential for both individuals and organizations to achieve their potential.

In the individualistic culture of the United States, it is the individual's right to autonomously think, act, debate, and discuss as well as to enter and leave groups that is paramount. In the United States, the role of organizations including the government is to serve the needs of each individual. Additionally, mainstream individualistic behavior may be somewhat more boisterous, assertive, direct, and egalitarian in its characteristics.

Confucian values provide a backdrop for understanding the communication patterns of Asian Americans today. With this in mind, managers should be better able to place the behavior of Asian Americans into a larger and more comprehensible context.

MANAGEMENT PRACTICES

Four factors characterize the general behavior of Asian Americans: hierarchy, interdependence, cooperation, and indirectness. These four qualities have a significant impact on interpersonal relations and, therefore, the management practices of Asian Americans in the workplace. The contrast of Asian American behaviors with other cultural behaviors in the workplace can lead to major misunderstandings. Our objective here is to place these behaviors and values in the context of the workplace to provide a better understanding of those differences.

As Grant Ujifusa's grandfather taught him, Japan is a vertical society. This means that the behavior of individuals tends to vary with particular hierarchical relationships. Therefore, one acts differently with a superior than with a subordinate.[58] Asian Americans are positively inclined toward hierarchical relationships. To varying degrees, Asian Americans may expect that superiors will exercise some care for subordinates. They also may expect that proper distance will be maintained between superior and subordinate and that interactions will be more formal than informal, thus, maintaining a vertical hierarchy rather than a horizontal egalitarian relationship. Furthermore, in the Asian American collectivist culture individuals tend to be interdependent. The group is primary and endures; the individual is secondary and serves the group. One is dutiful and selfless in discharging one's obligations to the group. Harry Kitano and Roger Daniels relate how this value persists in contemporary Japanese American basketball leagues. Individual oriented hot doggers, who shoot too frequently, soon find that their group-oriented teammates repress their behavior by simply not passing them the ball.[59] The model organization is one in which self-effacing individuals readily accept their status while working hard and harmoniously in the name of the group. According to the Chinese proverb: "The nail that stands out highest is hammered down first." As one Chinese American professor stated: "'Us' is the center of importance, not 'me.'"[60]

Cooperation is a highly valued attribute among Asian Americans, however, cooperation has limits. Generally one interacts and cooperates primarily with the members of one's group. In the interest of group harmony, one is self-controlled, restrained in openly expressing feelings, frequently silent, and does not openly argue or forcefully express one's views. Talking about oneself or boasting of one's accomplishments signals a lack of self-control. Again, the group is paramount and its harmonious survival and success cue individual behavior.

The Asian American trait of indirectness pervades almost every aspect of interaction. One scholar has suggested that lines and points are metaphors for interpersonal communication in mainstream U.S. culture, but for Asians and Asian Americans it is the circle and curve.[61]

The line and the point are metaphors for the clarity and directness that are expected in everyday interactions in the workplace. White managers exhort each other to follow a clear line of reason in getting to the bottom line of a discussion or decision. In this process, one should get to the point, stay on the point, and not beat around the bush.

Indirection characterizes the interactions of Asians and Asian Americans with each other. Whites may be discreet and indirect when feelings are at stake, but, for Asian Americans, indirectness is a way of life. A study of U.S. and Japanese organizational behavior highlights some basic differences in the communication styles of their respective employees. Americans exert a great deal of overt effort to communicate as clearly and as accurately as possible. In contrast, Japanese employees consciously speak in an ambiguous and roundabout way.[62] We can better understand these differing cultural behaviors by examining the logic that undergirds them.

The logic may differ for Asian Americans and whites. According to the mainstream norm, logic is assumed to be linear, clear, and sequentially lead to a point. Only communication behavior that corresponds to such an unconscious structure of logic is deemed satisfying in many business settings. That is why the indirect Asian American verbal behavior may frustrate colleagues who criticize its ambiguity and its lengthy process.

To some Asian Americans, such a conceptualization is viewed as simplistic and immature. In Asian culture, words or ideas do not have an existence separate from the speaker. Therefore, to criticize words or ideas is to attack the person who utters them. In such a culture, the words used cannot be extricated from their user. Therefore, the Western agonistic approach of dispassionate and logical criticism that is objectively separate from the speaker may be difficult for some Asian Americans to understand, let alone practice. This may be why one of the most influential nineteenth-century Japanese minds, Yukichi Fukuzawa, could not comprehend how Western politicians could amicably argue and debate one another as enemies, and then eat and drink at the same table. To Asians, publicly disagreeing or expressing a contrary view means becoming a personal enemy of the other individual and his group.[63]

In the Eastern tradition, discourse evolves by maintaining harmonious affirmation between parties where each mutually validates and adjusts positions in a continuous circular process. The goal is not so much the logical attainment of truth as the maintenance of harmony in relationships.[64] In the Western tradition of agonistic polemics, discourse moves linearly by negation and contradiction. Argumentation is the tool for identifying and expanding upon differences in the objective pursuit of factual truth. The scientific methodology is based on this premise.

Knowing this, perhaps, the manager in the diverse workplace will transcend the pitfall of stereotyping individuals whose behavior eludes one's understanding. It is erroneous to label the behavior of Asian Americans as inscrutable, shy, or uncommunicative given the Confucian or collectivist roots of their behaviors. Culture shapes us not only in terms of the behaviors we exhibit but also in the meanings we make of them. Given the fact that many Asian Americans have emigrated to the United States since 1970, it is important to keep in mind that differences in behaviors exist according to the individual's level of acculturation to American life.

NONVERBAL COMMUNICATION

Hawaii is the most Asian American state of the United States. It also is the melting pot of America. In 1990, two-thirds of Hawaiians identified and placed themselves in an Asian demographic category, but a 1987 survey found the following ethnic groups: mixed race, 31 percent; Caucasian, 24 percent; Japanese, 23 percent; Filipino, 11 percent; Chinese, 5 percent; black, 2 percent; Korean, 1 percent; Hawaiian, 1 percent; other ethnicities, 3 percent.[65] As some researchers discovered: "Although assimilation is evident in dress, style of home, and religious affiliation . . . in norms governing day-to-day interaction, the effects of the culture of origin remain influential."[66] Hawaii is a signal case for understanding ethnic differences, particularly in nonverbal communication. Hawaiians' knowledge of differing styles of behavior and expectations of role performance enables them to interact more successfully with one another.

Among Asian Americans, a number of nonverbal behaviors stand out. Depending upon the level of acculturation, the varying nature of eye contact, proxemics, and touch are all relevant cues in face-to-face communication.

Eye Contact

In Asian American culture direct eye contact connotes a range of interpretation from superiority to impoliteness or even rudeness, but in U.S. culture, looking someone in the eye is perceived as a sign of trustworthiness and character. Particularistic behavior pervades Asian culture, that is, one does not behave the same way with everyone. Superiors may establish more eye contact with subordinates than subordinates may with superiors. In addition, what is neutral or normal in one subculture may be perceived as negative or intense in another. For example, a researcher from the University of Hawaii studying Japanese Americans found that "The intense and concentrated staring that sometimes accompanies a Western counselor's communication of concentration and interest may be misinterpreted by Japanese Americans as disdain and contempt."[67]

When communicating across cultures, listeners should not misinterpret an Asian American's lesser level of eye contact toward them as disrespectful or indicating a lack of attention. In fact, it is exactly the opposite. While some eye contact is necessary in face-to-face communication with Asian Americans, it is important to remember that beyond a certain level Asian Americans may come to feel ill-at-ease and even anxious. Effective face-to-face communication with an Asian American is likely to involve less eye contact than with individuals from some other U.S. subcultures, especially with members of the opposite sex.

Proxemics

The proxemic behavior of Asian Americans may differ in certain ways with individuals from other ethnic groups.

Asian Americans tend to place themselves at greater distances from others than almost any other major U.S. cultural group. This is true whether they are standing or seated.[68] Individuals unaware of Asian American proxemics may misinterpret this behavior as being cold or removed. However a study of Japanese, Venezuelan, and American students in the United States discovered that when conversing in their own language, the Asian students sat furthest apart (40 inches), Venezuelans in closest proximity (32 inches), and Americans in between (35 inches). When speaking in English, students from Japan sat closer and students from Venezuela sat farther away, both approximating the proxemic distance of the U.S. students.[69] If simply speaking in English has an impact on the proxemic distance between individuals as these researchers found, one wonders about the impact of acculturation upon the proxemic behavior of a native-born, second, or third generation Asian American. Proxemic behaviors may vary depending upon the individual Asian American with whom we are dealing.

Touch

Asian Americans come from a low-contact culture. According to one cross-cultural study, U.S. students reported twice as much touching as Japanese students. A number of Asians reported the absence of any physical contact even with parents after age fourteen. No U.S. subjects reported such an absence of contact.[70] Another researcher advised that physical contact in the initial stages of a relationship is likely to create discomfort and apprehension among Asian Americans.[71] An illustration of this low-contact behavior is the Asian mode of greeting — bowing from the waist. Noncontact bowing is in sharp contrast to the U.S. mode of shaking hands. Some Asian American immigrants have had to learn not only to shake hands but also to do so with the firm grip that is expected in the United States.[72]

Asian American nonverbal communication can pose a paradox to others. What is apparently emitted is minimal, yet, its meaning is maximal. Among Asian Americans there tends to be less eye contact, greater proxemic distance, less touch, and nearly absent facial expression. To a non-Asian American, the absence of nonverbal cues can be bewildering. One Japanese scholar predicates that, in his culture, only 10 percent of a message is overtly verbal with the remaining 90 percent being contextually nonverbal.[73] Thus, between the minimal messages sent and a culturally unprepared receiver emerges the regrettable basis for the stereotypically inscrutable Asian American. These barriers can be transcended by understanding the cultural basis of these behavioral patterns.

VERBAL COMMUNICATION

Asian American verbal communication, like its nonverbal counterpart, tends to be indirect and constrained. The maintenance of group and hierarchy remain primary social values. Thus, the purpose of verbal communication is to promote group survival through group harmony. Communication patterns are rooted in the socialization process and childrearing practices. Researchers have found that Japanese American and Chinese American parents talk less with their children than Caucasian parents. In addition, Asian American parents tend to restrain their expression of emotions and ideas, and are somewhat reticent in their expression of nonverbal and verbal messages.[74] One of the frequent complaints by American-born Asian American children of their immigrant parents is that there is too little verbal communication in their families and that what communication there is tends to be directive and top-down.[75] Children are taught to respect their parents and avoid divisive argumentation and debate at home, in the interest of family harmony. The same rules apply to interactions with peers while growing up. The net result is that the family experience does not always prepare Asian Americans for the classroom or business experience that agonistically pits one individual against another.

The bulk of Asian Americans who are immigrants face a compounding problem with their children. Many of these parents do not have a full command of English while their children do not have a full command of their parents' mother tongue. This is likely to create an additional barrier to their communication because neither parent nor child can convey the richness of their human experience to the other.[76]

Silence

Few areas of interpersonal communication differentiate Asian Americans from other Americans more than the use of silence. "One cannot *not* communicate" is an axiom of communication.[77] The airline passenger who closes her eyes and reclines in her seat is nonverbally communicating the message "Do not disturb." Likewise, the passenger in the next row who slightly rotates his upper body to face his neighbor, smiles, and makes eye contact wordlessly says "Let's talk."

Similarly, silence communicates. In the mainstream culture, silence communicates negativity — tension, discomfort, disinterest, awkwardness, and even rejection. Asians who negotiate with Americans know that, in many cases, if they remain silent long enough Americans will tend to make desired concessions without further effort.[78] Accordingly, a psychologist based in Hawaii counseled his peers that "greater acceptance of the positive aspects of silence is necessary when working with Japanese Americans. Within Japanese cultural traditions, a wise person uses silence as well as speech to communicate."[79] If this is true, what does silence mean to Asian Americans? What does it communicate?

To Asian Americans, silence is a noncommittal posture one takes while reflecting upon what has been said and how to respond. In one study Japanese and Americans were asked to interpret expressionless faces in a series of settings. Japanese saw them as being neutral but Americans described these faces as critical or worried.[80] Silence is more likely to wordlessly signify agreement with the other party, a potential meaning of silence that non-Asian Americans might keep in mind.

Cross-cultural communication scholar Dean Barnlund posits that because the Japanese sphere of the private self is smaller their communication style renders them less accessible to others.[81] Conversely, because the American sphere of the private self is larger their communication style renders them more accessible to others. Where one enshrouds, the other is open. Thus, for Asian Americans silence serves the double function of limiting access to one's private self while limiting the domain for interaction.

Use of Questions

Questions reflect the central value of group harmony in Asian American culture. One should be polite, indirect, considerate, and minimalist in one's communication because to speak little is to run the least risk of offending another. Asian Americans tend to ask few questions, especially closed questions, because to do so is considered impolite.[82] When asked direct questions, they may reply indirectly for fear that a direct and honest response could offend.[83]

The use of questions and silence are intertwined. Should a question be asked of an Asian American, silence is more likely to ensue. The silent person may be pausing to reflect upon the question or considering an appropriate response. The questioner, feeling uneasy, rephrases the question again or, even worse, poses another. Such a situation increases the stress for the respondent who now has two responses to contend with when, in fact, he or she might prefer to deal with neither. Thus, to the Asian American the questioner appears to be prying while to the questioner the responding Asian American may appear to be uncooperative. To both, this scenario is frustrating. Let us consider Chris and Mieko's conversation when they first encounter one another in a business context.

CHRIS: It's great to meet you. I am looking forward to working with you on this deal.

MIEKO: I, too, am pleased to meet you. (silent pause)

CHRIS: There is so much to talk about, where do you want to begin?

MIEKO (silent pause, breaking eye contact. Before Mieko has had the chance to respond, Chris asks a second question.)

CHRIS: Do you think we should start by looking at the proposal, or do you want to spend a few minutes talking about our approach?

MIEKO (pauses again): Thank you for asking me. But I think we can begin where you think we should.

CHRIS: Well as a matter of fact, what's on my mind is to let them know that they have to go through us to get this deal rolling.

MIEKO (nods her head in agreement): I see.

CHRIS: I think we should go in together and straighten them out, right?

MIEKO: That's one way of doing it.

CHRIS: I agree 100 percent.

This dialogue epitomizes two cultures talking with one another to the exclusion of the individuals involved. One wonders if Chris was aware that Mieko deferentially avoided answering his direct questions or at best was noncommittal for fear of offending him. In fact, Chris asked the questions in rapid tempo, one after the other, seemingly unaware that his questions had gone unanswered to begin with. The more formal and careful Mieko felt pressed to respond to these questions before she could determine where Chris stood on these matters, hence, her silent pauses. Furthermore, the nature and number of Chris's questions violated her personal boundaries and put her at risk of appearing confrontational. For Mieko, confrontation is a situation to avoid at all costs.

Expression of Emotions

Among the most prevalent comments one hears about Asian Americans is that they are intelligent, hard working, and technically proficient but that they are quiet and inscrutable. In fact, the literature substantiates the point that Asian Americans generally are less likely to express their emotions than are individuals from other cultures.[84] When Asian Americans do express emotions, they are likely to be subtle and understated.[85]

Asian American culture is rooted in the value of interpersonal harmony that is achieved through personal self-control. Research indicates that the childrearing practices of Asian Americans place a high value upon self-control. Asian American parents are more likely to exhibit affection through indirect actions, such as self-sacrifice for children or hard work for family, rather than through direct actions, such as touching or embracing.[86] Within the family, children are encouraged to preserve positive relationships by refraining from expressing negativity or criticism.[87]

When Colin Watanabe taught English at the University of California, Berkeley, he found that Asian American college students suppressed the expression of emotions in their writings.[88] Furthermore, Asian Americans find it difficult to express emotions even within the security of the family, particularly toward higher status or older individuals.[89] In general, Asian Americans tend to be guarded in their expression of emotions. Many report frequent discomfort in group situations where other individuals may be more expressive. Some scholars report that Asian American students feel they are unable to express themselves easily in a classroom setting and that assertiveness training might help them become more expressive.[90] Other research indicates that the Asian American behavior of deference is heightened in group settings, such as business meetings. Under such pressure their involvement actually lessens.[91]

Confrontation

The Asian American attitude toward confrontation marks one of its major differences with the agonistic style of the mainstream mode of communication. Just as the agonistic mode of communication is historically rooted in Western civilization, so the Asian American approach originates in Confucian-influenced Asian cultures. Hierarchy and status are two of the central values of Asian society. They bring order to society and render it harmonious. Within this hierarchy each person occupies a position and, if they act in accord with it, social order is assured.

Hierarchy, status, and language are the antecedents of harmony. The linguistic constructions of the Japanese and Chinese languages promote harmony in conversations between individuals. Dean Barnlund points out that in Japanese the frequent utterance of *ne* (isn't it?), *yo* (a subtle way of emphasis), or *ka* (to avoid making too definitive a statement) not only make statements softer and less direct but also change declarative sentences into less challenging questions.[92]

Similarly, in Chinese sentence structure, speakers tend to front-load sentences with large amounts of justifying information and place the main idea at the end of the sentence. The Western linguistic structure consists of the subject-verb, thesis first, and supportive data later pattern.[93] In both Asian languages, the goal of verbal communication is to dispel dissonance and create a validating and affirming conversational exchange. This is in stark contrast to the Western agonistic tradition where one is more challenging and polemical, thus, creating the imminence of a more confrontational interchange. While the essence of the agonistic communication mode is one of contradiction, that of the Asian American mode is of affirming confirmation: "Conversation proceeds not by negation or contradiction as in the West, but by affirmation where the speaker seeks continual confirmation and approval from the listener." Where one leads to more interpersonal conflict, the other leads to more interpersonal consensus.[94]

One should not surmise that Asian Americans never become involved in heated discussions or confront one another, especially if one is a superior or elder. However, the context in which they do so is important. The guiding principles are hierarchy and status. A younger person should not confront an older person, nor should a subordinate confront a superior. No individual should violate the basic organizing principles of society.[95]

CONCLUSION

Asian American communication patterns manifest themselves in America today. A number of research studies indicate that the communication paradigm of Asian Americans continues in diminishing ways to reflect traditional ethnic patterns. Even in private and affirming settings, the typical patterns of cautiousness, indirectness, and unassertiveness occur in conversations with Asian Americans. If these patterns persist in private situations, it should come as no surprise that these behaviors, rooted as they are in cultural values, will surface again in the public interactions of the workplace. Individuals who are aware of these cultural characteristics will find themselves better able to communicate and manage.

NOTES

1.   Grant Ujifusa, on receiving an award from an Asian American Society in Washington, D.C., September 27, 1990.

2. Peter L. Rose. (1985). Asian Americans: From pariahs to paragons. In Nathan Glazer (Ed.), *Clamor at the gates: The new American immigration* (pp. 181–212). San Francisco, CA.: ICS Press, cited in Harry Kitano, & Roger Daniels. (1988). *Asian Americans: Emerging minorities*(p. 48). Englewood Cliffs, NJ: Prentice-Hall.

3. Stanford Lyman. (1974). *Chinese Americans* (pp. 71–72). New York: Random House.

4. Thomas Sowell. (1981). *Ethnic America: A history* (p. 137). New York: Basic Books; Kitano, & Daniels, *Asian Americans: Emerging minorities*, p. 22.

5. Kitano, & Daniels, *Asian Americans: Emerging minorities*, p. 22.

6. Lyman, *Chinese Americans*, p. 61.

7. Page Smith. (1995). *Democracy on trial: The Japanese American evacuation and relocation in World War II*. New York: Simon & Schuster; see also S. Frank Miyamoto. (1973). The forced evacuation of the Japanese minority during World War II. *The Journal of Social Issues, 29*(2), pp. 11–32.

8. Sowell, *Ethnic America: A history*, p. 138.

9. Ibid., pp. 144–145.

10. Ibid., p. 175.

11. U.S. Bureau of the Census. (1994). No. 233. Educational attainment by race, ethnicity, and sex: 1960–1993. In *Statistical abstract of the United States*. Washington, DC: Government Printing Office.

12. Dana Takagi. (1990, November). From discrimination to affirmative action: Facts in the Asian American admissions controversy. *Social Problems, 37*(4), pp. 578–592.

13. U.S. Bureau of the Census. (1994). No. 712. Money income of households — Percent distribution by income level, race, and Hispanic origin: 1992. In *Statistical abstract of the United States*. Washington, DC: Government Printing Office.

14. U.S. Bureau of the Census. (1993). *1990 Census of the population: Asians and Pacific islanders in the United States* (CP-3-5) (pp. II-1–II-3). Washington, DC: Government Printing Office.

15. Rose Hum Lee. (1960). *The Chinese in the United States of America* (p. 9). Hong Kong: Hong Kong University Press.

16. Sowell, *Ethnic America: A history*, p. 139.

17. Harry H. L. Kitano. (1981, March). Asian-Americans: The Chinese, Japanese, Koreans, Pilipinos, and Southeast Asians. *America as a Multicultural Society: The Annals of the American Academy of Political Science, 454*, p. 129.

18. Kitano, & Daniels, *Asian Americans: Emerging minorities*, pp. 23–24.

19. Lyman, *Chinese Americans*, p. 6.

20. William Peterson. (1971). *Japanese Americans* (pp. 51–58). New York: Random House; Harry H. L. Kitano. (1969). *Japanese Americans: The evolution of a subculture* (pp. 17–18). Englewood Cliffs, NJ: Prentice-Hall.

21. Sowell, *Ethnic America: A history*, p. 175.

22. William Peterson. (1978). Chinese Americans and Japanese Americans. In Thomas Sowell (Ed.), *Essays and data on American ethnic groups* (p. 84). Washington, DC: The Urban Institute.

23.   Bill Hosokawa. (1969). *Nisei: The quiet Americans* (p. 410). New York: William Morrow; Peterson, *Japanese Americans*, p. 87.

24.   Setsuko Matsunaga Nishi. (1995). Japanese Americans. In Pyong Gap Min (Ed.), *Asian Americans: Contemporary trends and issues* (p. 128). Thousand Oaks, CA: Sage Publications.

25.   Pyong Gap Min. (1995). An overview of Asian Americans. In Pyong Gap Min (Ed.), *Asian Americans: Contemporary trends and issues* (p. 13). Thousand Oaks, CA: Sage Publications.

26.   Min, An overview of Asian Americans, p. 11; U.S. Bureau of the Census. (1994). No. 11. Resident population — selected characteristics, 1790 to 1992, and projections, 1995 to 2050. *Statistical abstract of the United States.* Washington, DC: Government Printing Office.

27.   Min, An overview of Asian Americans, p. 13; Morrison G. Wong. (1995). Chinese Americans. In Pyong Gap Min (Ed.), *Asian Americans: Contemporary trends and issues* (p. 64). Thousand Oaks, CA: Sage Publications.

28.   Sowell, *Ethnic America: A history*, p. 135.

29.   William P. O'Hare, William H. Frey, & Dan Fast. (1994, May). Asians in the suburbs. *American Demographics, 16*(5), pp. 32–38.

30.   Wong, Chinese Americans, pp. 77–78; Min, An overview of Asian Americans, p. 28.

31.   Min, An overview of Asian Americans, p. 25; Wong, Chinese Americans, p. 87.

32.   Min, An overview of Asian Americans, p. 28; Nishi, Japanese Americans, pp. 118–119.

33.   Nishi, Japanese Americans, p. 128.

34.   Ibid., pp. 114–118.

35.   H. Brett Melendy. (1977). *Asians in America: Filipinos, Koreans and East Indians* (pp. 121–126). Boston: Twayne Publishers.

36.   Kitano, & Daniels, *Asian Americans: Emerging minorities*, pp. 105–111.

37.   Min, An overview of Asian Americans, p. 16.

38.   Kitano, & Daniels, *Asian Americans: Emerging minorities*, pp. 116–117.

39.   Melendy, *Asians in America: Filipinos, Koreans and East Indians*, pp. 139–144.

40.   Pyong Gap Min. (1995). Korean Americans. In Pyong Gap Min (Ed.), *Asian Americans: Contemporary trends and issues* (p. 209). Thousand Oaks, CA: Sage Publications.

41.   Ibid., pp. 218–221.

42.   Ruben G. Rumbaut. (1995). Vietnamese, Laotian, and Cambodian Americans. In Pyong Gap Min (Ed.), *Asian Americans: Contemporary trends and issues* (pp. 239–240). Thousand Oaks, CA: Sage Publications.

43.   Rita Chi-Ying Chung, & Sumie Okazaki. (1991). Counseling Americans of Southeast Asian descent: The impact of the refugee experience. In Courtland C. Lee & Bernard L. Richardson (Eds.), *Multicultural issues in counseling: New approaches to diversity* (p. 109). Alexandria, VA: American Association for Counseling and Development; Rumbaut, Vietnamese, Laotian, and Cambodian Americans, p. 241.

44.   Rumbaut, Vietnamese, Laotian, and Cambodian Americans, p. 241.

45. Ibid., pp. 242–245.

46. Ibid., p. 247.

47. June Ock Yum. (1991). The impact of Confucianism on interpersonal relationships and communication patterns in East Asia. In Larry A. Samovar & Richard E. Porter (Eds.), *Intercultural communication: A reader*, 6th ed. (pp. 66–78). Belmont, CA: Wadsworth Publishing Company.

48. Min, An overview of Asian Americans, p. 16.

49. June Ock Yum. (1988). The impact of Confucianism on interpersonal relationships and communication in East Asia." *Communication Monographs, 55*, p. 376.

50. Ibid., pp. 377–378.

51. John C. Condon. (1984). *With respect to the Japanese: A guide for Americans* (p. 9). Yarmouth, ME: Intercultural Press.

52. Frank Johnson, Anthony Marsella, & Collen Johnson. (1974). Social and psychological aspects of verbal behavior in Japanese-Americans. *American Journal of Psychiatry, 131*, pp. 580–583.

53. Edward T. Hall, & Mildred Reed Hall. (1987). *Hidden differences: Doing business with the Japanese* (pp. 78–79). New York: Anchor Books/Doubleday.

54. Laura Uba. (1994). *Asian Americans: Personality patterns, identity, and mental health* (p. 47). New York: Guilford Press.

55. Lian-Hwang Chu. (1988). Locus of control differences between American and Chinese adolescents. *Journal of Social Psychology, 128*, pp. 411–413; Theodore Hsieh, John Shybut, & Erwin Lotsof. (1969). Internal versus external locus of control and ethnic group membership: A cross-cultural comparison. *Journal of Consulting and Clinical Psychology, 33*, pp. 122–124.

56. Alexis de Tocqueville. (1981). *Democracy in America* (p. 395). New York: The Modern Library.

57. Robert N. Bellah, Richard Madsen, William M. Sullivan, Ann Swidler, & Steven M. Tipton. (1985). *Habits of the heart: Individualism and commitment in American life*. Berkeley: University of California Press.

58. Chie Nakane. (1970). *Japanese society*. Berkeley: University of California Press; Dean C. Barnlund. (1989). *Communicative styles of Japanese and Americans: Images and realities* (p. 31). Belmont, CA: Wadsworth Publishing Company.

59. Kitano, & Daniels, *Asian Americans: Emerging minorities*, p. 72.

60. Hwei-Jen Yang. (1993). Communication patterns of individualistic and collective cultures: A value based comparison. Paper presented at the seventy-ninth annual meeting of the Speech Communication Association, Miami Beach, Florida, p. 4.

61. Condon, *With respect to the Japanese: A guide for Americans*, pp. 42–44.

62. Richard Tanner Pascale. (1978). Zen and the art of management. *Harvard Business Review, 56*, pp. 153–162.

63. Carl B. Becker. (1986). Reasons for the lack of argumentation and debate in the Far East. In Larry Samovar & Richard E. Porter (Eds.), *Intercultural communication: A reader*, 6th ed., (pp. 234–243). Belmont, CA: Wadsworth Publishing Company.

64. Dean C. Barnlund. (1975). Communicative styles in two cultures: Japan and the United States. In Adam Kendon, Richard M. Harris, & Mary Ritchie Key

(Eds.), *Organization of behavior in face-to-face interaction* (pp. 450–451). The Hague: Mouton.

65.   Kathy Bodovitz, & Brad Edmondson. (1991, July). Asian America. *American Demographics*, pp. 16–17.

66.   Colleen Leahy Johnson, & Frank Arvid Johnson. (1975, December). Interaction rules and ethnicity: The Japanese and Caucasians in Honolulu. *Social Forces, 54*(2), p. 453.

67.   Anthony J. Marsella. (1993, April). Counseling and psychotherapy with Japanese Americans. *American Journal of Orthopsychiatry, 63*, p. 203.

68.   Nan M. Sussman, & Howard M. Rosenfeld. (1982). Influence of culture, language, and sex on conversational distance. *Journal of Personality and social Psychology, 42*(1), pp. 66–74.

69.   Ibid., p. 203; Darold Engebretson, & Daniel Fullmer. (1972). Cross-cultural differences in territoriality: Interaction distances of native Japanese, Hawaii Japanese and American Caucasians. In Larry A. Samovar & Richard E. Porter (Eds.), *Intercultural communication: A reader* (pp. 220–226). Belmont, CA: Wadsworth.

70.   Barnlund, Communicative styles in two cultures: Japan and the United States, pp. 444–447.

71.   Marsella, Counseling and psychotherapy with Japanese Americans, p. 203.

72.   James Morishima. (1981). Special employment issues for Asian Americans. *Public Personnel Management Journal, 10*, p. 389.

73.   S. Yotsuka. (1977). Ethnolinguistic introduction to Japanese literature. In W. C. McCormack & S. A. Wurm (Eds.), *Language and thought: Anthropological issues*, The Hague: Mouton, cited in Susan A. Hellweg, Larry A. Samovar, & Lisa Skow. (1991). Cultural variations in negotiation styles. In Larry Samovar & Richard E. Porter (Eds.), *Intercultural communication: A reader*, 6th ed. (p. 188). Belmont, CA: Wadsworth Publishing Company.

74.   Jing Hsu, Wen-Shing Tseng, Geoffrey Ashton, John F. McDermott, Jr., & Walter Char. (1985). Family interaction patterns among Japanese-America and Caucasian families in Hawaii. *American Journal of Psychiatry, 142*(5), pp. 577–581.

75.   Colin Watanabe. (1973, February). Self-expression and the Asian-American experience. *Personnel and Guidance Journal, 51*(6), pp. 393–394; Kitano, & Daniels, *Asian Americans: Emerging minorities*, p. 72.

76.   Shi-Jiuan Wu. (1994). An ethnography of Chinese families in America: Implications for family therapy. Paper presented at the fifty-second annual conference, American Association for Marriage and Family Therapy, Chicago.

77.   Paul Watzlawick, Janet Beavin, & Don Jackson. (1967). *Pragmatics of human communication: A study of interactional patterns, pathologies and paradoxes* (p. 49). New York: W. W. Norton.

78.   Joel P. Bowman, & Tsugihiro Okuda. (1991, December). Japanese-American communication: Mysteries, enigmas, and possibilities. *The Bulletin of the Association for Business Communication, 48*(4), p. 19.

79.   Marsella, Counseling and psychotherapy with Japanese Americans, p. 204.

80.   Milton Wayne. (1973). An experimental study of the meaning of silence

in three cultures, Master's thesis, International Christian University, cited in Dean C. Barnlund. (1989). *Communicative styles of Japanese and Americans: Images and realities* (p. 142). Belmont, CA: Wadsworth Publishing Company.

81.   Barnlund, Communicative styles in two cultures: Japan and the United States, pp. 429–436.

82.   Johnson, & Johnson. Interaction rules and ethnicity: The Japanese and Caucasians in Honolulu, p. 456; Kitano, *Japanese Americans: The evolution of a subculture*, p. 104.

83.   Bowman, & Okuda. Japanese-American communication, p. 19.

84.   Frederick T. L. Leong. (1986). Counseling and psychotherapy with Asian-Americans: Review of the literature. *Journal of Counseling Psychology, 31*(2), p. 197; Karen Huang. (1991). Chinese Americans. In Noreen Mokuau (Ed.), *Handbook of social services for Asian and Pacific Islanders* (p. 91). New York: Greenwood Press.

85.   Marsella, Counseling and psychotherapy with Japanese Americans, p. 205.

86.   Uba, *Asian Americans: Personality patterns, identity, and mental health*, pp. 37–38.

87.   Stanley L. M. Fong. (1973). Assimilation and changing social roles of Chinese Americans. *Journal of Social Issues, 29*(2), pp. 116–117.

88.   Watanabe, Self-expression and the Asian-American experience, p. 390.

89.   Steven P. Shon, & Davis Y. Ja. (1982). Asian families. In Monica McGoldrick, John K. Pearce, & Joseph Giordano (Eds.), *Ethnicity and family therapy* (p. 227). New York: Guilford Press.

90.   David Sue, & Derald Wing Sue. (1991). Counseling strategies for Chinese Americans. In Cortland C. Lee & Bernard L. Richardson (Eds.), *Multicultural issues in counseling: New approaches to diversity* (pp. 86–88). Alexandria, VA: American Association for Counseling and Development.

91.   Leong, Counseling and psychotherapy with Asian-Americans: Review of the literature, p. 200.

92.   Barnlund, Communicative styles in two cultures: Japan and the United States, pp. 450–451.

93.   Linda Wai Ling Young. (1982). Inscrutability revisited. In John Gumperz (Ed.), *Language and social identity* (p. 79). Cambridge: Cambridge University Press.

94.   Barnlund, Communicative styles in two cultures: Japan and the United States, pp. 450–451.

95.   Allen E. Ivey. (1994). *Intentional interviewing and counseling: Facilitating client development in a multicultural society*, 3rd ed. (pp. 194–195). Pacific Grove, CA: Brooks/Cole Publishing Company; Michael O. Watson. (1970). *Proxemic behavior: A cross-cultural study* (p. 105). The Hague: Mouton.

10

The Communication Paradigm of the United States in the Twenty-first Century

"It used to be that America had a center that was white, and everybody else was on the margins," he said during our last interview. "The people on the margins didn't have the power, they didn't become judges, they didn't become city council members, they didn't run the school boards, they were just out there, sort of like the forgotten people. Well, it's a little different now. If you look around L.A., for example, you see companies that are full of Asian engineers, and Hispanic woman managers, and black computer programmers. These are all people who have simply gone about their business, moved on and up, got an education, found jobs, bought homes. They aren't kicking up a ruckus, so it's easy to miss what's going on, but they've fanned out across America, and they're building businesses, and getting tenure, and being successful. The truth is that in some ways it's not a big deal anymore. There used to be the white center, and then just a few recognizable categories of 'other' — the Jews, the blacks, the Hispanics. But now there are hundreds of categories of 'other,' and their numbers and proportion are growing. What happens when they are suddenly a quarter, a third, a half of the voting population? When I was growing up, people didn't make a big deal about acknowledging the difference between, say, Presbyterians and Baptists. Everyone's attitude was, So what? In terms of American public life, it mostly didn't matter whether you were a Methodist or a Lutheran. I think it's getting to be that way about more and more kinds of people. I think there's a whole lot of cultural mixing going on among people who aren't making a stink about it. I sometimes want to pat myself on the back for being the white half of a venturesome interracial marriage. But the truth is, it's not venturesome, it's old hat, it's no big deal."

— Peter Norton, Norton Utilities[1]

Quietly and without fanfare, a powerful dynamic is unfolding across America. As Norton points out, individuals who have simply gone about their business without kicking up a ruckus are transforming America. More than ever before, individuals in the United States are respected for who they are as individuals and for what they contribute to our society rather than the gender or ancestry groups from which they come. More and more, America is realizing the two most significant founding values that have characterized our history — the inherent worth of the individual and the progressive unfolding of equality.

These ideals, plus the more hard-nosed need to hire and promote the best talent, whatever the gender, ethnic, or race, drive U.S. organizations toward inclusion. In today's high velocity environ-ment of global competition, corporations without the best human talent can nosedive and disappear. Therefore, U.S. organizations have sought to address diversity through new and different training approaches.

DIVERSITY: DEVELOPMENTS AND TRAINING APPROACHES

Several developments and training approaches characterize the efforts of U.S. organizations to deal with diversity. They are affirmative action, beyond affirmative action, demographic awareness, valuing diversity and differences, social justice, and managing diversity.

Affirmative Action

Three government actions were critical to the development of affirmative action in the workplace. They originated in all three branches of the government.

Congress's Civil Rights Act of 1964 outlawed discrimination in employment. For the first time in our history government held employers responsible for the development of timetables and targets in order to diminish ethnic and gender discrimination in the workplace. In 1965 President Lyndon Baynes Johnson's Executive Order 11246 prohibited discrimination, on the basis of race, religion, or national origin, by the federal government and the contractors that did business with it. In 1967 discrimination on the basis of sex also was prohibited. These executive orders mandated gender and racial parity goals and timetables in the hiring and staffing areas.

In its 1971 decision, *Griggs v. Duke Power Company*, the Supreme Court ruled that discrimination suits and substantial settlements against employers could be won without having to prove disparate treatment, but merely by demonstrating disparate impact among categories of employees. Henceforth, organizations were legally liable not only for the unequal treatment of employees but also for the statistical employment levels of employees that might be discrepant with a gender or ethnic group's representation in the general population.

These and other government actions spurred organizations to meet goals by reaching out to recruit and promote more women and minority individuals. While minority men comprised only 12 percent of public and private managers in 1990, such efforts have dramatically increased the number of women managers. These recruiting efforts are largely responsible for the fact that in 1990 white women comprised 36 percent of managers, black women about 5 percent, Hispanic women 5 percent, and Asian American women about 1 percent. So women make up 47 percent of U.S. managers.[2]

In its 1995 *Adarand Constructors v. Pena* decision, the Supreme Court narrowed the grounds upon which affirmative action programs give preference to race. This decision held that affirmative action programs must be specifically tailored to justify compelling governmental interest in dealing with racial preference. The broad and general grounds for affirmative action programs laid out by *Griggs v. Duke Power Company* were restricted by this and other court decisions.

Affirmative action came to the political forefront as an issue in California. In 1995, the California state government ended many state-mandated affirmative action programs. The California Board of Regents also ended gender and race as factors in hiring and in student admission to the California public college system. California voters may decide in 1996 whether to maintain or terminate affirmative action programs in state education and government. Affirmative action also could be an issue in the 1996 presidential election.

Beyond Affirmative Action

A number of forward-looking companies have voluntarily instituted programs that go well beyond what has been mandated by affirmative action. Companies like Xerox and California's Pacific Bell have established successful programs to recruit and promote qualified female and minority individuals.[3] What have been the results?

By 1990, white women comprised 30 percent of Xerox's sales personnel (the U.S. work force contained only 18 percent women), while 23 percent of its technicians were minority men (as opposed to 13 percent minority men in the U.S. labor force). At Pacific Bell, minority managers increased from 17.5 percent in 1980 to 28.2 percent in 1990. How did this happen?

During the early 1980s California's Pacific Bell diversified its work force by increasing programs to recruit and promote top quality women and minorities. Program director Nancy Gutierrez urged managers to seek out, hire, and develop the best and the brightest candidates. It worked. After watching ten minority candidates in a management exercise, the previously reluctant managers of one department increased their request from three to seven hires.

Xerox has always had an extraordinary social conscience. Chester Carlson, xerography's inventor, gave much of his vast fortune to charities, many of them black, in part because of his belief that "America could never repay the Negroes for what it had done to them."[4] Joseph C. Wilson, founder of the Xerox Corporation, evidenced his moral commitment to fairness with his belief in valuing and respecting people. Such ideals are seen as essential contributors to the bottom line by Xerox's chief executive officer, Paul Allaire, who believes that Xerox derives a competitive edge from its diverse work force.[5] By 1965 Xerox had established its Step-Up program to hire, train, and promote more minority workers. In 1984, Xerox initiated a balanced work force strategy to transform itself from a primarily white male organization to one whose work force was more clearly diverse. By envisioning affirmative action not as a plan or as a program but as a natural management process, Xerox, today, is not only more diverse but also more successful and profitable than many of its Fortune 500 competitors.

Such efforts have foreshadowed the approaches that more and more far-sighted corporations are taking to establish and maintain high quality work forces in an increasingly diverse society. Many of the largest U.S. corporations have announced that they will voluntarily retain their own affirmative action programs. The experience of these two companies makes the point that, when motivated by a pragmatic blend of values and profit, voluntary affirmative action programs can both enrich their participants and be profitable.

Demographic Awareness

The 1987 Hudson Institute study, *Workforce 2000*, first identified the demographic shifts taking place in society and the workplace. Years later, it's best-known forecast continues to be widely misquoted and misunderstood. *Workforce 2000* forecast that between 1985 and 2000, only

15 percent of the net work force entrants would be native-born white males. Many writers and executives have dropped the word "net" or misunderstood its significance and erroneously assert that only 15 percent of entering workers will be white males. In actuality, between 1985 and 2000 approximately 34 percent of total work force entrants are forecast to be native-born white males.

Sensationalized by this misunderstanding, *Workforce 2000* was read by executives across the country and was the catalyst for many diversity training programs. Those who carefully read *Workforce 2000* discovered that its forecasts required no hyperbole — managers faced tighter competition for educated and skilled workers in an increasingly diverse labor force. This labor force was unlike any that business had known since 1945.

After World War II the relaxation of religious discrimination, the GI Bill, and a growing economy induced corporations and institutions, which until then had been largely run by WASP males, to begin recruiting educated Catholic and Jewish white males. The conformity of U.S. culture, coupled with the power of WASP managers, induced the new ethnic white male managers to conform to their corporate culture in order to secure their jobs and careers. Then changes began to occur.

The percentage of white males in the labor force started decreasing while that of women and minorities began increasing. The Civil Rights movement and the Women's Liberation movement changed attitudes. Astute corporations began to realize that it was in their interest to hire and promote the best talent, regardless of gender, race, or ethnicity.

Valuing Diversity and Differences

Years before the publication of *Workforce 2000*, Digital Equipment Corporation was breaking new paths in diversity training. No one knows for sure, but Digital, a globe-girdling computer and network systems producer, may have invented the term "valuing diversity." At that time Digital had manufacturing plants and sizable numbers of minority employees in Massachusetts and Puerto Rico as well as an ongoing commitment to respect individuals and do the right thing. So Digital found good reason to address the issue of diversity. It was one of the first corporations to recognize the paradox involved in trying to deal with group differences without openly talking about them or talking openly about group differences and running the risk of dangerous emotional blowups between employees. Digital's valuing diversity program came to include training in cultural awareness, celebrating ethnic traditions and holidays, gender and racial support groups, and small group discussions.

These efforts made it possible for Digital employees to celebrate and value the differences that elsewhere drove workers apart.

In the 1980s, Lennie Copeland, a U.S. diplomat's daughter who had lived in foreign cultures, and her husband, Lewis Griggs, recognized that if cultural diversity were a growing fact of life then valuing that diversity was a logical next step. With impeccable timing, Copeland and Griggs produced a video training program that was so successful that it helped name that next stage of the diversity movement — valuing diversity or, as it has evolved, valuing differences.[6]

Coming on the heels of *Workforce 2000*, the valuing diversity approach contended that, in a more diverse society and work force, those organizations that "achieve a true multicultural environment will have a competitive edge."[7] Therefore, organizations should train their employees to recognize, talk about, and, most important, value gender, racial, and ethnic differences that, heretofore, had been unrecognized, ignored, or perceived as negative. Unless differences were valued, previously white male organizations would become subject to misunderstandings, miscommunications, and management breakdowns as they became more diverse. The goals of valuing diversity both complemented and were broader than affirmative action.

Affirmative action focused on numbers. Similarly, valuing diversity aimed at providing women and minorities with a better chance to earn promotions by creating a more supportive organizational climate.[8] Valuing diversity sought to heighten gender and ethnic awareness, acceptance, and pride through films, small group discussions, and training as well as ethnic menus in cafeterias and company-sponsored celebrations of ethnic days.

Valuing differences aimed at changing organizational cultures. With training, organizations could be transformed from being neutral, uncomfortable, or hostile toward gender, racial, ethnic, or other differences to becoming supportive of and even celebrating those differences. Only then could the increasing numbers of women and minorities who were newcomers to the system feel comfortable and eventually attain positions of equity and profit.

Social Justice

Some prominent scholars and trainers in the diversity field propound what they term the "social justice" approach to diversity training. They see the social justice approach as being:

About the struggle against oppression in organizations and the promise of diversity. . . . Our institutions have failed to eliminate harassment and ongoing discrimination against women of color, men of color, white women, gays, lesbians, people with disabilities, older workers, younger workers and others who are systematically excluded. . . . The volume of these voices indicates the magnitude of change required to answer their call. We must dramatically shift the power dynamics in our relationships and change many of our policies and practices. . . . The promise of diversity cannot be achieved through simplistic means. Achieving the promise of diversity requires much more than: Eating ethnic food. . . . Understanding different cultures. . . . Developing more-effective listening skills. . . . Establishing networks and support groups. . . .Attending awareness workshops. . . . We must address issues of oppression through actions that will eliminate racism, sexism, heterosexism, classism, abelism, and other forms of discrimination at the individual, identity group, and systems levels. The promise of diversity and the struggle against oppression in organizations call for redefining, reexamining, rethinking and restructuring many aspects of our institutions and our lives.[9]

The social justice approach tends to be exclusionary because it envisions organizational change as part of a broad struggle that includes all except those who oppress others. It ultimately focuses on power issues. The hands that control the levers of power are seen as vital to the kind of total change felt to be requisite for moral and just organizations.

Managing Diversity

Perhaps, more than any other individual, R. Roosevelt Thomas, Jr., has popularized the term "managing diversity." His work at the American Institute for Managing Diversity at Atlanta's Morehouse College has more of a management focus than some other approaches to diversity training. Thomas urges a broader, more inclusionary approach that includes white males who, he writes, may be "as odd and as normal as anyone else."[10] He compares the problem that changing demography poses to organizations to an engine running on a new blend of fuel. He asks how we can "get from a heterogeneous work force the same productivity, commitment, quality and profit that we got from the old homogeneous work force."[11] His response is to realize each individual's potential through changes in corporate culture and management:

Managing diversity is a holistic approach to creating a corporate environment that allows all kinds of people to reach their full potential in pursuit of corporate objectives. It is *not* a prepackaged set of solutions. It is *not* a program for addressing discrimination.[12]

Dealing with diversity is not about civil rights or women's rights; it is not about leveling the playing field or making amends for past wrongs; it is not about eliminating racism or sexism; it is not about doing something special for minorities and women. Rather it is about enhancing the manager's capability to tap the potential of a diverse group of employees.[13]

This vision sidesteps the question of equality, ignores the tensions of coexistence, plays down the uncomfortable realities of difference, and focuses instead on individual enablement. It doesn't say, "Let's give *them* a chance." It assumes a diverse work force that includes us and them. It says, "Let's create an environment where everyone will do their best work."[14]

The goal of managing diversity is profound organizational change. Future organizations will have more talented employees with unassimilable differences, such as gender and color, who might not be as willing or as able to conform to a corporate mold as might have been true in the past. Managing diversity aims at change through companywide cultural audits and other interventions that are designed to change the root causal factors of an organization by altering its basic cultural assumptions. Thomas recognizes that managing diversity requires not only systemic and cultural changes at the organizational level, but also profound attitudinal changes among individuals.[15] Here managing diversity appears to provide more guidance for change at the organizational level than at the individual level.

EVALUATING PREVIOUS DIVERSITY TRAINING APPROACHES

Each training approach is a partial response to an extraordinarily refracted, multileveled human and organizational problem. Each has made valuable contributions to dealing with diversity, but each also carries baggage. Let us examine the contributions of these approaches as objectively and fairly as possible. Each approach provides solutions to a different aspect of the challenge of diversity.

Affirmative action and other approaches have helped more women, blacks, Hispanics, and Asian Americans enter and rise in America's workplaces at a faster pace than ever before. Affirmative action not only provided a means for the first skilled group, primarily white women, to enter the organizational hierarchy but also helped them attain higher-paying and more powerful positions. In the past three decades under affirmative action, the number of women managers has increased substantially while minority managers have made fewer gains. In 1990 white males comprised 39.8 percent of all executives, administrators, and managers in the private and public sectors; white females 36.3 percent; blacks 8.5 percent; Hispanics 11.4 percent; and Asian Americans 2.8 percent.[16]

Efforts to make the work force more diverse have had a positive effect. It is a well-established fact in social science that heterogeneous groups are much more creative and better at solving problems than are homogeneous groups.[17] In keeping with reflexive communication, the more positions from which a problem is viewed, the more varied are the perspectives on it and the more creative and rich are the solutions. Diversity already is widely recognized as a valuable asset that helps U.S. organizations meet the challenges of the globally-competitive, high-velocity informational era.

There are downsides as well as problems to each approach. As one diversity trainer wrote, everyone seemingly embraces diversity training: "And why not? . . . If we don't do it, we are avoiding very obvious shifts in the population and hence, the workforce. If we ignore demographic realities, the complex systems that make up the organization will certainly suffer. . . . But diversity, as an agenda topic and lesson plan, is like a new drug. Its capabilities and benefits are highly touted, but its inescapable side effects are hidden in the small print of a cumbersome text — if they are known at all."[18]

What are some of the side effects of previous approaches to diversity training? The disadvantage of the affirmative action dilemma is that, although it has opened opportunities for minorities, it has also bred resentment. Affirmative action deals mainly with numbers and helps more with entry than with promotion to top levels. It is criticized for emphasizing goals and targets rather than standards and performance. Substantial numbers of individuals from every ethnic group are both opponents and supporters of affirmative action. Some whites support continued affirmative action while others feel that it amounts to reverse discrimination. Some minorities believe that it stigmatizes their individual performance while others hold that affirmative action is the only path to social justice.

The add-on nature of affirmative action has accomplished less than expected toward changing the normal or regular operations of the organization. In too many cases, minorities find themselves in such areas as public relations or community relations rather than in key line or staff positions that provide qualifying experience for top level jobs. Affirmative action programs do not necessarily provide models of how individuals can, through merit incentives, rise in organizations nor do they necessarily generate any of the fundamental or systemic changes in the organization that a diverse work force may require in the years to come.[19]

There is a growing recognition of diversity awareness. Whatever one's personal feelings toward any diversity approach or the disposition of any diversity law or policy, Americans are increasingly aware of the demographic challenges they face and their common need to respond.

Many outcomes of the valuing differences approach have been positive and helpful. However, as Thomas stated, "You can accept, understand, and appreciate differences, even be free of racism and sexism, and still not know how to manage diversity — how to create an environment that naturally taps the potential of a diverse group of people in pursuit of organizational objectives."[20]

The managing diversity approach has much to offer. Its chief goal is to establish a context that allows a diverse array of workers to realize their potential while pursuing organizational objectives. It seeks to provide the strategies to manage the increasing diversity of the U.S. work force. Managing diversity proposes a realistic, long-term approach to the difficult problems of diversity rather than any quick fix or magic bullet solution. It focuses heavily on changing the organization and its culture at the systemic level. However, the managing diversity approach has less to say about how to effect the desired change at the individual level.

Jack Gordon addressed some outcomes of the social justice approach to diversity training when he wrote:

It makes no sense any longer to pretend that the answer to the . . . (race) . . . problem — or the sexism problem or the homophobia problem — is to tell white males one more time, or 1,000 more times that they are 'bad guys and oppressors and that they have a debt and better make good on it." They've all heard the message. *If anything, the message now seems to be exacerbating the very problems it's supposed to solve.* . . . If we want to build a society with equal opportunity and justice for all — and businesses that function effectively with diverse employees and customers thrust upon them by demographic changes and the global economy — the road of guilt and blame looks increasingly like a dead end.[21] (emphasis added)

According to Frederick R. Lynch, as much as half of all diversity training may be tied to averting or minimizing lawsuits. In the event of court action, corporations with diversity training in place can demonstrate good faith efforts that might help win a case or at least reduce the cost of settlement. He writes: "This may be a source of the grumbling among consultants about management being 'stuck in the one-day training mode' rather than moving on to more sweeping organizational reform. Employers may be buying only as much protection money as they think they need."[22]

Another outcome of some affirmative action, valuing diversity, and social justice programs has been to strain and polarize relationships between majority and minority workers. This has resulted from the focus on selected groups, particularly women and minorities.[23] One survey found that conflicts among employees increased after diversity training.[24] As the title of a journal article indicated "Training Can Damage Diversity Efforts."[25] Polarization and divisiveness is usually attributed to ineffective training or unprofessional trainers. However, such an assessment may be too narrow. This is not to detract from the many competent professionals who are in the diversity training field or the many positive benefits of each diversity training approach.

Diversity training has never recognized or come to grips with the twin natures of diversity. Increased contact alone, among members of a heterogeneous group, can easily lead to greater creativity in problem solving, or it can lead to greater tension and even conflict.

Diversity scholars and trainers have trumpeted the undeniably greater creativity of heterogeneous over homogeneous groups. To date, however, there is much less said about the tensions, difficulties, and conflicts that might be inherent in diverse or heterogeneous groups. Indeed, too much diversity and too few commonalities have been found to increase communication problems and interpersonal discomfort in the areas of problem solving and decision making.[26]

Harry Triandis, a leading scholar of cross-cultural psychology, sees both creativity and conflict as inherent in heterogeneous groups. He writes: "I value creativity and history tells us that creativity is maximal when thesis and antithesis are in clear view. . . . I realize, of course, that heterogeneity has a price; it means interpersonal conflict. But I believe that there are ways to teach people to deal with it."[27]

The fundamental question that we all may be asking ourselves is How do we deal with the creativity that diversity can engender as well as the tension and conflict that can plague it? This may be the critical question that confronts diversity training. There are two possible answers to this question. First, the types of change that various approaches have sought to implement may not have met the requirements of diversity. Second, diversity training may have focused more on the role of the group than on the role of the individual in bringing about change.

We should not forget the dynamic context for this change. In 1950, white males made up 65 percent of the work force. In 1990 they comprised 43 percent and that figure is declining.[28] In 1990, Hispanics were 9 percent of the U.S. population. In 2050, census forecasts indicate that Hispanics will be nearly 25 percent of the U.S. population with blacks and Asian Americans totaling another 25 percent.[29] A pragmatist, if not an idealist will realize that such demographic shifts prompt extraordinary degrees of change to and for the United States. Perhaps, change of this magnitude necessitates a transformation of personal attitudes as much as, if not more than, does the passage or enforcement of laws.

FIRST- AND SECOND-ORDER CHANGE

In 1973 communication theorists Paul Watzlawick, John Weakland, and Richard Fisch published a quietly influential book. It focused precisely on the issue that is central to resolving problems of diversity in the workplace. It held that there are not one but two types of change — first-order and second-order. Much diversity training to date has brought about first-order change. It may be that resolving the problems of diversity demands second-order change.

The basic difference between these two types of change is that first-order change does not alter the system in which it occurs while second-order change does.[30]

Watzlawick and his coauthors suggest that one example of first-order change is a nightmare — jumping, hiding, screaming — while continuing to dream. A second-order change shifts the state in which it occurs from sleeping to waking up. First-order change follows two rules — the rule of opposites and that of more of the same.

According to the rule of opposites, the solution to a room's winter cold requires heat and to the evening's darkness requires light. If the desired correction or equilibrium in the room has not been realized, the second rule is then applied — more of the same (more heat, more light). In such cases, the solutions of first-order change solve the problem. But in so doing, they do not alter but rather maintain the system.

We all have commonsensically and successfully applied the rules of opposites and more of the same to everyday problems. First-order change is appropriate in many situations where it is all that is needed. However, it is in the nature of first-order change that the solution effected can, in some instances, become part of the problem. This is particularly true of complex problems that involve human behavior. No solution is more guaranteed to become part of the problem than to tell an introvert to be spontaneous, someone who is shy to just be one of the gang, or someone who is depressed to cheer up. In fact, first-order changes may have been unintentionally implemented in previous attempts to deal with diversity.

For example, in applying first-order change to the problem of discrimination, one automatic response has been to institute the rule of opposites. In the case of discrimination, the rule of opposites may have led to affirmative action — from discriminating against women and minorities to discriminating in their favor. Affirmative action may have addressed just one part of the problem. It has opened the doors to many career opportunities hitherto unjustly denied women and minority Americans. When affirmative action programs were first instituted they were frequently the only means by which those who previously had been excluded could be hired. The current controversy surrounding it reflects the degree to which the solution may have become the problem. In fact, the subheading of a New York *Times* article on affirmative action was entitled "A Remedy Becomes A New Problem."[31]

In one instance, diversity trainers divided employees of a midwestern manufacturer into two groups — the Caucasian oppressors and the minority oppressed — who then vented their frustration and anger at their exploiters. Is it any wonder that, after the training, Caucasians felt outraged while minorities felt vulnerable and work relationships were worse than ever?[32]

As a respected observer of training has noted:

Learning to respect or "value" differences cannot be a matter of everybody exchanging and memorizing lists. . . . Joe learns that he must never . . . use a term like "salesman" or "chairman" around Betty, and he must always refer to Maya as a "woman of color," to Diana as "black," and to Sam as a "Chinese American" rather than an "Asian American." Betty, Maya, Diana and Sam learn to call Joe a European American but never to call Bob one. . . . These are not people who will like one another, trust one another, be comfortable with one another or do any creative work together. . . . If the goal of diversity work is a high-performance organization rather than just a climate in which nobody's feathers are ever ruffled, *we need a different way to talk about the problem of differences.*[33] (emphasis added)

Perhaps, this is why Griggs, co-producer of the widely-used training film "Valuing Diversity" said: "We've got to go back and come in through a different door."[34]

Perhaps, diversity approaches to date have dealt in first-order solutions that have not resulted in the intended change. Consequently, some of these solutions may have become part of the problem and even intensified it. Some may feel that such resentment is merely the price of change. Yet, in the contemporary case of affirmative action the level of such resentment threatens this program's survival and, in certain cases of diversity training, worsens relationships among colleagues in the workplace.

To illustrate the difference between first-order change and second-order change, try to connect the nine dots below in four straight lines *without lifting your pencil from the paper.*[35]

```
   •     •     •


   •     •     •


   •     •     •
```

Most people cannot solve this problem because they become mired in the assumption that they should not go outside the square that the dots comprise. They become frustrated, running through all of the many first-order solutions to this problem always leaving at least one dot unconnected. Until one leaves behind the assumption, that one should not go outside the square, the problem cannot be solved.

Solving the puzzle through first-order change becomes what Watzlawick and his coauthors call a "Game Without End" — running through endless repetitions of the same behavior without ever solving the problem. They write: "A system which may run through all its possible internal changes (no matter how many there are) without effecting a systemic change, i.e., second-order change, is said to be caught in a *Game Without End. It cannot generate from within itself the conditions for its own change*"[36] (emphasis added).

In such instances, second-order change is required, but change efforts are stuck at the first-order level. Therefore, the failed first-order solutions become more and more a part of and exacerbate the problem. First-order change involves "a change from one behavior to another within a given way of behaving."[37] Only by engaging in second-order change, that is, changing one's assumptions by going outside the square with one's pencil, can one solve the puzzle. Only by perceiving and defining the problem differently and taking a different approach can the problem be solved. The successful solution of a problem often involves understanding and delineating the process by which it has been created and maintained. Only then can the Game Without End cease and new solutions be generated. Second-order change is change that occurs at another and higher level. Second-order change induces us to shift "from one way of behaving to another."[38]

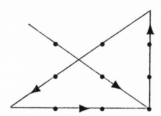

This is the case with our puzzle. To successfully connect the nine dots, you must go outside the square. This involves shifting one's assumptions. Extending the line outside the square involves a second-order change, and only then can you solve the problem.

We are suggesting that previous approaches to diversity training have been attempts at first-order change. Their unintended consequence often has been to maintain the problem rather than effect the change that was desired. Beyond anecdote, there is no overwhelming substantiation that much of what has been termed diversity training has effected the desired change in the desired direction.[39] Reviewing recent efforts, one diversity trainer summed up the mixed bag of outcomes: "Diversity training can spark new ways of thinking and working. It can also cause confusion, disorder, and hostility. . . . We preach the evils of stereotyping, while exalting the value of the growing ethnicity and other types of diversity within the workforce . . . we should not and cannot attempt to alter or eradicate deeply embedded perceptions in the space of a two-day session. Because diversity training usually involves some sort of participatory activity by class members, the process can begin to resemble group therapy. It should not."[40]

The problems attendant to diversity training will not improve until a new approach is undertaken that brings us to a new level, one beyond conflict and polarization. By developing a second-order solution to the problem of diversity, we open up whole new vistas for action. There may have been too much of a cultural focus in previous approaches to diversity.

To focus upon culture primarily, whether it is to increase the awareness of ethnic subcultures or to change the culture of the organization itself, is a necessary but insufficient step in the process of mutual adjustment that is key to diversity training. To emphasize culture alone heightens the awareness of group differences at the cost of the individual. By focusing exclusively upon the issues of group differences and historical discrimination, diversity training paradoxically may have emphasized the problem that it sought to diminish. In so doing, it is possible that the solution may, indeed, have become the problem.

Previous training approaches may have fostered first-order change that is inadequate to deal with the complex and refracted issues of diversity. Perhaps, the challenge that diversity training faces was summed up best by Susan E. Jackson and Eden B. Alvarez:

Cultures have consequences that are easily experienced but more difficult to describe . . . exotic customs, religions, foods, clothing, and life-styles that make foreign travel — as well as trips into the ethnic enclaves in our local cities — both stimulating and enjoyable. These aspects of a foreign culture can be experienced without ever engaging in conversation with someone from that culture. It is also easy for businesses to accommodate these aspects of cultural diversity — the cafeteria can offer a variety of ethnic foods and flexible policies can allow employees to observe whichever holidays they choose.

However, the deeper consequences of culture — such as values and ways of interpreting the world — cannot be handled merely by changing menus and policies. And it is these deeper consequences that organizations are struggling with today.[41] (emphasis added)

It may be that a vital link has been left out: accessing the individual at his or her level according to one's freely self-induced pace and direction and by means of a self-generative, interactive process.

REFLEXIVE COMMUNICATION AND DIVERSITY

The issues of diversity in the workplace become more critical the further America moves into the twenty-first century. The more diverse the United States becomes, the more prone we are to misunderstandings and conflicts with colleagues who have differing worldviews and expectations.

A new approach to managing diversity is necessary. Reflexive communication embodies the principles required for a second-order change. Through the recursive feedback loops it engenders, reflexive communication induces individuals to move beyond the limits of old assumptions. Furthermore, by flattening the hierarchy, its egalitarianism encourages the participation that unfolds to find new and creative solutions.

This new approach to communication delineates how individuals can come together to work on constructing mutual realities. The process of reflexive communication establishes commonalities rather than magnifying differences. It provides individuals with the opportunity to come to know one another through a continuous process of mutual interchange. Such an approach inclines us to modify our subjective meanings and to create the common grounds that are the bases for common understanding. The reflexive process of sharing information creates the recursive loops by which we clarify and reduce the uncertainties we all have about each other. Therefore, the nature of this change is both organic and evolutionary.

The second-order change induced by reflexive communication is not the result of external injunctions by trainers to change one's assumptions about groups, as may have been true of some previous training approaches. Rather, the change produced by reflexive communication is the result of a volitional, egalitarian, and mutually-induced process. The continuous interchange of reflexive communication creates the fertile ground where individuals working together co-create solutions of a second-order change.

This change emanates from newly-developed assumptions based on newly-generated realities. In effect, reflexive communication induces greater convergence in the thoughts, beliefs, perceptions, and meanings of the individuals who engage in it. As Johns Hopkins linguist Lawrence Kincaid puts it, an effective communication process logically leads to the "state of greater uniformity, or the successive reduction of diversity."[42]

Kincaid's insight resonates with the essential task undertaken here; that is, to create more overlapping common ground between individuals. The resultant mutual understanding forges the only path that allows individuals to come to know and work with one another, thereby transcending the existing barriers of diversity. As Harvard sociologist Orlando Patterson stated: "Universities and businesses should return to the principle of integration, to the notion that diversity is not something to be celebrated and promoted in its own right, but an opportunity for mutual understanding and the furtherance of an ecumenical national culture."[43]

In an increasingly diverse America, we should expect that an African American and an Asian American each may see the same reality from different positions and that, so long as they are uncommunicated, their different views of this reality will divide them. A process of communication that encourages the mutual exchange of these realities will progressively engender understanding through the mutual clarification of each others' values and meanings. Thus, the process of reflexive communication encourages the folding over of different perspectives that gradually overlap and transform individuals by drawing them closer together.

Thus, applying reflexive communication in the diverse workplace can lead us to a place where the construction of new realities is possible. This is where cultural issues and cultural differences meld, and a new reality ensues as a result of the information-sharing process. Hence, myths about differences begin to diminish and common realities begin to evolve. From these emerge the common ground, the convergence that is essential for the shared understanding that common action requires.

Reflexive communication is the missing link of diversity training. It is the second-order process by which individuals can mutually change themselves and each other according to their own pace and direction, thereby satisfying the requirement that "it . . . generate from within itself the conditions for its own change."[44]

THE DISTINGUISHING CHARACTERISTICS OF REFLEXIVE COMMUNICATION

What are the distinguishing characteristics of reflexive communication? First, it addresses not only the level of cultural or organizational change but also the level of human relationships — the missing link of diversity training. As two experienced trainers put it: "At the heart of diversity work is a fundamental question about the individual's ability to build interdependent relationships with people he or she regards as different."[45] Once participants learn and engage in the process, reflexive communication erodes stereotypes while it builds relationships. Once participants learn the how's of the process, they open up to the who of the individual before them.

Next, it focuses on the individual, not the group. In this respect, reflexive communication distinguishes itself from every previous diversity approach. Further, it aims at melding cultural differences by changing the basic building blocks — individuals and their views of each other.

Third, reflexive communication is a learning process. We change only when we learn. We cannot truly change if we do not communicate. The elemental problem with diversity has been how to dialogue and, more specifically, how to talk about some of the deepest and most sensitive topics. Reflexive communication proposes a learnable, step-at-a-time process by which we can learn to transcend each other's cultural differences and come to know each other as individuals.

Unlike other approaches to diversity training, reflexive communication offers no prescriptions or solutions. Rather, it generates change by encouraging individuals to learn from each other so that they can find their own solutions. Its interactive nature helps individuals determine their own place and relationship rather than feel they must change in accordance with the injunctions or prescriptions of others. Indeed, injunctive change, no matter how well-intentioned, is, perhaps, most assured of failure because of reactance. Psychologists Sharon and Jack Brehm suggest that when humans are pressured by another's demands they often respond by "reacting back" to reaffirm their own free will.[46] Could reactance help explain some of the difficulties experienced by previous diversity training approaches?

Reflexive communication is nonhierarchical and collaborative. It sparks involvement and establishes a sense of ownership. Participants are assumed to be democratically capable of learning from each other whatever particular truths apply. Anything less is likely to lead to the conflictual us versus them polarization that sometimes has been characteristic of diversity training. Instead, reflexive communication volitionally generates change from the inside out and bottom up rather than imposing it from the outside in and top down. Such change is more likely not only to be accepted but also to be acted upon. It is the only possible approach with any chance for attitudinal transformation in an area as refracted as cultural diversity.

Reflexive communication is inclusive. It does not focus on some groups to the exclusion of others. As the 1995 Glass Ceiling Commission Report points out, diversity training is most effective when it is inclusive of all groups.[47] In this approach, after a period of meaningful conversation bonding begins to occur. Ongoing conversation maximizes the affinity between individuals and minimizes the differences between groups. Thus, the process of mutually discovering false assumptions about each other is accompanied by the realization of the differences within one's own group. As conversation unfolds, group and individual differences are explored and then supplanted by the realization of shared commonalities. Significant relationships begin to develop. Exchanging multiple points of view, thus, enables participants to begin relating to one another at new and deeper levels. Reflexive communication becomes the means to transform relationships.

Generally, there is little resistance to reflexive communication. Once involved, participants are attracted by the interactivity of reflexiveness. Dialogue that is not confrontational, hierarchical, or aimed at particular goals has a peculiar power. It not only draws people into the process but also provides a place where participants can examine their own perceptions and assumptions while learning about those of others and, if they are convinced as individuals, change them.

Just as it enables us to realize more about the individuality of others, reflexive communication enables us to realize more about ourselves. Because it provides steps to enhance communication, it also enhances relationships. Reflexive communication is a process of personal growth as well as individual change — at one's own pace and for reasons one oneself discovers. Only then can transformational change of a second-order nature occur.

CELEBRATING THE INDIVIDUAL

The best antidote to stereotyping and discrimination is to know one another as individuals. Reflexive communication values the uniqueness of the individual. The basic assumption of reflexive communication is that separate individuals view and express, from their own positions, their unique perspectives on reality. These perspectives are reciprocally validated and affirmed through communication. It is at this point that a deeper dialogue evolves between individuals. Greater understanding of one another is likely to occur and a change is likely to ensue.

Transformational or second-order change is an organic, intrinsic, developmental process. It is based on a cardinal principle: The mind is best convinced by reasons it itself discovers. The self-generated change that diversity requires is based on conclusions one intrinsically arrives at. This is the most effective way to dispel myths and alter erroneous assumptions. The process that gets us there is reflexive communication.

We believe that diversity training needs to celebrate the individuality and uniqueness of each person. We see the purpose of diversity training as enabling people to look at each other as individuals and to see individual strengths and individual weaknesses instead of stereotypical group differences.

The participants in reflexive communication are separate individuals who perceive the world from the separate positions they occupy. Even among individuals who share the same gender or cultural heritage, one's beliefs, perceptions, and behavior are not necessarily predictable. Each person comes equipped with a unique genetic makeup and set of life experiences that account for the variations and differences that are exhibited by each one of us. Such factors as class, education, occupation, religion, and region not only contribute to our uniqueness but also give each one of us a different position from which to view the world. We should be aware that at best cultures provide the shared patterns necessary for common collective action. At worst, these patterns may be perceived as stereotypes. It is imperative that, when we encounter diversity, we hold our expectations of these behaviors lightly, always ready to discard them in favor of the individual we come to know.

Learning about each others' cultural and historical backgrounds is a necessary first step in celebrating the individual. Although necessary, it is not, by itself, sufficient. Individuals are the building blocks of American organizations and society. It is imperative that we focus on understanding the individual.

OUR INCLUSIONARY JOURNEY

The story of America is the story of ever-increasing inclusion in society and the workplace. Our story began with the first ethnic group to run America's major businesses and institutions — WASP males of English ancestry. Being different in eighteenth- or nineteenth-century America meant being of German or Scandinavian rather than English ancestry or being a Baptist or a Methodist instead of an Episcopalian or a Presbyterian.

It was not until after World War II that non-WASP males began to attend college in large numbers and learned the appropriate skills to be hired by U.S. businesses. Lee Iaccoca and others like him acquired the experience to step into top executive positions by the late 1960s and 1970s. Any individual who grew up in America remembers that, until then, Jewish, Catholic, and Orthodox males of southern or eastern European ancestry held about as many positions of power and influence as blacks, Hispanics, and Asian Americans do today.

Discrimination on the basis of religion has virtually disappeared from the contemporary U.S. workplace. Today, white males, regardless of religion, are commonly found and accepted in executive suites. Discrimination, sexism, and racism persist in American society today.

They will not disappear soon. Every political and legal means to combat them should be used. Our intent has been to propose a process by which individuals can understand each other better and change. As we approach the twenty-first century, we must address and conquer discrimination on the basis of gender and color. Perhaps, there is historical precedent to believe that this, too, will occur.

White females are following the same trajectory as ethnic white males did before them. We hold that white women are at the point where white ethnic males were, perhaps, during the 1960s. Having earned the requisite undergraduate and graduate educational credentials and acquired the lower and middle management experience, more women are now middle managers acquiring the seasoning for senior management positions.

We believe that the accelerating American dynamic of inclusion will expand over time to include more and more educated and skilled Americans who are women, black, Hispanic, and Asian American. As they become better educated these Americans are joining large and small organizations and will acquire the experience to attain top management positions. We fear that this hope will not be realized because of the comparatively low college graduation rates of some ethnic groups. Unless these graduation rates improve, there will not be a sufficient number of all Americans to compete for and secure their fair share of tomorrow's management and executive positions in the informational economy.[48]

The inclusionary trend of the workplace is driven by the core American values of individuality and equality. These preeminent values are deeply rooted in our heritage. The power of these values should not be underestimated. Individuality and equality played an important role in abolishing the enslavement of blacks by a white population in the nineteenth century and in bringing an overwhelmingly Caucasian state to end the internment of Japanese Americans during World War II. These values also undergirded the many executive actions, court decisions, and laws by white male–dominated government that have benefited women and minorities since the 1950s.

Americans are individuals first. Individualism is deeply embedded in our heritage. It is no accident that every American can cite his or her inalienable right to life, liberty, and the pursuit of happiness according to the Declaration of Independence. The individual has been and remains one of the preeminent American values.

Americans believe in the value of equality. All Americans. Especially Americans who are immigrants. Abraham Lincoln explained why equality is such an important value to them in a speech he gave in Chicago, Illinois, on July 10, 1858. With immigrants in mind, Lincoln said: "(When) they look through that old Declaration of Independence they find that those old men say that 'we hold these truths to be self-evident, that all men are created equal,' and then they feel that that moral sentiment taught in that day evidences their relation to those men, that it is the father of all moral principle in them, and that they have a right to claim it as though they were blood of the blood, and flesh of the flesh of the men who wrote the Declaration, and so they are."[49]

Individuality and equality continue to characterize Americans and have driven America's inclusionary past. These values will continue to drive its inclusionary present and future. Drawing upon the power of these ideals will help meld diversity issues in the workplace. To create the finest America of the future, we should draw upon the best of its past.

Megatrends author John Naisbitt wrote that genuine social change occurs only when personal values and economic necessity are in alignment, and not until then.[50] Similarly, we hold that genuine organizational change will occur only when the core American values of individuality and equality are aligned with the economic values of organizational self-interest and survival. Robert J. Samuelson captured the economic imperative when he wrote: "No major newspaper now wants only white men as reporters or editors; no sensible company wants to exclude blacks, women or Hispanics."[51] As journalist Nardi Campion put it: "I've found the Times good about women. So many talented women have worked on the paper by now that it couldn't be otherwise. No women deputy or foreign editors, but just wait."[52]

WASP males; ethnic males; white males; white women; black, Hispanic, and Asian American men and women — one day all will join in their society and in their workplaces to create a culture biased against none, open to everyone, and the common creation of all. This is the American solution to diversity.

NOTES

1. David Owen. (1995, January 30). The straddler. *The New Yorker*, p. 42.

2. U.S. Department of Labor, Glass Ceiling Commission. (1995). *Good for business: Making full use of the nation's human capital* (p. 79). Washington, DC: Government Printing Office.

3. Loriann Roberson, & Nancy Gutierrez. (1992). Beyond good faith: Commitment to recruiting management diversity at Pacific Bell. In Susan E. Jackson and Associates, *Diversity in the workplace: Human resource initiatives* (pp. 65–88). New York: The Guilford Press; Valerie I. Sessa. (1992). Managing diversity at the Xerox Corporation: Balanced workforce goals and caucus groups. In Susan E. Jackson and Associates, *Diversity in the workplace: Human resource initiatives* (pp. 39–40). New York: The Guilford Press; see also U.S. Department of Labor, *Good for business*, pp. 47–53, for highlights of pioneering programs by corporations like Xerox, Proctor & Gamble and IBM; Harold Orlans, & June O'Neil (Eds.). (1992).

Affirmative action revisited: The annals of the American Academy of Political and Social Science, vol. 523. Newbury Park, CA: Sage Publications.

4. Sessa, Managing diversity at the Xerox Corporation, p. 39.

5. U.S. Department of Labor, *Good for business*, pp. 47–48.

6. Lennie Copeland. (1988, June). Valuing diversity, Part I: Making the most of cultural differences at the workplace. *Personnel*, pp. 52–60.

7. Stona Fitch, vice-president of manufacturing, Proctor & Gamble, quoted in ibid., p. 54.

8. R. Roosevelt Thomas, Jr. (1990, March–April). From affirmative action to affirming diversity. *Harvard Business Review*, p. 108.

9. Elsie Y. Cross, Judith H. Katz, Frederick A. Miller, & Edith Whitfield Seashore (Eds.). (1994). Editors' introduction. In Elsie Y. Cross, Judith H. Katz, Frederick A. Miller, & Edith Whitfield Seashore (Eds.), *The promise of diversity: Over 40 voices discuss strategies for eliminating discrimination in organizations* (pp. xxi–xxii). Burr Ridge, IL: Irwin.

10. Thomas, From affirmative action to affirming diversity, p. 109.

11. Ibid.; R. Roosevelt Thomas, Jr. (1991). *Beyond race and diversity* (p. 9). New York: AMACON.

12. Ibid., p. 167.

13. R. Roosevelt Thomas, Jr. (1992). Managing diversity: A conceptual framework. In Susan E. Jackson and Associates, *Diversity in the workplace: Human resource initiatives* (p. 311). New York: The Guilford Press.

14. Thomas, From affirmative action to affirming diversity, p. 114.

15. Thomas, Managing diversity: A conceptual framework, p. 314.

16. U.S. Department of Labor, *Good for business*, p. 79.

17. Harry C. Triandis, Eleanor R. Hall, & Robert B. Ewen. (1965). Member heterogeneity and dyadic creativity. *Human Relations*, *18*, p. 52; L. Richard Hoffman, & Norman R. F. Maier. (1961). Quality and acceptance of problem solutions by members of homogeneous and heterogeneous groups. *Journal of Abnormal and Social Psychology*, *62*(2), p. 407.

18. Victor C. Thomas. (1994, January). The downside of diversity. *Training and development*, p. 60.

19. Thomas, From affirming action to affirming diversity, pp. 107–110; Thomas. *Beyond race and diversity*, pp. 21–26; Thomas, Managing diversity: A conceptual framework, pp. 306–315.

20. Thomas, Managing diversity: A conceptual framework, p. 314.

21. Jack Gordon. (1992, January). Rethinking diversity. *Training*, p. 28.

22. Frederik R. Lynch. (1994, February 21). Workforce diversity: PC's final frontier? *National Review*, pp. 34, 36.

23. See, for example, Gordon, Rethinking diversity, pp. 23–30; Linda S. Gottfredson. (1994, November). From the ashes of affirmative action. *The World and I*, pp. 365–377.

24. Lynch, Workforce diversity, p. 34.

208 Reflexive Communication in the Culturally Diverse Workplace

25. Shari Caudron. (1993, April). Training can damage diversity efforts. *Personnel Journal*, 72(4), p. 51.

26. Taylor Cox, Jr. (1994). *Cultural diversity in organizations: Theory, research & practice* (p. 39). San Francisco, CA: Berrett-Hoehler Publishers.

27. Harry Triandis. (1976). The future of pluralism. *Journal of Social Issues*, 32(4), p. 181.

28. U.S. Department of Labor, *Good for business*, p. 12.

29. U.S. Bureau of the Census. (1994). No. 12. Resident population characteristics — Percent distribution and median age, 1850 to 1992, and projections, 1995 to 2050. *Statistical abstract of the United States*. Washington, DC: Government Printing Office.

30. Paul Watzlawick, John Weakland, & Richard Fisch. (1974). *Change: principles of problem formation and problem resolution* (p. 10). New York: W. W. Norton.

31. Rich Bragg. (1995, August 21). Fighting bias with bias and leaving a rift. New York *Times*, pp. A1, A10.

32. Caudron, Training can damage diversity efforts, p. 51.

33. Gordon, Rethinking diversity, pp. 29–30.

34. Ibid., p. 29.

35. Watzlawick, Weakland, & Fisch, *Change*, p. 25.

36. Ibid., p. 22.

37. Ibid., p. 28.

38. Ibid.

39. Gottfredson. From the ashes of affirmative action, pp. 365–377.

40. Thomas, The downside of diversity, pp. 60–61.

41. Susan E. Jackson, & Eden Alvarez. (1992). Working through diversity as a strategic initiative. In Susan E. Jackson and Associates, *Diversity in the workplace: Human resource initiatives* (pp. 22–23). New York: The Guilford Press.

42. D. Lawrence Kincaid. (1988). The convergence theory and intercultural communication. In Young Yun Kim & William B. Gundykunst (Eds.), *Theories in intercultural communication* (p. 286). Newbury Park, CA: Sage Publications.

43. Orlando Patterson. (1995, August 7). Affirmative action, on the merit system. New York *Times*, p. A13.

44. Watzlawick, Weakland, & Fisch, *Change*, p. 22.

45. Barbara A. Walker, & William C. Hanson. (1992). Valuing differences at Digital Equipment Corporation. In Susan E. Jackson and Associates, *Diversity in the workplace: Human resource initiatives* (p. 129). New York: The Guilford Press.

46. Sharon S. Brehm, & Jack W. Brehm. (1981). *Psychological reactance: A theory of freedom and control* (pp. 1–7). New York: Academic Press.

47. U.S. Department of Labor, *Good for business*, p. 40.

48. See, for example, the much less widely known follow-up study to *Workforce 2000*, U.S. Department of Labor, Hudson Institute. (1988). The dilemma: Unemployment in a sea of opportunity. In *Opportunity 2000: Creative affirmative action strategies for a changing workforce* (pp. 66–69). Washington, DC: Government Printing Office.

49. Roy Basler (Ed.). (1953). *The collected works of Abraham Lincoln*, vol. 2 (p. 499). New Brunswick, NJ: Rutgers University Press.

50.   John Naisbitt. (1984). *Megatrends: Ten new directions transforming our lives* (p. 203). New York: Warner Books.

51.   Robert J. Samuelson. (1995, August 14). Affirmative action as theater. *Newsweek*, p. 51.

52.   Nardi Reeder Campion. (1955, September–October). Women of the times: Radcliffe rampant at the *New York Times*. *Harvard Magazine, 98*(1), p. 59.

Name Index

Subject Index

ABOUT THE AUTHORS

JOHN F. KIKOSKI is Professor of Political Science at Sacred Heart University, Fairfield, Connecticut. For more than 15 years he has taught, published, and given workshops on face-to-face communication in the workplace, and is a past president of the Section on Professional Organization and Development of the American Society for Public Administration.

CATHERINE KANO KIKOSKI is Professor and Director of the Graduate Program in Marriage and Family Therapy at Saint Joseph College, West Hartford, Connecticut. A licensed psychologist and family therapist, she has been involved for the past two decades in researching, writing, and teaching in the field of cross-cultural communication.